Unleashing Leadership

Aligning What
People Do Best
With What
Organizations
Need Most

By

John Hoover
and
Angelo Valenti

CAREER
PRESS
Franklin Lakes, NJ

UNLEASHING LEADERSHIP
EDITED BY KRISTEN PARKES
TYPESET BY EILEEN DOW MUNSON
Cover design by DesignConcept
Printed in the U.S.A. by Book-mart Press

ComposiTeam™ is a trademark of Valenti & Hoover, LLC

To order this title, please call toll-free 1-800-CAREER-1 (NJ and Canada: 201-848-0310) to order using VISA or MasterCard, or for further information on books from Career Press.

The Career Press, Inc., 3 Tice Road, PO Box 687,
Franklin Lakes, NJ 07417
www.careerpress.com

Library of Congress Cataloging-in-Publication Data

Hoover, John, 1952-
    Unleashing leadership : aligning what people do best with what organizations need most / by John Hoover and Angelo Valenti.
        p. cm.
    Includes index.
    ISBN 1-56414-787-8
    1. Leadership. 2. Vocational qualifications. 3. Personality and occupation. 4. Performance. 5. Success in business. I. Valenti, Angelo. II. Title.

HD57.7.H664 2005
658.4'092--dc22

                                                                2004058456

Acknowledgments

The authors would like to thank Cindy Wilson, who continues to support and encourage our ComposiTeam Leadership System staff. Our success is in no small way a result of Cindy's dedication and resourcefulness. Thanks to Sandy Wilson and Gayla Zoz, who read and commented on early manuscripts and related materials. Thanks also to Jay Herrick and Duthie Associates of Nashville, who were instrumental in first putting the functionality of our system online at *www.compositeam.com* and making it so user-friendly. At Career Press, publisher Ron Fry and his staff, including Stacey A. Farkas, Kristen Parkes, Michael Pye, and Laurie Kelly-Pye made this book possible.

Contents

Foreword by John Bracewell   7

Introduction   9

Part I: Culture and Leadership
11

Chapter 1: Meet Your Dragon   13

Chapter 2: Leadership as an Expectation   28

Chapter 3: Personality: The Invisible Hand   44

Part II: Alignment Tool Kit
65

Chapter 4: The Inventories   67

Chapter 5: The Initiative Profile   96

Chapter 6: Managing the Team   125

Chapter 7: The Fear Factor   137

Part III: Leadership Styles
153

Chapter 8: The Control Specialist   155

Chapter 9: The Compliance Specialist   175

Chapter 10: The Social Specialist   187

Chapter 11: The Stability Specialist   198

Part IV: Leadership Motivations
211

Chapter 12: Courage   213

Chapter 13: Confidence   229

Chapter 14: Concentration   246

Chapter 15: Passion and Values   264

Index   279

About the Authors   285

Foreword

When I met Dr. John Hoover and Dr. Angelo Valenti, I had a working knowledge of many leadership models but still no real game plan of how to make them work in real life. Like most businesspeople, I've been Drucker-ed, Covey-ed, One Minute Managed, and Who Moved My Cheese-d, to death. Despite reading countless books on leadership over the last 30 years, attending seminars, and sitting through keynote addresses where the *guru* was cheered like a rock star, little seems to have caught on universally.

Fighting back my growing sense of cynicism, I joined the team charged with launching Hoover and Valenti's ComposiTeam Leadership System, a leadership decision-tool based on concepts described in this book. The more I learned about their theories, their war stories (both have real-world experience as executives and consultants—with battle scars to prove it), and their ideas for a better way, the more I realized they were on to something. Little by little, a sense of hope and optimism began to crowd out the cynicism that I'd endured for so long.

If you've *done time* in Corporate America, don't be surprised if you find yourself uttering an involuntary "amen" or "you got *that* right!" as you read this book. You won't be alone. It's a head-nodder as you identify with the leadership quandaries the authors describe. You'll see that the authors *are* on to something that promises to forever change the way we approach leadership team development. Could it be that leadership is just as much a state of mind as it is the power to tell someone what to do? What if this state of mind, *if grasped by everyone in an organization*, unlocks new levels of energy and productivity, and finally cures corporate constipation?

Drs. Hoover and Valenti explain how asking employees to work outside their natural comfort zones blocks effectiveness, erodes productivity, and disables natural leadership abilities. We've all seen the real organizational and personal damage that can occur when associates and their responsibilities are misaligned. The authors urge us to acknowledge each person's unique styles and motivations, blend those with the unique styles and motivations of others, and align this newly released energy—this composite personality—with organizational goals, not just to do things, but to *get things done*. The ComposiTeam Leadership System unlocks hitherto imprisoned leadership potential as it aligns what your people do best with what your organization needs most.

Unleashing Leadership challenges us to stop trying to *train away* individual differences. It pushes us to acknowledge that team members do their best when they're asked to perform tasks within the comfort zone of their unique personal style. It promises liberation from the one-size-fits-all mindset that has been terrorizing American management for decades. *Unleashing Leadership* offers a practical, new vehicle for developing effective leadership teams; one that embraces rather than condemns uniquely natural leadership personalities. Each person has an inner leader yearning to break free. *Unleashing Leadership* shows you how to unlock the cage. Make the most of it.

JOHN BRACEWELL
PRESIDENT, COMPOSITEAM LEADERSHIP SYSTEM
www.compositeam.com

Introduction

*Leadership is a potent combination of strategy and character.
But if you must be without one, be without strategy.*

—Norman Schwarzkopf

The character of your organization is the composite character of your staff. If 20 percent of the people in your organization do 80 percent of the work and vice versa, does that mean 80 percent of your organization's population is lazy? Are 80 percent of your people lacking in virtuous character? We don't think so. It's much more likely that 80 percent of the people in your organization are not properly aligned with your expectations for, or the needs of, your enterprise. *Alignment* is the key.

The greatest potential of your organization is tied directly to aligning what your people do best with what your organization needs most. Choosing team members based on softball batting averages, golf and bowling handicaps, cookie recipes, fashion choices, or other equally inappropriate criterion is self-defeating behavior. But how would you know any better? Until you start asking the right questions, you won't.

How would your organization perform if *everyone* accepted leadership responsibility? How differently would your organization behave if leadership were an *expectation* of everyone, not an *exception* for the anointed few? The most distinguishing characteristic between thriving enterprises and struggling enterprises is the presence and quality of leadership at all levels.

You'll be happy to know that you have all the leadership potential needed in your organization *right now* to increase performance, productivity, and profits—and to sustain those increases. Unfortunately, the vast majority of your organization's leadership potential is probably locked up behind the bars of bureaucracy or staggering under the weight of organizational inertia. This doesn't happen by chance. The cultural dragon you're fighting feeds on old-school notions about leadership that grew out of a Napoleonic, hierarchical military organizational model.

Hierarchical organizations are typically run by...well...little Napoleons and Napoleonettes, especially at mid-organization level. They're cute, especially the way they prop their hands under the lapels of their jackets; but they're not good leaders for the 21st century. It's not their fault: The old leadership school taught that organizations are made up of officers and enlistees, the more powerful and the less powerful, superiors and subordinates. A hierarchical organizational design draws leadership focus and energy away from problem-solving and progressive thinking by encouraging those climbing the organizational food chain to focus on protecting their positions, perks, and territory.

Leadership is a circle, not a ladder. Inverting this traditional pyramid of institutionalized defensiveness and territoriality requires a premeditated, purposeful, intentional, and methodical *leadership system* that aligns what people do best with what organizations need most. The ComposiTeam Leadership System is designed to do exactly that, and finishes what the movement for flattened organizations, shared responsibility, and distributed leadership responsibility started. It does all this with remarkably sophisticated three-step simplicity:

1. Create a database that identifies the leadership styles and motivators of everyone in your organization.

2. Profile the jobs, tasks, projects, objectives, and initiatives your organization needs to execute.

3. Match the composite leadership profile of a leadership team to the initiative profile.

With that, the stage is set to focus everyone's unique talents and abilities on making your organization thrive as never before. Not by luck, chance, nor edict from on high; but from a well-designed and engineered leadership system that ties everyone in your organization to the truth of the past, the irreplaceability of the moment, and the promise of the future. Without these things, much in the way of time, energy, and resources will be wasted in an effort that might take you someplace to which you had no intention of going, at a price you had no intention of paying, and with more unintended than intended consequences.

An intentional, methodical, well-engineered leadership system is your best hope for taming your organizational dragon. The leadership system outlined in this book can unleash tremendous stored-up leadership potential in your organization. The same knowledge that will greatly diminish fear's power to hold people back will become a system for building and sustaining effective working relationships.

Culture
and
Leadership

PART I

Chapter 1

Meet Your Dragon

Puff the Magic Dragon is a familiar song to all of us. The character Puff is even familiar to our children and grandchildren. Yet, how many of us have asked the burning question: What happened *after* "Jackie Paper came no more?"

After Jackie dumped Puff for "other toys," we heard how Puff's "head was bent in sorrow;" how "green scales fell like rain," how Puff "no longer went to play along that cherry lane," how "Puff could not be brave," and "sadly slipped into his cave." But, "dragons live forever," remember? So, the story didn't end there.

Jackie grew up, earned an MBA, and became an executive—too busy for childish things such as dragons, enjoying life, and making work and play as enjoyable as possible for his customers and team members. Puff, meanwhile, stewed and ruminated in his cave. His sorrow turned to anger, his anger to resentment, and, before long, the dragon's thoughts turned to revenge. It was *get-even* time for Puff.

Puff didn't spend all of his time in the cave moping around. He surfed the Internet, researching what makes organizations thrive, so he could make sure they wouldn't. Puff emerged from the cave on a mission to destroy organizations whose executives had forgotten how to have fun, create happy customers, and develop enthusiastic team members. Having heard that "you are what you eat," he changed the name on his driver's license to *Org*.

Using his magical powers, Org has become a ubiquitous creature, and now resides in the custodial closets of every organization in the Western world. As a nocturnal dragon, Org sleeps all day, invisible and virtually undetectable (except for the snoring that everybody acts as if they *don't* hear). He ventures out at night, when the office hallways are dark and empty. People who work flextime into the wee hours to avoid the office idiot and hear those strange "after midnight" noises, know they're not alone.

A Well-Fed Dragon

Although not every dragon's diet is made up of organizational leadership's best intentions, Org's is. Org's Web research revealed that, among other successful characteristics, the highest performing organizations tend to make leadership everybody's business. The best companies believe that a leadership attitude should be an expectation of everyone, not an exception for a few. In the most productive and profitable enterprises, leadership responsibility is distributed and shared as much as possible across the organization, not merely used as a way to control labor and predict profits. It was clear to Org that, in order to slow down progress in organizations, to reduce their effectiveness and efficiency, and to make them resistant to change, he needed to keep the leadership potential of team members bottled up.

Org's research also taught him that change is inevitable, and the most successful organizations remain flexible by anticipating change, planning for it, and using it to their advantage. They proactively adjust to fluctuations in the internal and external marketplace. By making leadership a part of everyone's daily responsibilities, organizations are able to stay on the leading edge of change and to respond to it in real time.

To accomplish these things, organizations invest billions (with a capital *B*) on change initiatives, continuous process improvements, new leadership skills, and a wide variety of training and development programs intended to improve personal and/or organizational performance. It was an acquired taste, but Org developed an appetite for gobbling up change initiatives, continuous process improvements, new leadership skills, and any type of training and development program that threatened to improve personal and/or organizational performance.

Initiatives intended to achieve mastery and excellence have become the staples of Org's diet as he roams your darkened offices at night. Just before dawn, a bloated dragon waddles back to the custodial closet, curls up, belches, and goes back to sleep.

The next morning, the change management initiative has been replaced with organizational inertia; continuous process improvement has become a continuous meeting, supervisors, managers, and executives are flying by the seats of their pants and skirts again; customer service is as much an oxymoron as ever; internal customers aren't communicating effectively with each other—much less with anyone outside the organization—and the last time an incoming call was answered by a live voice was sometime in the second quarter of 1996. In short, the organization has become more user-*unfriendly* than ever. Bad dragon.

Got Corporate Culture?

The simple answer is, "Yes." The complex answer is, "More than you know." Whether you like it or not, any time two or more people get together to do anything, a culture emerges. Most people think corporate culture is the collective, underlying, mostly unspoken, beliefs, values, paradigms, etc., that James Belasco, Warren Bennis, Jim Collins, Stephen Covey, Peter F. Drucker, Gareth Morgan, Peter Senge, Margaret Wheatley, and others taught us about during the last quarter of the 20th century.

We agree. But what they call corporate culture, we call *Org, the Organizational Dragon*. If you try to initiate or, harder yet, *sustain* change that runs contrary to your organization's culture, the change will last only until Org gets hungry again. It doesn't matter how much you pay consultants, or how energetic and enlightened the training program is, attempts at change will wind up in Org's digestive tract. It won't help to merely throw money at your culture, go through the training and development motions, find nothing but crumbs the next morning, stand with your head thrown back, shake your fists in the air, and scream, *"Org!"* He's a sound sleeper.

What do we mean by change? Try a 10-percent increase in profits or cost savings. That's change. How about reducing turnover and intellectual capital leakage? That's change, too. Anything that produces improvement or digression from where you are at the moment is change. Any attempt you make to change your organization, its performance, or outcomes will be, by design, positive. Now, if we can only get things to consistently work the way we design them to. As any business professional knows, sometimes they do; often, they don't.

Got a cynical corporate culture?

Do some change initiatives work splendidly? Sure they do. Are there great training and development programs out there? Of course. Do many organizational change initiatives last over time? Indeed. Is there terrific leadership in many organizations? Without question. Why are you reading this book? Probably because you can't answer yes to the last four questions about *your* company with a straight face, *or* you have one of those super, high-performance organizations constantly looking to get *even better*.

Everybody involved in leading change begins at a real disadvantage. Org is going to wake up tonight with a growling tummy. Every change initiative, continuous process improvement, new leadership skill, customer service training, internal/external communication initiative, and OSHA compliance seminar that team members are exposed to or participate in—that their immediate bosses ignore, *don't* participate in, and/or simply don't support—is a recipe for dragon delight.

Many people in leadership positions consider their jobs finished when they send their people to be trained. They don't understand that their jobs as leaders is only beginning; in fact, it's never done. When a change initiative is undertaken, only to be abandoned later, people won't be *more* eager to embrace the next one. When people's hopes and expectations are built up only to be demolished, they become a lot harder to motivate the next time, and the time after that. Cynicism builds cumulatively, like a callous.

The thicker defensive skin becomes over time, the more difficult it is to penetrate. We're consultants. We know what it is to be introduced to a room full of middle managers, or executives, as "the guys who are going to change things around here." Right. Where's that loud snoring coming from? The custodial closet? Who could that be? Org is alive and well in the sallow complexions and vacant stares we get from the managers and/ or executives. After an endless stream of consultants and change management initiatives, they have become zombies—the living dead.

We don't blame them. How would you like to be a square peg being pounded through a round hole? Classical management theory would have us believe that the fastest way to get a square peg through a round hole is to use a bigger hammer. Time is money, after all. Long-time middle managers can be easily identified by their flattened heads. New hires still have rounded domes.

Why is Org cynical?

Org is cynical because he assumed Jackie Paper would keep frolicking forever. Jackie didn't, and Org got ticked. People in organizations get ticked and become increasingly cynical every time a new change initiative, continuous process improvement, leadership development program, customer service seminar, internal and/or external communication initiative is brought in, and nothing improves.

Whose fault is that? Bosses blame unmotivated team members. Team members say it's their idiot bosses. We know where to place the blame because we work with unmotivated team members *and* idiot bosses. We've *been* unmotivated team members *and* idiot bosses. We've played the role of oppressor and the oppressed at different times in our careers. We also assumed, like Org did, that the people we relied upon would never fail us. But, it happens. Some learn to get over it. Some, such as Org, get even. We loaded up our wagons with questions and set out looking for answers.

When we slip into our collective worst selves—uninspired, defensive, and selfish—cynicism becomes a self-fulfilling prophesy. Then we all share the blame for our own cynicism and the loss in personal and organizational performance. Clinging to unrealistic expectations, we can become our own worst enemies.

The temptation to become cynical and leave our motivation in the parking lot is understandable, but we know it doesn't have to be that way, no matter how much the organization stumbles over its own feet. It ultimately boils down to personal choice, and saying no to cynicism and negativity. When you do, the first person to benefit is you. A more proactively motivated organization will follow.

It takes a new skill set, to be sure. Such personal and organizational improvements call for a new paradigm. If this sounds complicated, difficult, or bothersome, remind yourself that, a few minutes ago, you didn't even know you had a dragon living in your custodial closet. See how your thinking has changed already?

Good and Bad Luck

Don't be fooled by thinking luck is the same thing as successful change. Many executives, us included, have benefited from upswings in the market, unexpected shifts in customer demands (in our favor), fortuitous timing, and luck of the draw. Of course, we called it brilliant executive leadership at the time. We didn't worry about the dragon in the custodial closet because he couldn't eat enough to keep up with and overcome our run of good luck. At times, we succeeded in spite of Org—until he caught up with us. But dragons not only live forever, they *eat* forever, and luck eventually changes.

What happens when business is off? Is it because leadership has lost its edge? Are supervisors, managers, or executives being exposed as phonies whose luck has run out? People don't learn much about themselves or others while they're succeeding in spite of poor practices. When the real outcomes reflect the real work being done, the real learning begins.

Org knows when organizations are living in a fool's paradise, and he just keeps eating. When earnings tank, have you ever noticed how productivity and morale seemed to have found their way into the tank first?

Most executives bring in a consultant or a new training program for course correction *after* they've steered the ship into an iceberg.

Why are they suddenly concerned with efficiency, productivity, and performance issues they didn't give a second thought to when customers were beating down their doors and throwing money at them? Efficiency, productivity, and performance should *always* be priorities, through good times and bad. Everybody experiences bad times. You don't need to be visited by three ghosts like Ebenezer Scrooge to expect downturns now and then.

Org loves organizational policy-makers who act shocked and surprised when fortunes turn, because they're the most likely to shoot from the hip. Imagine executives cramming hastily acquired training programs and consultants down the barrel of an antique canon, pointing it at the problem, and lighting the fuse. The "boom" is loud and impressive. Although the cloud of smoke is majestic, it masks the fact that nothing hit the target; at least until it clears. By that time, the executives are off to blow up something else, leaving behind piles of dragon food.

Substance abuse

The same organizational cultural faux pas applies to hiring and keeping talented and knowledgeable people. We define substance abuse as throwing away substance in favor of a better-looking wrapper. Running off experienced people for cheaper labor makes as much sense as peeling a banana, throwing the fruit away, and eating the peel. It takes patience, persistence, and perseverance to make the most of what we already have going for us, especially if the wrapper is worn and tattered. Nevertheless, the financial and stability benefits that flow from better use of available human resources have been proven time and time again. Culling the benefits requires forming a coalition of the willing—dragons and team members alike. And so it comes back to culture.

Too often, executive leadership looks at people as digits on a profit and loss statement, or "overhead" on a cash-flow analysis. Have you ever heard anyone come right out and suggest, "Let's dump all those older men and women who know our business, our products, our customers, and the marketplace inside and out. We can replace them with kids who don't know squat, but will work twice the hours at half the pay."

We haven't heard anyone say that either...*aloud*. But that's the message echoing down many corporate hallways. What we *are* used to hearing in executive sessions is, "Retirement costs are skyrocketing. Labor and benefit costs need to be reduced substantially if we expect to show strong earnings on The Street." Then sinister solutions seem to formulate in the shadows until HR announces the latest "downsizing," "resizing," or "right-sizing." The dirty little secret most executives refuse to acknowledge is that the *real* cost in intellectual capital, the expense of training new-hires, and the productivity ramp up will eventually deflate earnings on The Street and another frenetic fire drill will begin.

Frenetic fire drills are attempts to stabilize organizations destabilized by "downsizing," "resizing," "right-sizing," or "reductions in force." Expenditures on consultants and new training and development initiatives contribute to the cost of these fire drills until the cost of "downsizing," "resizing," or "right-sizing" eclipses what it would have cost to unleash the pent-up leadership already inside the organization. Now you know why consultants have a reputation for pulling the fire alarm in your headquarters building. But we don't want to give away too many of our trade secrets. Org has to eat.

The substance abuse issue of sending away older, more experienced people in favor of younger ones is often not about money at all. When the veterans have become alienated by conflicting and/or disappointing company policies over time, the "new blood" is often an attempt to bring in fresh, untainted attitudes. Of course, the same inconsistent policies and lack of follow through that turned the veterans cynical to begin with will have the same effect on the newcomers. Just give them time. Org is a patient dragon.

Whatever happened to boosting earnings by getting more out of the intellectual resources currently available? Sending intellectual capital out the door with a gold watch, a hail, and hardy farewell just makes Org's foraging for food easier. With all of that valuable knowledge and skill heading for retirement, training and development efforts must be stepped up for the new kids on the block. Org says, "Bring it on."

Changing Culture

If the desired culture is inconsistent with the real culture, Org will continue to snarf up the desired culture every night, belch, and go back to sleep. Organizational executives will scratch their scalps until they're bald or scream until they're hoarse, and Org will snore. Team members will mutter under their breath, "Another training and development program mysteriously disappears, never to be heard from again. Remind me to take a personal day when it's time to start another one."

The only organizations able to successfully defy this cultural consistency challenge are those that have managed to actually *change* their corporate cultures, or *align* their desired cultures with their existing culture. Changing a culture—*really* changing it, not just redecorating the old one and pronouncing it changed—requires taming your dragon and making him a part of your team. To align a desired culture with an existing culture requires at least learning to coexist with your dragon. Both approaches can work. Sometimes the best solution is a combination of both.

Changing Org's diet

We would never suggest anything so cruel as to starve Org by cutting off his food supply. Yet, that's what happens when you make change, professional growth, and organizational development issues personal. New knowledge and skill sets that people acquire through change initiatives, continuous process improvements, leadership, and a wide variety of other training and development activities intended to improve personal and/or organizational performance must be *personalized* if they're to be *internalized*. They become internalized only when people believe and buy into the knowledge and information presented to them. Improved efficiency, productivity, and performance, all necessary for increased profitability, require adjustments and adaptations from you *and* your team members.

When new knowledge and skill sets are internalized, Org can't eat them. People don't leave internalized knowledge and skill sets lying around the office when they go home. Because they've been internalized, new knowledge and skill sets are carried in the hearts and minds of the learners wherever they go. That's where real organizational culture exists—in the hearts and minds of the organizational population. Org can't eat what's carried inside a person's heart and mind.

If you, as a policy-maker, haven't invested in developing and consistently supporting your people, what they believe about you in their hearts and minds can be counterproductive. "It doesn't matter if they feel good about the organization and their role in it," you might say. "I don't pay people to feel good." We know you'd never say anything so short-sighted. But some do, in spite of the fact that organizational performance, productivity, and profitability depend more on the emotional investment people have in meeting organizational objectives than any other factor.

What you want your people to carry in their heats and minds are positive, proactive intentions about your organizational mission and agenda. That way, they'll leave the useless, irrelevant, negative junk behind when they go home at night. When the real culture is as positive as the *desired* culture, all that's left for Org to eat is the stuff you don't want contaminating your organizations. Faced with hunger, Org will eat what he can get; this time, doing us a big favor in the process. He's a dragon on a mission, but when it's time to eat, it's time to eat. After all, *voracious* is Org's middle name.

Organizations are voracious, too. People participate fully, with the best they have, when they feel necessary to the outcome. People want to participate, but only if they'll feel good about what they're doing. They're hungry for encouragement, growth, and a sense of ownership. Either feed your organizational population stuff they can put to good use or they'll eat *you*.

Tumbling Traditional Towers

Many people reading this book have struggled long and hard to get their dragons working on the same page as organizational leadership, and our hats go off to them. Many of those same people are organizational designers and appreciate how Napoleonic, military-style hierarchical organizational structures make it practically impossible to change anything, much less organizational culture. Org is particularly fond of hierarchical organization charts. They're like a road map to dinner.

Traditional hierarchies make foraging for dragon food easier. When leaders are separate and definitely not equal, they tend to become ensconced in corner offices, or at least offices with windows. All Org needs to do to find a rich diet of discarded change initiatives, customer service, diversity, or communications training, is work the interior of the building, away from corner offices and windows.

Classic, Napoleonic, hierarchical organization charts look good on paper, but rarely translate into efficient work practices. They are, in fact, those designs that really don't work as designed. The biggest problem is that human beings are just too, well, *human.* As a result, traditional organizational charts tend to institutionalize inefficiency, and misalignment of natural talents to job descriptions.

Silos and subversion

The only thing silos are good for is storing grain or intercontinental ballistic missiles. As we help companies distribute leadership responsibility throughout their organizational populations, we also help them rethink their traditional concepts of hierarchy. We sometimes refer to the time-honored organization chart as the *money* chart, because, more than anything else, it maps who gets paid the most. In terms of form and function (that is, getting things done), the traditional money chart doesn't account for the many techniques people have devised to subvert it.

People in intermediate organizational positions quickly learn how they can influence decisions at the top by filtering information as it makes its way up the ladder and back down again. If top executives are making decisions based on heavily censored information, they are not as powerful as they think they are. Neither are they as effective as they could be if they received clear and complete data and an uninterrupted way to communicate unfiltered information back to the worker bees.

Another hidden problem with the traditional money chart is the *silo effect*. Department heads zealously protect their dominance over the column of names beneath their own. If someone in Ralph's silo wants to contact or work with someone in Helen's silo—not necessarily for betting in the office football pool or debriefing weekend reruns of *Trading Spaces* on Monday morning—there are immediate political implications. When it comes to taking initiative and forming strategic alliances to get things done, one must first honor the silo and go through channels; if one goes by the book, that is.

Going through channels means seeking permission from those above you. Then (if they're helping you) they do the same, and so on until your request reaches the top of your silo. Then Ralph contacts Helen (maybe) and the request starts working its way down her silo to the person you wanted to deal with in the first place. Everyone's played the party game where you whisper something in a person's ear and that person whispers the information to the next person, and so on, until it comes full-circle back to you. By then, the information has significantly changed simply by the way it was repeated over and over. Imagine how much more distortion there will be if the information is screened each time based on each person's political agenda.

The traditional organization chart, with its well-defended silos, is a major contributor to organizational inertia. When the number-one priority for supervisors, managers, and executives becomes protecting their territory, is it any wonder that efforts to shake it up and change things are fed to the dragon almost as fast as they arrive? Thus, organizations with traditional, Napoleonic, military-style hierarchies tend to remain static. To loosely paraphrase Sir Isaac Newton's *law of inertia,* organizations at rest tend to stay at rest. Fortunately, organizations in motion will tend to stay in motion, as long as you keep doing the things that got you moving in the first place.

An end to isolation

Ideally, in organizational life, no one works in isolation. Unfortunately, cynicism and lack of meaningful engagement often result in people withdrawing into their own safe spaces. The organizational money chart enables people to isolate because they can always point upward when someone asks, "Who's in charge?" which is another way of asking, "Who's responsible?" which is another way of asking, "Whose fault is it?" which is another way of asking, "Who's going to take the fall?" The one taking the fall is usually *not* the person who is truly at fault, and, over time, the motivation to do well dwindles. It's hard enough keeping attitudes and motivation high without throwing structural roadblocks, such as hierarchical organization charts, in the way.

Behavior and relationship expectations in most organizations are based upon the organizational money chart, which illustrates who makes the most dough and has the best benefits. But a dollar paid to a line worker or a computer programmer is worth the same as a dollar paid to an executive vice president. The executive vice president merely gets paid more of them. This makes sense as long as the executive vice president is contributing proportionately more to the organization's earnings.

This is the theory behind most compensation schemes and organization charts. As the playing field becomes increasingly leveled and leadership responsibility is distributed based on natural ability and inclination to shoulder responsibility (as we're going to show), the compensation scheme must adjust accordingly. If compensation is merely tied to the organizational money chart, the real contributions of many in the organization are not being recognized or rewarded. Such neglect kills enthusiasm and effort.

Rings of responsibility

Unless the autocracy has absolute power to punish or imprison subordinates, hierarchical, militaristic-style leadership models seldom produce genuine excellent performances. When in doubt, we offer a three-word reminder: former Soviet Union. A more realistic and functional way to think of leadership responsibility in organizations is concentric rings. At the core are individuals who are encouraged to take leadership responsibility for themselves and their specific tasks.

Moving outward are rings of increased responsibility that tend to become more complex as you move farther from the core. The more area contained within a ring, the higher the demand for effective leadership performance, and the more responsibility assigned to the leader. Although everyone is expected to accept collaborative leadership responsibility for all they are able and qualified to lead, they must also respect the ringleaders.

Within each ring, people should be allowed to move freely without regard for political boundaries or territoriality. One of the things ringleaders encourage is the uncensored free-flow of information and ideas, both within their circles and within the biggest circle of all, the one drawn around the entire organization. Think of a leader orbiting around a single team as a *team leader*. Responsibility for several teams is given to a *group leader*. Responsibility for several groups is give to an *area leader*. And so on. The specific language you associate with the position needs to reflect the organizational function, so as to reinforce the nature of the relationships. (If you insist on keeping your silos, then at least be honest and call department heads "silo lids.")

Each ring, regardless of its size, represents a cell that is formed around initiatives the organization needs to execute to achieve the organization's overall strategic goals and objectives. That's a whole lot different than merely saying that Frank is the vice president of marketing, which means Frank sits atop the marketing silo. If Frank is orbiting around a marketing cell, formed around a specific purpose, Frank is earning his money. Sitting on top of the silo, he may or he may not be. One thing is for sure, sitting on top of the silo, Frank's not moving very fast, and any effort exerted by Frank, or his staff, is a sitting duck for Org, the dragon.

The Molecular Organization

Think of your organization as a molecule instead of a field of silos. Silos are static. Molecules are in constant *motion*. A molecular design can help release your organization's pent-up energy and speed past inertia. Orbiting around his marketing cell, Frank and his team are a moving target. Org is a lot less likely to devour moving targets. As the saying goes, slow rabbits get shot first. In a molecular organizational model, Frank and his team members are changing and adapting constantly, so that what they do reflects the most current realities of internal and external market factors.

As a leader in motion, Frank is aware of Org and his cynical bent. Frank also knows that team effort, strengthened by a sense of ownership and the enthusiasm that comes with it, is dragon-proof. Proper alignment of initiative and team players make genuine progress possible in spite of the snoring coming from the custodial closet.

To release the stored leadership energy in your organization and turn it into increasingly productive and profitable kinetic leadership energy, think structurally. In a molecular organization the rings of responsibility are round and easily maneuvered. Power is handed off, shared, and reassigned as the need arises.

Figure 1.1

When you stop looking at your organization as a hierarchy and start looking at it as a molecule, you can see how it becomes more dynamic and responsive to internal and external changes. Org won't be able to keep up with how fast the organization adjusts to fluctuations in the internal and external marketplace. When people are engaged at the level where they can contribute most, there's no stopping the motion.

As we strive to engage more people at every level of the enterprise, we try to make levels disappear, or at least become seamless. We want the levels to cease functioning as a caste system between the haves and have-nots. Change initiatives, new leadership skills, and professional development programs will cease to be dragon food as Org begins to look at the fast-moving, ever-changing organization as a playful environment, every bit as much fun as the Honalee of his childhood. The more fun Org has, the more likely he'll be to join the team and work for you instead of against you.

Leadership development as a system

As you might have guessed, this book is not primarily about structuring the organization to maximize traditional leadership opportunities for everyone, although that helps. Instead, we deal more with the more urgent challenge of leadership design. We seek to identify strengths and essential natures within *everyone* in the organization so they can fully participate with a leadership attitude, regardless of their positions. A systemic approach to leadership is not only effective in enhancing individual leadership performance in every nook and cranny of the organization, it is also provides the foundation and the methods for building strong and effective leadership *teams,* which are the core of any effective and dynamic organization.

Adopting a molecular model for your organization aligns structure with the nature of getting things done. It also gives individuals better opportunities to contribute on those projects where their unique talents and abilities are most appropriate. Not everyone's leadership style is appropriate for every leadership challenge. All of the elements we're describing are components of a systemic approach to leadership that includes organizational structure, leadership style, and alignment of purpose with unique talents and abilities.

You've no doubt heard recommendations to make everyone in the organization reapply for their job each year to prove they still deserve it and/or they're still qualified for it. That's how a molecular organization works. Cells are formed around initiatives and tasks created from initiatives. When the need for a specific initiative or task ceases to exist, the cell ceases to exist. The people in the leadership team executing that task or initiative are reassigned to new tasks and initiatives, or absorbed into other cells that are expanding or otherwise changing in composition.

The strong, enduring, positive culture you want will stand the best chance of surviving and thriving in spite of Org's appetite when the activities people engage in are tied to a specific organizational purpose. More than that, the achievement of organizational goals and objectives will come much more swiftly and efficiently when the organization is in motion, rather than stagnant.

Chapter 1 Summary: Keys to Unleashing Leadership

- **Org, the voracious dragon:** Organizational culture, we call him Org, reflects the shared values and beliefs among members of the organizational population, but it can be tainted by mishandled conflicts and cynicism that accumulate over time. The first step is to accept that the dragon exists...and he's *hungry*. Engineering the best way to deal with him comes next. Assuming you want a positive, productive, profitable organization, you can make it happen by managing Org's diet.

- **Don't let Org eat intentional efforts to change:** If a change initiative contradicts the underlying beliefs, values, and experiences of the organizational population, it's not likely to last till morning. The dragon will only be tamed when solutions resonate with the shared values and beliefs among members of the organizational population. Internalized new ideas, beliefs, and principles are safe from Org's nightly ravaging.

- **Don't abuse your substance:** Doing more with the human resources you have, rather than discarding them, makes far more financial and operational sense than engaging in frenetic fire drills every time things get shaky. The reasons that people become hesitant and cynical are clear enough. So too are the solutions to turn those attitudes around. Do the things that will encourage people to embrace new information and knowledge, not yawn and go to sleep.

- **Fire the hierarchy:** Long live the molecule! Tethers to old hierarchical organization charts must be loosened. If possible, severed. Flat-footed notions of hierarchical leadership need to be replaced with agile attitudes. This might sound like a pep rally, but the real and practical benefits of flexibility, agility, and unbounded thinking will become increasingly evident as we move forward.

- **Leadership is a system:** As we'll discuss more in Chapter 2, leadership should not be synonymous with higher pay, more power, or a corner office. Leadership is an attitude that needs to permeate every fiber of your organization. Rather than portray leadership as an exception for an anointed few, it must be acknowledged as an expectation of everyone, regardless of their positions. Your organizational culture must consistently and unflaggingly support that notion. And keep it out of Org's reach.

Now you've been introduced to Org and have learned how he makes arbitrary attempts at change and organizational improvement disappear. We move ahead to deal with how old notions of leadership have kept Org well fed over the years, while keeping most of the leadership potential in your organization under lock and key. We'll also explore how new leadership concepts can change Org into a vital and positive member of your team as they unleash the captive leadership potential in your organization.

Chapter 2

Leadership as an Expectation

No executive has ever suffered because his subordinates were strong and effective.

—Peter F. Drucker

As we prepare for a systemic approach to unleashing leadership held captive by your organizational dragon, it's important to clarify what we believe to be the essential nature of leadership. Leadership is like energy: it's neither created nor destroyed. It exists in one of two states: stored or kinetic. In teams of people that have been organized to accomplish predesignated goals and objectives, everybody has leadership potential. Although you've heard that before from the new-school advocates, our slant is slightly different. The new school almost has it right. But they're still looking at leadership as something some people do, but not others.

We believe *everyone* needs to assume leadership responsibility for what he or she does, be it simple or significant. In the highest performing organizations, leadership attitudes are not only encouraged in everyone, they're no longer optional. Consider how your organization would perform if everyone demonstrated leadership responsibility for his or her job?

Those stuck in old-school thinking might say, "That would be chaos and pandemonium. With everybody acting like a leader, we'll have nothing but chiefs and no warriors. Everybody will run around telling each other what to do." To us, this argument indicates the whole concept of leadership is misunderstood. This reasoning reflects a narrow definition of leadership in the Napoleonic military school. The military model is good, if you're running an army.

No sooner do we say that than we realize that the new, volunteer army in the United States is an example of engaging leadership enthusiasm and responsibility at the troop level as never before. The proof is in the performance. American military personnel have always had a reputation for accomplishing things most other militaries could not. Never has that been more evident than in recent years.

We think that's because, as a voluntary force, the vast majority of U.S. military personnel are voluntarily subordinating themselves to a larger concept of excellence. Voluntary submission is the essence of popular authority. Leaders whose team members have embraced popular authority have more influence and loyalty than they could ask for.

Who's the Subordinate?

Leadership is not about telling other people what to do. As long as leaders see themselves as order-givers, Org will remain fat, dumb, and happy. The first thing an effective and enlightened leader does, whether leading only his or her individual activities, or the activities of a thousand, is subordinate him- or herself to the greater good of the organization and the cause it serves.

In the traditional military hierarchical organization chart, it's assumed that the rank and file will subordinate to leadership. In the new, *new* leadership school textbook (from which we teach), individuals in positions of leadership voluntarily subordinate themselves to the principles of distributed leadership, common interests, and shared values. When persons in positions of organizational leadership surrender to the greater good of the organization and all of its internal and external customers, the invitation is extended for others to do the same. The primary role of leadership expands to include the development of leadership attitudes in others.

Some call this servant leadership. Some call it leading by example. Some call it leading through learning. We call it leading the way we like to be led. No matter what it's called, we've never seen chaos when people are given genuine responsibility for their jobs. When participation and sense of ownership are high, Org takes on the proportions of a pet dragon, no longer to be feared.

Lead the Way You Like to Be Led

The first rule of effective leadership is: *Lead the way you like to be led.* (This really hacks off Org.) Each one of us is living proof. If leadership attitude and ability are bottled up inside of us (that is, the desire to do something meaningful, something that really makes a difference), the first thing we want from someone in a position of influence is to be appreciated for who we are and the unique contributions we bring to the table. If that's done consistently, over time, we'll step forward confidently to pick up our share of leadership responsibility.

The next thing we want from someone in a position of influence is to align our tasks and responsibilities with activities that produce the greatest sense of participation and ownership. Once that's done, we step forward *enthusiastically* to *seize* our portion of leadership responsibility. That sense of participation and ownership is where enthusiasm comes from. Enthusiastic, highly motivated people don't cast aside important stuff for night-foraging dragons to eat.

Org prefers it when people in positions of institutional authority make decisions with little or no input from others. He likes it when supervisors, managers, and executives issue edicts that are heavy on effort and low on incentive. Giving assignments to subordinates without proper guidance or adequate information to get the job done guarantees frustration, resentment, friction, and growing cynicism.

The more cynicism and hostility generated around the organization, the more training and development initiatives are ordered to remedy the situation. More high-priced motivational speakers are hired. More inspirational books are purchased. But it never fails: The new ideas and principles that the organizational population is supposed to swallow like multivitamins, no matter how credible or potentially helpful, wind up in Org's tummy. All this because people in positions of authority didn't lead others the way they, themselves, like to be led.

When we are asked, as consultants, to assess a poorly performing business unit, we study the gap between the way organizational executives believe their enterprises should be performing and reality. Without exception, we find that vast amounts of leadership talent are bottled up, caged, secured under lock and key, only to be released one individual at a time through traditional leadership development programs.

Invariably, this results in people being led in ways the policy-makers would never accept for themselves. The first mistake is the policy-makers' belief that becoming a leader means changing into something or someone different than who they are. We say everybody's a leader, even if it's for their own activities and responsibilities, and nothing more. Becoming a better leader means becoming a better you. If you're supposed to become transformed into something other than who you are, and then inspire others to do the same, the organization will wind up with the specious leading the spurious.

The Tip of the Iceberg

A 1971 study by UCLA psychologist Albert Mehrabian revealed that words account for only 7 percent of interpersonal communication; voice quality and tone accounts for 38 percent; and 55 percent was nonverbal, characterized by gestures, posture, and facial expressions. A good portion of the relationships between people in positions of broad authority and those within their rings of responsibility exist subsurface and are unspoken. By "a good portion of the relationships," we don't mean some relationships are above the surface and others are below the surface; even though it sometimes seems that way. We mean that what is visible and conscious about virtually all workplace relationships is like the tip of an iceberg: seven-eighths of each relationship is below the surface. If you don't believe that what's below the waterline is real and to be reckoned with, type the word *"Titanic"* in your Google search.

Most hiring and promotion decisions are based on what the tip of the iceberg looks like. In most cases, that leaves seven-eighths of the issue to chance. When people don't work out in positions of expanded responsibility, it's probably due to some subsurface issue that wasn't identified or anticipated, even by the person hired or promoted. Understanding the nature of subsurface workplace issues is a building block for more effective leadership at any level, and it begins with understanding the difference between being a leader in name vs. a leader in fact.

Leader in name vs. leader in fact

In any organization, there are those who have been formally appointed to positions on the organization chart (leaders *in name*), and leaders informally anointed by their peers (leaders *in fact*). Those appointed by executives higher on the organizational food chain have institutional authority. Those who are anointed by coworkers tend to have earned a place in the hearts and minds of their peers, otherwise known as popular authority.

Left to his own devices, Org's authority is purely popular, and unsanctioned. Without a premeditated, systematic, and methodical leadership system in place, your organization's dominant culture will likewise be purely popular, informal, and unsanctioned. Armed with only institutional authority, leaders in name who try to defy the popular authority of a fire-breathing dragon will retreat into their offices with singed clothing and smoldering hair.

The fastest and longest-lasting way to win the hearts and minds of people within *your* ring of responsibility is to devote yourself to their personal and professional growth and development. That's the ticket to popular authority. The amount of additional responsibility *they* are able to prove themselves worthy of is a matter of behavior over time. But it starts with you. Zig Ziglar said it years ago and it's truer than ever: "People don't care how much you *know* until they know how much you *care* about them" [emphasis added]. In proving our commitment to the growth and development of others, actions speak much louder than words. Actions reveal what's beneath the waterline.

Supervisors, managers, and executives can cast individuals in roles of leadership responsibility. But the true title of leader is earned. As leadership author and authority Danny Cox has written numerous times, only the individuals and groups of individuals within the leader's ring of responsibility can bestow the genuine honor of *leader in fact*. Most appointed leaders in name, such as vice presidents, directors, managers, supervisors, or coaches, possess institutional authority and influence over others. But they're not true leaders in fact until those within the bounds of their responsibility buy in.

In a perfect world, persons with expanded responsibilities are both appointed *and* anointed. Alas, most leaders in name are not leaders in fact. We could say a leader's not a leader until the rest agree to follow. But we won't. We don't like the concept of a leader vs. follower relationship any better than we like the concept of a superior vs. subordinate relationship. Ideally, everyone picks up his or her leadership responsibility, such as it is, and moves together.

In their 1994 book *Flight of the Buffalo* (Warner Books, 1994), James A. Belasco and Ralph C. Stayer made the best case we've heard about the lead position being shared regularly the way the lead goose changes frequently in flight. The best leaders take turns following. If you lead like a buffalo, always holding onto the lead position, your team members will (a) follow you off any cliff you happen to stumble over, or (b) peer over the edge and watch you fall alone. Neither scenario will win you a spot in the leadership hall of fame.

Leadership as an Expectation, Not an Exception

> "Leadership is action, not position."
>
> —Donald H. McGannon,
> author and historian

The new leadership school maintains that people don't need to be separate and special to be leaders. The more inclusive thinking of the new leadership school, while not perfect, is a step in the right direction.

Graduates of the old leadership school say that leaders are not born, they're trained and developed. We agree that training and development increase the value of anything. However, the new leadership school's agenda is to develop the leadership potential in everyone so they will be at the ready when the call comes.

We agree with the new school approach and challenge it to go further. Those of us in the *new*, new leadership school believe in developing the leadership potential in everyone so they can adopt leadership attitude and behaviors right where they are, *right now*. When we refer to a leadership system, that's what we mean: making leadership an expectation for everyone, not an exception for a few.

We not only believe that people in organizations have the answers to whatever is challenging the enterprise, we believe the people in organizations *are* the answer. If it's true that everyone possesses leadership potential, why isn't the leadership potential in everyone being systematically unleashed? Instead of continuing to single out individuals for leadership, even those who wouldn't have been considered under classic criteria, why not extend the expectation of leadership to everyone, right where they are?

The old military notion that leadership is a rank given to a few in order that they be distinguished from and exercise power over the many often leads to the passing of responsibility like a hot potato in non-military situations. Those not in a position of leadership can rationalize poor performance by claiming lack of direction, information, and/or leadership in general. In an effective organization, responsibility is shared—not begrudgingly, but eagerly.

Former manager of the world-champion Los Angeles Dodgers, Tommy Lasorda, once told his good friend, Robert H. Schuller, that he preferred players that *wanted* the ball. Lasorda didn't care for timid players that lamented what bad things might happen if the ball were hit in their direction on the next pitch. He wanted players that eagerly anticipated the next pitch and chanted under their breath, "Hit it to me. Hit it to me." When team members enthusiastically seek maximum participation and contribution, organizational performance takes off like a home run over the center-field fence.

Joe Albertson's supermarket

When we refer to a leadership attitude, we're talking about a sense of ownership and pride. There is no person in a successful organization who should be without a leadership attitude. A memorable radio and television grocery-store advertising campaign once featured a produce manager proudly singing, "It's Joe Albertson's supermarket, but the produce department is *mine*." The seafood manager sang, "...but the seafood department is *mine*," and so on. The jingle was a clever way to say that, at Albertson's, people take ownership of, and feel pride about, their work.

More than simply promoting the virtues of pride and ownership, the commercials revealed how the organization's culture was intentionally built upon the concept of leadership attitudes at all levels. That's how to tame Org the dragon. Don't just talk about people being involved and participating, preach it. Shout it from the mountaintops. Do everything in your power to ensure that your team members feel so strongly about what they do that Org gets put on a strict diet. If you keep it up long enough, and if Org becomes the organizational mascot and suits up for your team, you want a lean, mean reptile wearing your company's jersey.

Moments of truth

Wherever examples of distributed leadership appear, excellence also appears. In his book *Moments of Truth* (Ballinger Publishing Company, 1987), Jan Carlzon, former president and CEO of Scandinavian Airlines, described how the same concept of leadership at all levels helped turn the struggling airline around. Carlzon made everyone leaders and empowered them to solve customers' problems, instead of seeking permission and authorization from supervisors and managers. Carlzon set the airline on its head by genuinely empowering those near the bottom of the traditional money chart. Many organizations have since found success by encouraging their folks in the trenches to set the customer service standards for those *up the chart* to follow. The Ritz Carlton even put their team members on the same footing as customers when they referred to them as "Ladies and gentlemen serving ladies and gentlemen."

Rule #1: The customer is always right

Dairy store mogul Stew Leonard believed so strongly that the customer is always right that he placed an enormous boulder in the entry of each of his stores. The boulders are inscribed with the "rules" of his company: "Rule #1: The customer is always right. Rule #2: If (you think) the customer is ever wrong, re-read Rule #1."

The incredible customer service that led to the equally incredible success of Stew Leonard's dairy stores in the Northeast is based on the *expectation* of leadership throughout the organization—an expectation that Stew's staff meets and exceeds day in and day out. Stew Leonard's team members, like team members everywhere, *want* the potato. Stew Leonard, Jan Carlzon, and other great business leaders make sure their people *get* the potato.

If you work hard to assemble a good team, why wouldn't you put them in the game and keep them there? They can't score points for you without the ball. Just handing them the ball and telling them to run with it isn't enough. If they're not sufficiently inspired and personally invested, they will not only drop the ball, they'll leave it laying around after work for Org to eat. The next day you'll be handing them yet another ball.

Chosen year after year as one of *Fortune* magazine's Top 30 Companies to Work for in America, Stew explained it like this: "Customers cannot have a great place to shop unless the company first makes it a great place to work. I believe with all my heart that, if you take good care of your people, they will take good care of your customers."

Blueprint for Leadership

Leadership is not a *ladder*. It's a *circle*. As soon as people at all levels of the organization are invited into the great circle of leadership, attitudes, performance, and productivity improve almost instantly, and dragons have to get used to a new diet.

Org will stop eating the good stuff and simply snarf the leftover residue of trials and errors that erred. There is always plenty of that to go around. Not everything we try works out the way we want it to. As long as we're making a wish list, how about if our bosses create and sustain an environment that challenges us, yet does not place us in uncomfortable and unfamiliar circumstances that will cause us to become fearful and anxious? In other words, an environment that challenges us to grow and develop the best of our potential without demanding that we give up who we are or abandon our essential nature in the process. Org is starting to slim down already.

This is not fantasy. Industrial research has repeatedly proven that self-actualized people are significantly more creative and productive when given the unimpeded opportunity to grow and develop. A sense of pride, participation, and ownership increases performance and productivity even more. The best results occur when personal and professional growth and development are encouraged and supported as a matter of organizational *policy* and *practice*.

Organizations are systems of human beings and functions. Involvement of those people and execution of those functions must be approached systemically. At this moment, everyone in your organization is capable of making valuable contributions to organizational leadership. What the organization, in all likelihood, does *not* have is a leadership *system* to take maximum advantage of what the organizational population has to offer and to encourage the most widespread and enthusiastic participation possible.

Leadership is revealed in *followership*

In traditional organizational design, there are far fewer leaders in an organization or a society than there are followers. In classical leadership scenarios, the faces of those under the influence of a person in a position of power are like a mirror that reflects the genuine face of the leader. The best way to distinguish between leadership that resonates with the hearts and minds of people in the leader's sphere of influence vs. those who feel forced, coerced, or have no choice but to comply is to study *followership.*

Old notions of hierarchical leadership led to the creation of leadership development programs that focused on transforming raw material with "leadership potential" into effective leaders. This cookie-cutter approach was based on conformity to preordained definitions of leadership. What these programs actually did was to effectively *carve away* much, if not most, of what individuals had to offer as uniquely talented leaders.

The old leadership school approach was to identify top performers in the organizational population, tap them out, and send them to get an MBA, to the Disney Institute, National Training Labs, or some other intensive preparation from which they were expected to return a week later as leaders. While the anointed ones were sent away to become effective leaders, those left behind were supposed to, by osmosis, be transformed into equally effective followers. We haven't seen many training and development programs designed to teach followership and subordination.

The leader vs. follower disparity of power

What's the relationship between leadership and followership? If we play the role of organizational detectives and examine the evidence, some interesting behavioral patterns and facts begin to emerge. Would you like to work for a CEO who motivates with threats rather than encouragement? We wouldn't. Who wants to work for an executive who promises the moon, but only delivers the mud puddle it's reflected in? Sometimes the CEO tries to encourage and uplift, while middle management operates with threats and intimidation. The ultimate message to the worker bees is that the CEO doesn't have a clue what's really going down in his or her own organization. Credibility is lost either way.

Wherever there is a presupposition of leader vs. follower—as in superior vs. subordinate—there is a disparity of power designed into the organization. If the leaders coercively misuse their power, they're considered abusive. If they simply can't manage to get anything good done, they're considered ineffective. Either way, the more concentrated power is in an organization, the more likely it will come to no good, unless, as Dwight Eisenhower said, you have a benevolent dictatorship.

Are there executives in corporations, not-for-profits, and government agencies that use the power given to them to empower others, encourage, and support the personal and professional growth of everyone in their organizational population? Fortunately, yes. Unfortunately, there are many who don't. Is it intentional mismanagement of human resources, or lack of awareness that there are better ways to distribute responsibility and share leadership? We think it's usually the latter.

Are there executives in corporations, not-for-profits, and government agencies who focus their individual power and resources on defending and maintaining their positions at the expense of promoting the growth and development of everyone in the organization? Yes. An increasing number of exploitive executives are having the whistle blown on them; not just because they're abusive, but because they're costing stakeholders megabucks in real cash and squandered human capital. It seems that many are getting the message, and looking for new ways to approach the challenge of organizational leadership. That's good news for us, no matter how much it shrinks Org's smorgasbord.

As always, the human character and essential motivations of followers reveal the truth about a leader's sincerity. If you're in a position of power and influence, what do your team members' faces reflect about the quality of your leadership? True leadership is a continuous cycle of leading *and* following, like the geese. More than anything else, when a person in a position of power chooses to follow a team member's lead, he or she pays that person ultimate respect.

The blame game

When things don't get done, or get done poorly, workers frequently blame the bosses for not being better bosses. Just as frequently, the bosses blame the workers for not being better workers. Around and around it goes. As the leader/follower discontent spirals even deeper into the organization, Org starts to get really pudgy around the midsection. As the disconnect grows wider between superiors and subordinates, roles and expectations are poorly communicated, if they're communicated at all. Critical conversations, between people with vital information and others who need that information, deteriorate into grumbling. The very people who need to be working in concert with one another wind up avoiding each other in the hallway.

We know much of this might sound sinister and hopeless. But it's not, of course (the hopeless part, that is). The dysfunctional part is all too real in more organizations than care to admit it. Where leadership is looked upon as an exception for an anointed few, there will be disconnect. Count on it.

Willingness Trumps Competency

Many people ask, "What about competencies?" To us, the core competency for any job is willingness to do what needs to be done. Such willingness comes from a desire to play an important role in the success of the organization. Individual ego urges us to look to the organization to play an important role in our *individual* success. Ideally, it works both ways. But the individual submission comes first, and comes from the ringleader with the most institutional and popular authority.

So much has been written about leadership over the years that certain assumptions have become common and much leadership language has become ambiguous. Here are some of the most important characteristics we believe effective leaders must possess, whether she or he is a leader of one, or someone with broad and far-reaching responsibility:

> › Genuine concern for the good of the organization as well as the individual.

> › Willingness to pay a personal cost to bring about success in self and others.

> › The ability to accept and act upon the truth of the past, the irreplaceability of the moment, and the inevitability of the future, with all of its promise and potential.

Leadership Is a Specialization

Competency is on our list of important leadership characteristics. But it's not at the top, because taking an individual who is comfortable at doing one thing and putting him or her in charge of other people doing the same thing is not a guarantee that you've done anyone any favors. Success in one thing does not necessarily lead to success in all things.

This is especially true of leadership. Success with an individual endeavor, or in a specific field, does not guarantee that the successful individual will be an effective leader in that field or inspire others to similar achievement in a similar endeavor. More often than not, however, organizational executives and business owners still cling to the competency myth as they look to an individual's success in his or her discipline or designated activity as the primary qualification for leadership selection.

In organizational life, people are often assigned positions of broad responsibility before they have a chance to experience what expanded leadership responsibility entails, much less know if their subsurface issues will become an impediment. Regardless of an individual's demonstrated ability to perform a specific task, doing a task alone—even when naturally gifted at it—can be very different from motivating, inspiring, and guiding others to perform to the best of his or her abilities.

This is a natural trap in which to fall. Take sales, for example. As the saying goes, marketing makes the telephone ring, but it takes a sale to make the cash register ring. If an individual is the hottest salesperson in the organization, executives and owners start to salivate at the thought of elevating the performance of other salespeople to the top performer's level. "What better or faster way to do that," they reason, "than to put the top salesperson in charge?"

Pulling a super salesperson out of the field or off line accomplishes two things. First, the organization loses the services of the highest performing salesperson, and sales figures will show it. Second, a sales force in need of an effective, inspirational leader probably now has an unqualified person at the helm. A top salesperson placed in a position of leadership is qualified to sell, but, in all likelihood, will be unsuited to be an effective leader with broad responsibilities for the performance of other salespeople.

The qualities that comprise successful selling are usually not the same qualities that lead to inspiring others and bringing out the best in them. Strong salespeople have a well-developed ability to shed rejection like water off a duck's back. Other, less waxy salespeople develop other, sometimes extremely creative, ways to disassociate from the discomfort of rejection. Either way, deflecting, denying, or defending against feelings is one of the last qualities you want in a leader, especially a leader of salespeople.

The same principle applies to other disciplines as well. The best software writer won't necessarily be the best manager of software writers. The best external customer representative might not be the best boss of internal customers. The most gifted engineer might not be the best vice president of engineering.

The Power of Empathy

The ability to empathize is essential to effective leadership. If they are going to have any success as motivators, teachers, and/or coaches, leaders must have the ability to understand and appreciate the core causes of human behavior. Top salespeople will tell you that the most influential leaders in their careers are those most able to welcome battered, beleaguered salespeople; build them back up; and restore them to their former glory as inspired, lean and mean selling machines.

As a servant to his or her people, a person in a position of broad responsibility actively identifies strengths and tailors assignments and responsibilities that best match an individual's ability, suitability, and essential nature. Furthermore, the leader seeks to transfer as much leadership responsibility and sense of ownership to the ones doing the work, regardless of that work is. Willingness trumps competency every time. Competency can be taught—it dwells in the head. Willingness dwells in the heart.

Regardless of an individual's demonstrated ability to perform a specific task, doing the task alone—even when naturally gifted at it—can be very different from motivating, inspiring, and guiding others to perform at their best. If we're really lucky, the person we promote will be good at both. There are some ways to shift the odds in our favor. One way is to read the paths worn in the carpet.

There is usually someone in the department who everyone else seeks out for encouragement and wise counsel. This person is probably not the manager or the top performer. If we're talking about salespeople, this individual probably lacks the pure killer instinct to sell or function at full throttle and take no prisoners. But he or she empathically appreciates the importance of the sales function, or any other function in the organization, and the tough road that any successful professional must travel.

Follow the worn-out path in the carpet and you'll find that leader *in fact* at the end of the path. Behind the neat, well-ordered columns of the *money chart* is the real ant-colony-like labyrinth of popular authority being exercised, and cow paths being worn into carpet where senior executives would least expect to find them, even if they looked for them, which, as a rule, they don't.

Ideally, organizational executives or business owners will leave top performers in the environment where they perform best, whether in the field or their cubicles. The key is to reward them handsomely for their lucrative efforts without removing them from their area of greatest strength. When looking for a leader of salespeople, or any other discipline, look for the type of individual who has it in his or her nature to eagerly provide, emotionally and tactically, what people need most to do their jobs.

Let salespeople sell, and people builders build people. Identify the persons in your organization naturally suited and quick to help others find solutions and strategies to succeed. That requires people that keep the needs of both the organization and other team members in mind at all times. Although success in one thing does not necessarily lead to success in all things, previous success is a great indicator of future success, as long as you keep that person within his or her demonstrated strengths and abilities. Don't assume that high performance in any specialization is synonymous with leadership in that specialization. Leadership requires specialization of its own—it's called people.

Chapter 2 Summary: Keys to Unleashing Leadership

☞ **Leader in name vs. leader in fact:** Leaders in name have institutional authority. There is nothing wrong with that. In fact, being given institutional authority can position you to immediately win popular authority among those in your ring of responsibility. The trick is in how you use it. Are you consistent, fair, and willing to use your institutional power to hack a path through the bureaucratic jungle for your team members? Be a leader in name *and* a leader in fact.

- **Make leadership an expectation, not an exception:** Remove the potential for an *us vs. them* disconnect. Whether a person is responsible for only his or her immediate tasks or a person has expanded responsibility for the performance of a business unit, he or she needs to approach his or her day's work with a leadership attitude. The narrower an individual's focus is, the more his or her success will depend on pure competency. The broader an individual's leadership responsibility grows, the more important it is that the person be skilled with growing and developing others. Competent leadership starts with one.

- **Lead the way you like to be led:** It's an incredibly simple, but powerful test. If there is cynicism in the organization, are people being led the way you would like to be led? If motivation is low and performance is sluggish, the same question applies. We'll be shocked the first time we're called to study and assess poor performance in an organization where people are being led the way their policy-makers like to be led. People will always measure and compare the quality of leadership they're receiving against the way they want to be led.

- **Leadership is a circle, not a ladder:** A primary purpose of leadership is to increase and strengthen connections between people inside and outside of the organization, and to avoid potential disconnects. As rings of responsibility are formed around essential organizational functions and initiatives, the need for participation and a sense of ownership on everyone's part becomes more critical. People standing in a circle aren't looking up or down at one another, they're looking straight at the task.

- **Old and new school leadership theories:** Old school subscribers look for leadership potential. That is to say that they look for extraordinary, exceptional qualities in individuals and separate them from the herd to be anointed as leaders. New leadership school theorists believe that everyone has leadership potential and can be groomed to rise above the herd and to lead, under the right circumstances. The *new* new school of leadership we've founded maintains that organizations can't afford to separate the leaders from the organizational population. Everyone must take up the mantle of leadership, including leadership attitudes and responsibilities, right where they are.

Org isn't just anybody's dragon, he's *everybody's* dragon. Org is, at the same time, each of us and *all* of us. He is a mighty dragon that can make your organization work better or keep your organization from working. The choice is yours. Making him a friend rather than a foe requires committing to a consistent, systematic, methodical, and strategic agenda that will convince him he's better off working for you and not against you. It will take time and effort. But what things truly worth having don't?

Recognizing the invisible-but-powerful nature of your dragon is the first step. Taking leadership responsibility to its most functional and effective level, as close to the work as possible, is the second step. You work during the day. Org works at night. You make things happen. Org makes things un-happen. It's up to you to win him over. If, perchance, you're working late some night, perhaps into the wee hours, and you hear strange noises in the darkened hallways, keep repeating under your breath, "Nice dragon."

Chapter 3

Personality:
The Invisible Hand

The meeting of two personalities is like the contact of two chemical substances: if there is any reaction, both are transformed.

—Carl Jung

In his 1776 book, *An Inquiry into the Nature and Causes of the Wealth of Nations,* economist Adam Smith wrote about his theory of the "invisible hand" determining economic reality. If Smith can have an invisible hand, we can have an invisible dragon. Nothing that has transpired since 1776 has dispelled the invisible hand theory (or the belief in dragons). If you don't believe an invisible hand is at work in global economics, just ask anyone who has been heavily invested in the stock market for the past 10 years. Yowza. If you don't believe there is a dragon operating out of your custodial closet, when it comes to predicting individual and organizational performance, productivity, and profit, check the definition of "stock market."

The invisible hand takes an active role in many things beyond economics. It motivates some people to do extraordinary things that others don't bother to try. It changes a great round of golf one day to a disaster the next. It gives the gambler a lucky streak one day and a run of bad luck the rest of the year. Is it God? Is it the luck of the draw? Is it inexplicable molecular vibration in the universe? The invisible hand comforts people in times of struggle and suffering, which leads us back to the God concept. Perhaps it is different things in different situations and circumstances.

Whatever the invisible hand is, it represents those mysterious components in phenomena that we can't explain. Some call them *intangibles.* Life and business are full of them. When it comes to individual and organizational performance, productivity, and profit, we call the invisible hand: *personality.* Personality is the most powerful determinant in the performance and productivity of individuals and organizations. Recognizing the nature of personality, and how it dominates individual and organizational attitudes and behavior, is the first step to understanding the difference between, what our strategic problem-solving friend Doug Ward calls, "Doing things vs. getting things done."

What You Don't See Can Hurt You

If Org feeds on fear or, more specifically, the abandoned junk fearful, intimidated, and/or cynical team members leave lying around, he can be equally nourished by the debris left behind by ignorance. We use the term *ignorance* as it applies to stuff that the average supervisor, manager, and executive just aren't likely to know. Although personality profoundly affects the quality of leadership at any level in any organization, most leaders know very little about it. Supervisors, managers, and executives can be brilliant in their disciplines and specializations and yet be completely clueless when it comes to personality and the role it plays in individual and/or organizational success, or lack thereof.

When we don't understand something, it's not uncommon to:

> Remain blissfully clueless.

> Pretend that it doesn't exist.

> If it does exist, pretend it's of little consequence.

> Focus on more important things, such as the office football pool.

> All of the above.

> None of the above.

If you chose "None of the above," we're on the same page. It's time to drag Org out of the closet, so to speak. When people have a cold, they talk about it. Everybody can empathize, because everybody has a cold now and then. Everybody also has a personality, not just now and then, but *always*—cradle to grave. Your organization as a whole has a personality, and every team in your organization has a personality. It's the most universal experience people can have, yet nobody talks about it.

Do people ignore the personality factor in their organizations because they're ignorant about the topic, or are they ignorant about the topic because they ignore it? In our experience, once supervisors, managers, and executives discover how much power there is in personality—power to increase productivity, performance, and profits—they don't ignore it anymore. Now that you've been told, you will no longer be able to ignore the evidence of your organizational personality.

"Who has seen the wind?
Neither you nor I:
But, when the trees bow down their heads
The wind is passing by."

—Christina G. Rossetti

Personality is like wind. It's invisible to the naked eye. Next time you're at 35,000 feet in a 350,000-pound Boeing 767, point a camera out the window and take a picture of what's holding you up. Chances are you'll photograph the mighty wing from which an enormous jet engine is suspended. Maybe some clouds, a UFO perhaps. Your photo of the wing and the engine, however, shows everything *except* what's holding you up. If the air wasn't there, creating lift as the wing passes through it, the 767 would never leave the ground.

It's equally impossible to photograph the personality of your organization, or the individuals within it. Of course we're talking about Org the organizational dragon here and the culture he represents. As we discussed in Chapter 1, the personality of your organization and its culture are one in the same. You can photograph some of what your organizational culture causes to happen, but not the culture itself. It's harder still to photograph what the culture is *keeping from happening.* It seems that Org, with his surly and pouting attitude, is more invested in keeping things from happening than in causing things to happen.

It's easy to undermine individual and organizational efforts with subtle, almost intangible raids on change advocacy and performance improvement initiatives under the cover of darkness. If Org were to come out in the light of day and breathe fire up and down the halls, the sprinkler system would go off and pandemonium would ensue.

It would be helpful if there were yellow crime scene tape strung up around the office or plant, and yellow plastic A-frame signs that read, "Change-Initiative-Eating Dragon at Work." If the personality/culture/dragon in your organization were to work out in the open, and make really awful things happen, it would call for immediate, and even drastic, remedies. When the personality/culture/dragon in your organization keeps things from happening, it doesn't automatically set off a frenetic fire drill and send panic up and down the hallways at headquarters. It's more likely that supervisors, managers, and executives scratch their heads and say, "We just can't seem to get up to speed around here. It's like we're not firing all cylinders."

If the organization spends a great deal of money on a spectacular motivational kick-off to a new initiative and comes out of the blocks fast, sooner or later people will start saying, "We were doing so well there for a while. Now everything seems to have tapered off. It's like we're not firing all cylinders. Let's wait and see if things don't get better tomorrow." By preventing things from happening, Org is a much more effective saboteur of organizational performance, productivity, and profit than if he lumbered around scaring and scorching people.

Measuring Personality: Making the Invisible Visible

Personality is not a new subject in business and industry. There have been industrial psychologists roaming the halls of organizations for well over half a century. Given the powerful role that personality plays in organizational success, it's amazing that psychologists aren't routinely promoted to executive status. Some organizations have made faint attempts at elevating the status of human behavior issues with the creation of the roles of Chief People Officers and Chief Knowledge Officers. We think that's great. But we're not pleased to report that, most of the time, organizational psychologists remain relegated to a dark, windowless corner in the HR wing, where they can hold private sessions with employees deemed to have *problems*; that is, if there's a psychologist on staff at all.

There's nothing wrong with using talented mental health professionals to counsel people struggling with emotional problems. That's great. But in organizations that claim they want to grow and prosper, the underuse of organizational behavior specialists is another case of peeling the banana, throwing the fruit away, and eating the peel. Use of available resources is not being maximized. Opportunities to improve performance and increase productivity and profit are being missed.

Fortunately, human resources and some training and development professionals venture into the personality arena through the use of personality assessment instruments. Instruments designed to measure personality were created to make the invisible *visible*; each instrument in its own way. They were also conceived as a way of classifying and organizing people into categories based on personality, which is the most effective method yet devised to herd cats.

The language of personality typology

Human behavior is complex, and the more complex a phenomenon is, the more difficult it is to predict. For centuries, people have attempted to find ways to understand why people do what they do, in hopes that if they could understand past behavior, they could better predict future behavior. Demonic possession was one such early attempt, or in the words of comedian Flip Wilson, "The devil made me do it!"

Other such attempts included astrology, as well as racial, cultural, and ethic stereotypes. Although some would argue that astrology is a systematic study, one of the first "scientific" attempts to understand human behavior was put forth by the ancient Greek Hippocrates, the father of medicine. Hippocrates believed that the balance of four bodily fluids, which he called "humors," determined personality. The four fluids, *phlegm* (related to the head), *blood* (related to the heart), *black bile* (related to the liver), and *yellow bile* (related to the gall bladder), are present in varying proportions within the body.

According to this theory, too much yellow bile leads to a *choleric personality*, characterized by aggressiveness, impatience, and quickness to anger. Too much blood leads to a *sanguine personality*, characterized by a love of people, talkativeness, and sociability. Too much phlegm leads to a *phlegmatic personality*, characterized by resistance to change, lack of emotionality, and a strong sense of responsibility. Too much black bile leads to a *melancholic personality*, characterized by a desire for accuracy, a strict adherence to the rules, and a tendency to be overly critical. Although many dismiss this approach today, the terms choleric, sanguine, phlegmatic, and melancholic are still in use. You'll find them in any dictionary.

Modern approaches to categorizing human behavior include the DiSC Profile and the Myers Briggs Type Indicator (MBTI). Both of these approaches were developed in the 1920s and 1930s, but were designed to measure different aspects of human behavior. The theory behind the DiSC Profile was developed by Dr. William Marston, a psychologist who was interested in the behavior of normal people. Just as Hippocrates developed a four-dimensional model centuries earlier, so did Marston. In Marston's model, people vary in how aggressively they deal with problems and challenges (the dominance dimension); how they respond to other people (the interpersonal dimension); how tolerant they are of change, and the pace at which they work (the steadiness dimension); and how concerned they are with rules, regulations, and doing things correctly (the compliance dimension). Marston also postulated that people adapt their behavior to fit the environment in which they find themselves.

The typology that evolved into the MBTI was developed by Carl Jung, a contemporary of Sigmund Freud. In Jung's typology, an individual tends to have either an external focus, in which the individual finds others energizing, or an internal focus, in which other people drain energy from that individual (this is the extraversion-introversion dimension). An individual also has a preference for gathering information, either using his or her senses or using his or her imagination, hunches, and intuition (this is the sensing-intuiting dimension). The third dimension deals with how an individual processes and evaluates information, either using logic and reason or subjectivity, fairness, and personal values (this is the thinking-feeling dimension). The fourth dimension was added later by Isabel Myers and her mother, Katharine Cook Briggs, to explain how an individual relates to his or her environment, either by taking action and making quick decisions or by seeking out possibilities and keeping options open (the judging-perceiving dimension). The combination of these four dimensions leads to the 16 types (ESTJ, INFP, and so on) that those familiar with the MBTI will immediately recognize.

Other typologies are in common use today, and the majority of them use a four-dimensional model. For example, Wilson Learning Assessments terms their four dimensions: Driver, Expressive, Amiable, and Analytical. Birkman International uses the terms Implementer, Communicator, Planner, and Administrator. Although there are variations in all of these approaches, the one thing they have in common is the desire to systematically categorize the behavior or preferences of individuals in order to better understand and predict their individual behavior and how they are likely to relate to others in relational situations.

Despite all the attempts to categorize human thinking and behavior, dragons can still change the rules on us overnight. A lot got blamed on dragons before Hippocrates, and dragons will be scapegoats long after we're gone. But that doesn't mean we should stop trying to get it right.

ComposiTeam

The ComposiTeam Leadership System draws on the same philosophical underpinnings as the typologies we've mentioned with regard to individuals. However, we've changed the focus from the individual personality to the team, or *composite*, personality; or the invisible hand, if you prefer. Many HR professionals, organizational behavior specialists, and consulting psychologists are good at examining individual personalities and how those individual personalities interact on teams. But the ways team members' personalities line up relative to one another was never the primary focus of traditional typology instruments. While *their* primary focus has always been on the individual, the *composite personality*, or leadership profile, of teams has been the primary focus of the ComposiTeam Leadership System from its inception.

In most cases, not long after traditional assessment data is gathered on an individual, it is stored in personnel files and never pulled out or dealt with again. This isn't because the assessment information isn't important. It's because the vast majority of supervisors, managers, and executives are not versed in its language or applications. First, they lack a systemic approach to leadership development; as in our *leadership as an expectation, not an exception* mantra. Second, they have no systematic methodology to make practical use of personality data in selecting team members and/or aligning them with initiatives or their component tasks.

The ComposiTeam Leadership System effects this information on tactical, planning, and operational levels. The more it's made functionally available to operational team leaders, group leaders, area leaders, and organizational ringleaders, the more they can use it to sharpen the organization's saw, and put Org on a diet. Unfortunately, most personality assessment data is used at seminars, workshops, or in counseling sessions to enlighten individuals about themselves and possibly others in the workshops. It's much less often shared with department heads and team leaders.

Personality as a Strategic Weapon

One of the complaints we hear most often about assessment instruments being used in organizational applications is their relevance to what needs to be done, or perceived lack of relevance. Some are better in one application vs. another. Yet there is no universal language to integrate all the typologies. Despite their richness in information on individuals, and even relationships between individuals, most typology instruments have limited direct application to achieving organizational goals and objectives.

The best we can tell, this is why assessment data information is relegated to HR files, some training and development applications, and almost never to operational activities. Left, for the most part, on the sidelines, psychological assessment instruments generate a lot of dragon food. Need we remind you again that a fat dragon means a sluggish and uninspired organization? Releasing leadership is a matter of transforming personality data into strategic and tactical tools.

Before we form a posse, surround the custodial closet, and *out* Org, it's important to understand a bit more about how personality dictates organizational productivity, performance, and profits. Not *your* individual personality, nor *our* individual personalities, but the composite personality that emerges when two or more people join together to get a project done. Invisible to the naked eye, personality is most evident in what we chose to say and do. It's even *more* evident in *how* we say and do what we say and do.

Our focus is on leadership and team performance, and in the best of all possible worlds: leadership teams. In the molecular organization, with its rings of responsibility and expectation that everyone will demonstrate leadership attitudes, leadership will be distributed and shared as much as possible. We don't recommend this strategy because we want everybody in your organization to have a warm, fuzzy feeling when they come to work (even though molecular organization is not a bad idea).

We don't suggest everybody join arms and sing "Kumbaya" around the watercooler. We believe that having a functional, practical system in place to share and distribute leadership authority is how you bring the most targeted and talented leadership ability to bear on any given initiative or task. The goal is greater efficiency that leads to increased productivity and profits. If that's how you sing "Kumbaya," sing till your heart's content.

Culture = Composite Personality

The same tip-of-the-iceberg problems discussed in Chapter 2 apply to leadership teams. In fact, they're multiplied. It's hard enough to make an individual hiring or promotion decision based on one-eighth of the puzzle. It's even harder when assembling a leadership team of four, six, eight, or more people. You now have seven-eighths of four, six, or eight icebergs under the surface with which to deal. The probabilities of initiative and team member misalignment are enormous, and Org is going to have a lot to eat.

But a corporate culture is not merely a collection of personalities. It's a composite personality produced by all of the individual personalities, pushing and pulling against each other all at once, above *and* below the surface. That's the level at which we've chosen to deal with personality in the organization: the composite personality of the organization as a whole, as in its culture, or dragon, if you prefer. Any combination of two or more individuals from the organizational population form a composite personality that is more than the sum of the individual personalities added together.

Like the air that holds up the 350,000-pound Boeing 767, most of what determines leadership effectiveness is invisible to the naked eye. The composite personality of your entire organization, including the teams within your organization, is completely invisible. The composite personality is only evident when it causes things to happen or keeps things from happening. Old school *and* new school leadership training and development deal predominantly with visible and conscious leadership behaviors and personality styles. Only individual psychological assessments such as the ones we mentioned earlier begin to scratch the surface of unconscious and invisible personality issues affecting leadership.

Composite personality made simple

It's not hard to give a simple and straightforward explanation of composite personality, because composite personality is a simple and straightforward concept:

> ‣ One person = One personality. (Hopefully. If one person has multiple personalities, consult the nearest mental health professional.)

> ‣ Two people = Two individual personalities and one *Composite Personality*.

> ‣ Three people = Three individual personalities and one *Composite Personality*.

> ‣ Four people = Four individual personalities and one *Composite Personality*.

> ‣ And so on.

To be technically correct, three people or more have their individual personalities, their overall composite personalities, plus the *composite personalities* of every subgrouping of two or more people. Trying to deal with all that personality would surely lead to paralysis by analysis. It's just not practical to go that deep, or get that specific. When we do surgical diagnostic work in organizations with major conflicts, succession issues, and turf wars, these factional and coalition studies become necessary. But that's rare.

If a person is working in isolation, his or her individual personality is all that matters. When people work in teams of two or more, the composite personality determines the outcome of the team effort. When people work in organizations of two or more, the composite personality, more than any other factor, determines the nature and performance of the organizational effort.

For example, a team of four people can go through the MBTI or Keirsey Temperament Sorter and wind up identifying, say, an idealist counselor (iNFj), a rational field marshal (eNTj), an artisan performer (EsTp), and a rational architect (iNTp). With each type identified, you can study how they will relate to one another, who is most likely to be aggressive, and who will be more passive. You'll know who will be more of a counselor vs. who will be more a field marshal. But who are all these people when acting as a group? What invisible hand is at work when this team is together and when it's apart?

You could have a whole group of artisan crafters (iStPs). In spite of their common type, they might act quite differently in various situations. It's one thing to deal with them as individuals, but what about the overriding composite personality that emerges when they're all drawn together as a team? That composite personality will explain their propensity for mob mentality, groupthink, and a variety of inertia-producing maladies that can creep up when people are put together.

As is the case with Org the voracious dragon, that which can work against you can also work *for* you. A leadership team that can freeze up on its inherent inefficiencies can also position its members to achieve greater efficiencies than they could while working as individuals. For example, individual leaders have energy. Leadership teams have *synergy.* The composite personality you manage when you're responsible for team performance is not each individual's personality, even though you continue to address them as individuals. It's the invisible connections, positive and negative, encouraging and discouraging, created by the combined personalities. Managing the air space *between* people is as important as addressing the people directly.

The power of composite personality

More than the individual personalities measured by even the most popular typology instruments, the composite personality of your organization as a whole and the composite personalities of the work cells within your organization, *rule.* If you're not dealing with and/or managing the composite personality in your organization, you're a leader in name only, and you're even lucky to be that. Sorry to bring you bad news, but attempting to lead effectively without an operational awareness of composite personality is like trying to steer the battleship without a rudder; or trying to fly a jumbo jet without hydraulic pressure to control the ailerons, flaps, and vertical stabilizer. You're lucky to be pointed in the right direction, much less stay afloat or aloft.

Why is the composite personality of your organization and the leadership teams within your organization so dominant? For starters, it's not seven-eighths below the surface, like an iceberg. It's completely invisible. Most people aren't aware it's there, much less able to deal with it.

Leadership Potential Held Hostage

> "There is a curious paradox that no one can explain: Who understands the secret of the reaping of the grain? Who understands why spring is born out of winter's laboring pain; or why we all must die a bit before we grow again?"
>
> —The Fantasticks

Assessing individuals and addressing the ways individuals interact is still important, but take it one step further as you consider the powerful-but-invisible dragon created by the composite personality of everyone involved. That's where untapped leadership is sleeping, like Org in the custodial closet. Unlike Org, leadership potential is locked up in cells, held hostage by old school notions of hierarchical, bureaucratic, and limited leadership. It's not enough to merely wake slumbering leadership potential. It must be *released.* It's up to you to wake up the leadership potential in your organization, break open the locks, and fling open the cell doors. Do we hear an a-men?

As we discussed in Chapter 2, many existing leadership development programs are designed to transform individuals into leaders, and/or develop the leadership potential in individuals. You could say they are attempting to release stored or inert leadership potential. We won't argue, and what we're preaching and teaching in this book is not intended to displace anything that promotes personal and professional growth and development.

The personality assessment tools we discussed earlier are also used extensively in evaluating leadership talent and developing it in a variety of ways. We, too, are focused on aligning individuals professionally with what is in their essential natures and best abilities. But our primary departure from existing leadership and development is the notion that everyone should be expected to demonstrate a leadership attitude.

Go Team

With our focus on leadership being a cultural expectation rather than the exception, we encourage the use of leadership teams as the work cells we described in the molecular organization (page 24). Everything should be considered the work of either a *macro team* or *micro team*. The same shared leadership concepts apply whether teams are large or small. In truly mobile and agile organizations, there will always be teams of varying sizes, as well as teams being formed and teams being disbanded, depending on the dynamic nature of the workload.

We're not trying to rewrite the multitude of books on team development any more than we're trying to discourage the use of leadership development programs. Our hope is to expand your thinking around the concept of organizational flexibility, shared leadership, and distributed responsibility; all in the context of composite personality. The concept of composite personality is like attaching a handle to a wet bar of soap. There is something to hang onto where there was only a slippery proposition before.

The composite personality of a group of two or more is most evident in how the team expresses itself in words and actions. Whether you go through the effort to fully measure and map the composite personality of your organization or the composite personalities of the teams within your organization, just knowing you're dealing with an overriding personality that's greater than, and different from, the sum of its parts is a giant leap for mankind.

Natural vs. unnatural teams

As with organizational culture, there are teams, whether you like it or not. The difference is whether or not they're naturally formed, or unnaturally formed teams. Naturally formed teams come together without anybody asking them to. The group that likes to go to Taco Bell for lunch is a natural team. The groups that stand around talking about the big game on Sunday, or the scrapbooking party Saturday night, are natural teams. The folks who e-mail each other with jokes are natural teams. Democrats, Republicans, and Episcopalians are natural teams. The common purposes they come together to pursue include eating tacos, discussing sports, scrapbooking, antiquing, poking fun with jokes, discussing politics, and tearing down the wall that separates church and state.

The teams you put together in the workplace are unnatural teams, almost any way you cut it. They probably wouldn't be working together if you hadn't assembled them for that purpose. This gives you an agenda in assembling the team best-suited to the task, objective, or initiative. You must make it as clear as possible how valuable each individual is in the composition of the composite personality. Giving every bit of meaning and purpose possible to someone's involvement will pay dividends in team performance. A team will never form naturally unless, left to their own devices, people come together. You're forming teams to get things done, which is why the tools and techniques we're teaching you are so important.

Leadership styles

Thinking of the composite personality in your organization as an invisible hand, you must still start with each team member's leadership style. If everyone is expected to demonstrate a leadership attitude, affecting his or her sense of participation, ownership, and involvement, it's essential to know who's who. Because we believe so strongly in distributed leadership and shared responsibility in organizational design, we've operationalized our concept of the composite personality in what we call the ComposiTeam Leadership System. ComposiTeam means what the clever, compound word implies. Teams are dominated by the composite personality of their members. The system we've developed makes that invisible hand visible, and puts it to work in your favor.

Every human being is unique and special in a number of ways. However, to explore how fear can best be mastered and leadership potential unleashed, we've identified the four most common leadership styles in organizational life. The first job is to examine each team member to determine which of the four leadership styles is dominant:

> ›   Control Specialist.

> ›   Compliance Specialist.

> ›   Social Specialist.

> ›   Stability Specialist.

Each of these leadership styles is described in it its own chapter in Part II of this book. For now, it's important to start thinking in terms of the functional nature of leadership and leadership teams in the context of composite personality. Individuals will have a dominant leadership style, further defined by their underlying leadership motivations. However, our primary focus regarding the selection and management of leadership teams, will be how the individual leadership styles and motivations of the team members create a composite personality that will dominate the team's productivity, performance, and overall effectiveness.

In a dynamic and mobile molecular organization, individual leadership positions and leadership teams are formed around initiatives, tasks, and objectives. In other words, individual jobs, work cells, and even the organization as a whole must be committed to a meaningful and practical purpose if they are to survive and thrive. There must be a *reason* for an organization and its component parts to exist, and there must also be a preferred methodological approach to operations.

Team leaders go first

Looking at leadership as only the responsibility of the anointed few disregards the vast resource of potential leadership energy in the rest of the organizational population. It's a much better approach to train people in positions of enhanced responsibility to see *their* roles as followers. Instead of saying, "Do it this way," skilled leaders find a way to align organizational needs with individual's natural talents and abilities.

The organization's needs don't become subordinated to the team members' natural strengths and abilities, the team members are selected based on the initiative, as you'll see in Chapter 5. The initiative, objective, or task itself is profiled, and teams are assembled based on the composite personality that best matches that profile. By the time a team leader is in position, most of the alignment is done.

We don't believe there is any such thing as a completely, absolutely, positively, self-directed team. At some level, the responsibility rests with whoever is orbiting the leadership team or work cell. The team leader's job, as well as the group leader's job, however, are not so much to give directions as they are to manage the variances between the team's composite personality and the initiative profile. Managing the variances is a matter of staying plugged into how each team member is contributing and how the composite personality is functioning.

All of the knowledge that can be acquired regarding the leadership styles and behavioral tendencies in an organization won't amount to a hill of beans unless the leader puts him- or herself under the microscope first. The team leader must demonstrate, based on his or her unique leadership style, why he or she is appropriate to play a part in the achievement of the organizational objective, or task, around which the team was formed.

Doing this begins the never-ending sequence of reminders: "This is what we're here to accomplish, and this is why each of us are part of this effort." Org gets a lot to eat when there is ambiguity and/or confusion about what you're trying to do. In such chaos, who knows what's important and what's not?

When leadership teams are operating, team leaders end up following a sometimes circuitous route to the highest performance and productivity possible. Instead of imposing rigid structure and process on everyone, the structure and process emerge from the team's natural talents and abilities. Attention to individual skills, talents, abilities, and preferences that dictate personal performance needs to be balanced with attention to the composite personality that is dictating organizational performance.

Becoming an effective leader, in the context of the organizational composite personality, requires replacing rigidity with flexibility. Narrow thinking must become expansive thinking. Tethers to old hierarchical organization (money) charts must be severed. Flat-footed notions of hierarchical leadership need to be replaced with agile attitudes. This might sound like a pep rally, but the real and practical benefits of flexibility, agility, and unbounded thinking will become increasingly evident as we move forward.

Aligning what people do best
with what the organization needs most

In Chapter 4 you'll learn how easy it is to determine what your leadership style is, as well as the underlying leadership motivations that you tend to use when adapting to various situations and challenges. You'll also learn how easy it is to use a peer review system to enrich that data and enhance its reliability. The composite personality, nonetheless, remains dominant over organizational and team performance. So, you'll learn the simple formula to calculate the composite personality of any grouping of people you select, using your database of individual assessments.

In Chapter 5 you'll learn how easy it is to profile your organizational initiatives. Profiling anything from your mission statement to a routine, daily, plant-floor task, we will frame it in the same language and context as the individual and team assessments. Once an initiative profile is completed, you can begin comparing it to various combinations of team members to create the best fit possible between what the initiative calls for and the composite personality best suited to execute it.

Creative tension

One of the myths of team dynamics is that everybody should get along. Yes, people should bring positive energy to the team. Everyone should, hopefully, be able to get outside of themselves enough to put the team's needs above their own, at least as far as getting the job done is concerned. We think of this type of behavior as being professional, and everyone on the payroll should behave in a professional manner.

But in order for everyone on the team to have a love-fest, usually requires having like-minded people. Having nothing but like-minded people on the team elevates the danger that you have amplified dysfunctions. If everyone is a salesperson that likes to play golf, team energy will be devoted to finding ways to the golf course. If the team is comprised solely of software writers who love to stay isolated with their code and microprocessors, they may never be coerced into meeting face-to-face.

Before we say that these can't be effective teams, it's important to remember that the team is a function of the function it's intended to serve. If planning a golf tournament is the team agenda, perhaps you have a good team with all those salespersons. If the team agenda is to write code, you might be on the money with all those code warriors. The initiative profile will determine the type of composite personality required from the leadership team. That's the whole reason to go through the profiling exercise.

Before moving on to Chapter 4, with its individual and peer leadership inventories, and Chapter 5, with its initiative profile exercise, it's important to plant the notion of *creative tension* in your head. Walt Disney wasn't comfortable with the notion of like-minded people getting together to be creative. It was his experience that the best creative outcomes emerged from brainstorming among contrary minds and opposing thoughts. Who are we to argue with Walt Disney?

It *is* easier to deal with a group of people who have no differences, walk in lockstep, and follow orders explicitly. But the quality of the work will leave much to be desired. The point of assembling teams by matching the organization's needs (initiative profile), and what people do best (team composite personality), is to combine complementary strengths that will balance the effort. By balanced effort we mean filling in the gaps that details usually fall through, plugging the leaks where energy and results seep out, and keeping the team effort pointed in the right direction.

3 Easy Steps to Composite Personality

To tame the dragon roaming the darkened hallways of your offices at night you need to grab the initiative by mastering the concept of composite personality. It's not difficult. Two chapters from now, you will be able to:

1. Create a database of leadership styles and motivations for everyone you want in your pool of potential leadership team members.

2. Profile every initiative, objective, and/or task you want to form a leadership team to address.

3. Match the initiative profile to the composite personality of the team that best fits.

Armed with that knowledge and information, you will have the ongoing ability to align what your people do best with what your organization needs most. Once your database of individual leadership styles and motivations is populated, the order in which you create the alignment will change slightly. Because the function, objective, initiative, or task represents the organization's needs, it comes first:

1. Profile the initiative.

2. Select the team members whose composite personality best fits.

3. Go to work.

The Art Is in the Application

Good to Great author Jim Collins urges organizations to make sure the right people are on the bus. But how are you supposed to know that? Profiling the bus is a good start. As we mentioned, some organizations use the ComposiTeam Leadership System diagnostically. Some senior executives even profile their mission statements. Then they study the composite personality of their executive teams to see if there is alignment. That's an eye-opener.

When the alignment of what the company needs most, as in the leadership styles and motivations to realize the mission statement, and what its executive team does best are out of alignment, there are some choices to make. Reshuffle the executive team, rethink the mission statement, and reorganize are on the list. But even if the team composition and the mission statement are locked, knowing the degree to which and specific areas where the two are out of alignment makes the invisible stumbling blocks and gaps visible. Now you can address the variances, because you can *see* the variances.

Take that same process to the plant floor or the sales call, and get the same results. How will you know if you have the right people on the bus if the task, objective, or initiative has not been profiled? Saying that you have the right person for the job, when the essential characteristics of the job are vague at best, is gambling with the organization's time and money.

Having a well-defined and documented job description without a way to match leadership styles and motivations in terms of language and context is another roll of the dice. When teams are involved, these problems are multiplied. If the team's composite personality is not purposefully and skillfully aligned with the task, objective, or initiative, getting something meaningful accomplished—in an efficient, effective, productive, and profitable way—is a crapshoot.

We have been in enough executive positions ourselves and consulted and coached enough other executives through the years to testify in court how, almost without exception, team-member selection is a loosely organized, low-priority activity. This is another way to say there's a lot of shooting from the hip going on out there. What the team members are supposed to do is (supposedly) important, so why isn't the alignment of profile and personality a higher priority? Go figure.

That's precisely why we developed the ComposiTeam Leadership System. It's not a radical departure from essential problem-solving skills. It's common sense. Organizations have needs. Team members have unique talents and abilities. As Yenta the matchmaker would say, "Match them up already." If you never engage in the computation of composite personality, and merely profile your tasks, objectives, and initiatives, you'll be way ahead of the business curve in Western civilization. If you pre-meditatedly align what your people do best with what your organization needs most, you will be among the few, the proud, and the increasingly profitable.

Chapter 3 Summary: Keys to Unleashing Leadership

- **The invisible hand:** It's there, constantly at work. Like a dragon that roams the darkened corridors of your offices at night, it's not seen, but its presence is felt. Like the wind, just because it can't be seen doesn't mean it won't blow your house down. Just ask half the population of Florida once hurricane after hurricane tore through the state in the summer of 2004. So, you want to recognize the invisible hand's existence and learn to deal with it in a positive way? You're reading the right book. You can make the unseen attitudes and motivations that fill your team members' heads work in your favor. The first step is recognizing that what you can't see *can* hurt you.

- **Measure the wind:** There are lots of ways to study personality, and measure skills and competencies. We're all for that. However, it's our goal to operationalize personality data and make it a tactical and strategic tool in your arsenal. As you endeavor to enhance efficiency and effectiveness, improve organizational performance, increase pro-ductivity and profits, you need to maximize everything that's working for you and minimize everything that's working against you. Aligning the best your people have to offer with the activities, tasks, and initia-tives your organization needs most is a place to start.

- **Composite personality:** The most common mistake people make when trying to identify organizational culture is looking at the individual pieces of the group puzzle (vis-à-vis their personality assessments), and think they're looking at the whole cultural picture. Doing this is like looking at the wing and the engine, not the air that's creating the lift (and the drag) that enables the aircraft to fly. The composite personality is the overriding dominance that's more than the sum of the individuals. Dealing with organizational culture and the dynamics of leadership/work teams means dealing with the composite person-ality as much as the individuals. You want the composite personality of your organization to be like the wind beneath your wings, not the drag that brings the company down.

- **Go team:** A naturally forming team is not going to be very effective at getting something done unless it miraculously and coincidentally matches the task, objective, and/or initiative profile. It's much more likely that aligning what your people do best with what your organization needs most will produce an unnatural team. That means all of the skills and dynamics in team development come into play. More than anything else, you need to make it clear why each team member is on the team in terms of his or her contribution to the composite personality. Then, each member needs to know what is expected of him or her, and how that assignment resonates with his or her leadership style and motivation.

- **The art is in the application:** Once you have gathered data, the alignment of initiative profile to teams is simple. The initial value comes in profiling the tasks, objectives, and/or initiatives. That exercise alone is worth the price of admission. Putting two and two together to see what they add up to in your unique organizational population comes next. Composite personality can be tricky. We often hear clients say, "I never would have thought those particular folks would produce a collective personality like that. But it explains a lot." Measuring and tracking progress based on the profile/personality alignment will only sharpen your skills as an organizational artist.

The surprises never cease. Just when you thought you had one aspect of your organization figured out and your leadership puzzle solved, the tip of the iceberg melts a little more and a little more of what was under the surface emerges into the light of day. That's a good thing, as long as you understand and anticipate it. Knowing what composite personality is and how it works is a great start.

Looking ahead, you're about to discover your leadership style and motivations, and learn the process for building a database of leadership styles and motivations for your team, department, or organization. That body of knowledge will become the foundation for aligning what your people do best with what your organization needs most. Sorry, Org. Your all-you-can-eat smorgasbord is about to change to a health-food diet.

Alignment
Tool Kit

PART II

Chapter 4

The Inventories

The essence of knowledge is, having it, to apply it;
not having it, to confess your ignorance.

—Confucius

Confucius had it half right when it comes to organizational leadership. If policy-makers have knowledge, there is a reasonable chance that they will apply it. But where knowledge is lacking, so, usually, is confession. We've already found that ignorance generates a lot of dragon food for Org. But reducing the debilitating effects of ignorance requires something to displace them. Knowledge and enlightenment are good for starters; more specifically, *functional* knowledge and enlightenment.

Most organizational leaders have financial, operational, and/or procedural knowledge. But in-depth knowledge about what makes their people tick and how to best equip and inspire them to increase productivity and performance is rare. A passion for building people up is even rarer. We'd say the latter represents true enlightenment, and we're thrilled and inspired when we meet and get the opportunity to work with such people.

Lack of Knowledge Can Freeze up Any Organization

What do you really know about the members of your organization? Do you know enough about your team members to make informed decisions about their abilities, tendencies, desires, and relational strengths? If you've never thought of these things as important, or never thought of them at all, you're missing an incredible opportunity to dramatically help them increase their performance and productivity.

What do you really know about yourself? Are you willing to undergo a searching self-inventory to discover and identify your own natural abilities, tendencies, desires, and relational strengths? Leadership is about relationships—relationships with your team members; with other leaders in positions of authority similar to your own; with leaders up and down and throughout the organizational food chain; with your customers; and with others who look to you to provide leadership. Do you know enough, and are you sufficiently eager to replace the organizational food chain with rings of responsibility and the molecular organization we've talked about?

Think of ignorance as going under the hood of your car to repair the engine knowing only that it stopped running. If you don't know what makes a car run to begin with, much less run *well,* you're not going to be very effective at diagnosing the problem, much less to repair it. Before you think this is a far-fetched idea, consider the experience of an American landscape architect that worked for a Middle Eastern government during the oil embargos of the 1970s.

During those days, some Middle Eastern governments were accumulating such vast fortunes that they eccentrically hired American landscape architects for their deserts. This particular architect came back to the United States with stories and pictures of his experiences. His job was to landscape the medians of the new superhighways. The highways were practically deserted, except for an alarming number of brand-new Cadillacs abandoned on the shoulders of the highways.

The rulers of that country were not only very wealthy, but also very generous. Thousands of families in the small nation were given new Cadillacs as gifts from the royal family as a way of sharing the wealth. Most of these people had never been inside an automobile before, not to mention a luxury automobile. They had no clue what made a car run. They were taught to put gasoline in their tanks, but not much else. They drove their Cadillacs up and down the new superhighways until they ran out of oil (of all things) and the engines seized up. They pulled or pushed the cars off the road, left them there, and returned to more traditional and familiar forms of transportation.

The fact that many organizations run as well as they do, for as long as they have, is remarkable, given the tremendous lack of knowledge regarding behavioral and cognitive styles of their leadership and operational populations. It's common for organizations to seize up and stop functioning, just like the Caddies in the desert. And the reasons are similar. Even if they don't seize up altogether, they often get sluggish and lose performance as they deteriorate into organizational inertia.

Most organizational leaders know how to put gas in the tank and step on the accelerator. But when the pistons start knocking, then missing, and then seize up, people in leadership positions often respond by putting more gas in the tank and stomping harder on the accelerator. When things start really heating up, many executives finally start taking calls from persistent and pesky headhunters and, before long, they're behind the wheels of other organizations with their feet on the accelerators.

Michael E. Gerber, best-selling author of *The E Myth* (HarperCollins Publishers, 1988), says that his entire career as a consultant began with the realization that just because someone owns a business doesn't mean she or he knows anything about running one. In his experience, the two are often mutually exclusive. The same is true about leading ourselves and others. Just because a person is in a position of authority doesn't mean she or he knows anything about leading other people, or self-leadership for that matter. In fact, the very thought of it might scare the heck out of him or her. When that happens, expect the avoidant and defensive behavior we've spoken of.

Tools for Gaining and Using Knowledge

As you're about to find out, gaining knowledge about the composite personalities of people in the organization is not difficult. Learning how to apply the knowledge is not hard, either. So, why don't more people in leadership positions do it? Like the Cadillac owners in the Middle Eastern desert, they don't know what they don't know. Moreover, they don't want to know there's something important out there that they don't know.

The tools we're about to introduce are the leadership style inventory (LSI) and the leadership motivation inventory (LMI). There are self-reporting versions of each and peer-review versions of each. Together, the LSI and LMI will provide you with enough core knowledge to keep your organization running like a well-tuned engine, and even improve power and gas mileage. The LSI and LMI database is the right hand, and the initiative profile in Chapter 5 is the left. Press your palms together, and they should match. *Ideally*, once you have profiled a job, task, objective, project, or initiative, the LSI and LMI data (otherwise known as a leadership profile) will overlay perfectly; whether it's an individual's job description and the individual's leadership profile, or the executive team's composite leadership profile and the organization's mission statement.

The leadership style inventory (LSI)

The leadership style inventory will help you gain knowledge about yourself and how you tend to think and behave. It's an indication of where we are most comfortable, regardless of the situation. No matter how linear, or left-brained, you are, emotions, or right-brain activities, influence your behavior. Many engineering and financial types, typical left-brainers, like to fancy themselves as cool, analytical, and logical as Mr. Spock on *Star Trek.* Nice try. Emotions determine much more of how you behave than you think. Your comfort zone—that place where you like to hang out—is an *emotional* container.

The LSI will help you learn why particular people, events, and circumstances trigger certain feelings within you, even if you don't acknowledge them. It's vital information to know, especially if you're serious about improving your personal performance and the performance and productivity of your team members. The LSI is personality viewed through the lens of leadership.

The leadership motivation inventory (LMI)

The information provided by the leadership style inventory is further enriched by the measurement of five motivational qualities that modify the basic Jungian personality concept. We believe that these character qualities apply to every phase of life and are inseparable from the concept of leadership. Merely knowing which of four fundamental types dominates your leadership style is helpful, but lacks significant additional criteria that will add critical dimension to your analysis and application. If you think of most four-temperament personality indicators as markers, the data gathered on the combined LSI and LMI is more like a precision ballpoint pen.

The richer and more precise analysis, made possible by the LMI data, reveals a more intricate personality pattern. Just as the LSI data shows the essential personality characteristics of an individual in any environment, LMI data indicates how individuals are likely to respond and adapt to their environments. However, depending on the degree of threat or temptation in dynamic environments, the LMI data is more likely to vary.

Honesty is the best policy

"Your vision will become clear only when you can look into your own heart."

—Carl Jung

Whether you are ranking terms on the LSI and LMI that apply to you, or you're completing the inventory as peer feedback for someone else, the results are only as valid as your honesty in responding. In our experience, people don't necessarily rate themselves dishonestly, but it's difficult to be completely objective when self-reporting. Sometimes we're too close to our trees to see our own forests. Try to avoid the twin traps of

(a) wanting to portray yourself in an idealized manner, and (b) attempting to portray yourself as the person you *think* your boss wants you to be. Answer in a way that best reflects how you behave in the real world.

There is no right or wrong way to respond to the qualities and characteristics listed on the LSI, except to intentionally respond incorrectly. We find that people have a strong desire to be recognized and acknowledged for their unique strengths and characteristics. Doctoring answers will only hide the real you.

Any self-reporting assessment can be fudged or manipulated. Assuming it's possible to manipulate answers to self-reporting inventories and successfully craft the image of yourself that you think is best, you might condemn yourself to a life of play-acting. That can keep you awake at night and lead to permanent anxiety over being exposed as a fraud. Much, if not all, of the personal and professional development investment your organization makes in you will be wasted if you don't own who you really are. All that personal and professional leadership development debris will be a feast for Org.

In all likelihood, you won't be able to overcome the internal reliability of the inventory to completely produce a false image anyway. It's more likely that you'll end up with an assessment that looks neither like you nor the fictitious image you wanted to portray. Our advice is to just be honest. Thankfully, the vast majority of people who use these instruments are honest. When the expectations of you, in leadership team assignments, are based on who you really are, you'll be operating inside of your comfort zone, and you'll be able to sleep better at night.

All of the terms listed on the leadership style and motivation inventories (Figures 4.1 and 4.3) are vital to organizational leadership. If the value of creative tension is promoted on leadership teams in your organization, *there is value in every leadership style.* The only way to be wrong is to be misaligned professionally with your essential nature. If you intentionally misrepresent yourself, the behavioral expectations others have of you will be misaligned with what you're most likely to do naturally.

Notice that none of the words have a negative connotation. Even though all four words in a single row might apply to you, or the subject of a peer inventory you're filling out, you must rank them from the most dominant (4) to least dominant (1) in your character, or the other person's character, as a leader. Depending on circumstances and situations, all 40 words are useful and positive qualities and characteristics. Ergo, there are no wrong answers. You will learn in Chapter 5 that every task, objective, and/ or initiative around which a leadership team is formed is unique as well.

There's no way to predict how your self-reporting or peer inventory rankings will position you or anybody else vis-à-vis future leadership teams.

Some scenarios and tasks call for powerful, confident leadership, whereas others might do better with a skeptical and inquisitive leadership style. Everyone is a leader at some level, and everyone has a unique leadership style that is tied to his or her individual personality, especially when modified by his or her rankings on courage, confidence, concentration, passion, and values, which will be measured next.

One-time colleague of Sigmund Freud, Carl G. Jung, upon whose work these types of personality indicators are based, made this clear when he said, "Knowledge rests not upon truth alone, but upon error also." Many things are learned by accident as we set out to learn something else. Using instruments such as the leadership style and motivation inventories, we intend to uncover as much truth as possible and, hopefully, capture additional knowledge at the same time.

Filling Out the Inventories: Leadership Style Inventory

"Knowledge of mankind is knowledge of their passions."

—Benjamin Disraeli,
former prime minister of England

You might want to read through the rest of the chapter before grabbing a pencil and filling out the self-reporting inventories. If you're familiar with other assessment instruments or feel adventurous, grab your pencil and go for it the first time through. Go with what makes you more comfortable. The leadership style inventory is a grid with 10 rows and four columns of descriptive words (Figure 4.1). Thinking of yourself (self-reporting inventories), or the subject of the inventory (peer inventories), as a leader, circle or highlight the number 4 beside the word that *best* describes you *in each row.* Circle or highlight the number 3 next to the word that *next* best describes you in that row, a 2 beside the word that describes you less accurately than 3, and a 1 beside the word that *least* describes you as a leader.

You will rank terms in each row and will have a single 4, 3, 2, or 1 next to each of the words in each row. No two words in the same row (across) can have the same number. If you added up each row across, the sum would always be 10. Once you finish ranking the terms in a single row across, drop down to the next row across and repeat the process for each of the 10 rows on the grid. Each of the four *columns* will total no more than 40 and no less than 10. The sum of the four columns will be exactly 100.

ComposiTeam Self-Reporting Leadership Style Inventory for: (Name)			
	Column A	**Column B**	**Column C**	**Column D**
Row 01►	Powerful 4-3-2-1	Analytical 4-3-2-1	Helpful 4-3-2-1	Capable 4-3-2-1
Row 02►	Fearless 4-3-2-1	Detailed 4-3-2-1	Friendly 4-3-2-1	Balanced 4-3-2-1
Row 03►	Controlling 4-3-2-1	Mathematical 4-3-2-1	Upbeat 4-3-2-1	Steady 4-3-2-1
Row 04►	Commanding 4-3-2-1	Accurate 4-3-2-1	Welcoming 4-3-2-1	Strategic 4-3-2-1
Row 05►	Impatient 4-3-2-1	Factual 4-3-2-1	Spontaneous 4-3-2-1	Patient 4-3-2-1
Row 06►	Determined 4-3-2-1	Careful 4-3-2-1	Caring 4-3-2-1	Reliable 4-3-2-1
Row 07►	Dominant 4-3-2-1	Precise 4-3-2-1	Agreeable 4-3-2-1	Rational 4-3-2-1
Row 08►	Competitive 4-3-2-1	Correct 4-3-2-1	Peaceful 4-3-2-1	Evaluative 4-3-2-1
Row 09►	Take Charge 4-3-2-1	Methodical 4-3-2-1	Social 4-3-2-1	Responsible 4-3-2-1
Row 10►	Vigorous 4-3-2-1	Systematic 4-3-2-1	Personable 4-3-2-1	Dependable 4-3-2-1
	Col. A TOTAL	**Col. B TOTAL**	**Col. C TOTAL**	**Col. D TOTAL**

Figure 4.1

Add up the columns and enter the number next to the TOTAL for that column. *Remember, the sum of the four columns must equal 100.* Transfer

Column A Total:		Control Specialist
Column B Total:		Compliance Specialist
Column C Total:		Social Specialist
Column D Total:		Stability Specialist
LSI Chart Total:	100	

Figure 4.2

the column totals to the list in Figure 4.2 and see what your dominant leadership style is, what your second most dominant style is, and what your lesser styles are. Put the appropriate numbers from Figure 4.2 into Figure 4.5 on page 76.

The higher the point total, the stronger the leadership style identified by that column. If one of the columns adds up to 40, that is as dominant as an individual style can be. If a column adds up to 10, that is the minimum dominance this instrument can measure. The range from high to low indicates the true dominance of a single style. Comparing the column totals to one another shows the relative balance between styles. It's possible, though unlikely, that a person could have 25 across the board.

If your dominant leadership style has 40 and the other three are tied at 20 each, the dominant style is twice that of the others, which is significant. It indicates how *strongly* you are disposed to certain thoughts and behaviors. Some individuals are balanced between each specialization.

Once again, it's not possible to know how your particular balance or imbalance of leadership styles will affect alignment of the *composite personality* of a leadership team to a future task, objective, or initiative profile. Other factors, such as number of team members and/or the profile itself make that a wild card. What's most important at this stage is to be as objective as possible, identify your comfort zone, or give the most accurate assessment of peers you've been invited to evaluate.

Filling Out the Inventories: Leadership Motivation Inventory

The grid for the LMI (Figure 4.3) is similar to the LSI, and serves a similar purpose. Again, you are describing yourself, or someone else you've been asked to assess, as honestly and accurately as possible, in the context of leadership. Note that there are now five columns instead of four, and there are still 10 rows. Beside each of the terms *in each row across*, circle or highlight a number from 5 to 1, with 5 being the term that describes you the *best*, and 1 being the term that *least* describes you as a leader.

Add up the total for each column and enter that total at the base of each column and on the chart (Figure 4.4 on page 75). It's possible that one column could total 50. It is also possible that one column could total as few as 10. As before, the totals are most important in relation to one another, showing which motivational characteristics are most dominant and which are the least dominant. The sum of all five columns must equal 150.

ComposiTeam Self-Reporting Leadership Motivation Inventory for [*Name*]				
Column A	**Column B**	**Column C**	**Column D**	**Column E**
Bold 5-4-3-2-1	Tenacious 5-4-3-2-1	Contemplative 5-4-3-2-1	Passionate 5-4-3-2-1	Honest 5-4-3-2-1
Backbone 5-4-3-2-1	Certain 5-4-3-2-1	Determined 5-4-3-2-1	Driven 5-4-3-2-1	Strong Beliefs 5-4-3-2-1
Brave 5-4-3-2-1	Cool 5-4-3-2-1	Logical 5-4-3-2-1	Eager 5-4-3-2-1	Fair & Just 5-4-3-2-1
Daring 5-4-3-2-1	Composed 5-4-3-2-1	Centered 5-4-3-2-1	Energetic 5-4-3-2-1	Principled 5-4-3-2-1
Defiant 5-4-3-2-1	Sure 5-4-3-2-1	A Finisher 5-4-3-2-1	Enthusiastic 5-4-3-2-1	Purposeful 5-4-3-2-1
Headstrong 5-4-3-2-1	Poised 5-4-3-2-1	Persistent 5-4-3-2-1	Excitable 5-4-3-2-1	Controlled 5-4-3-2-1
Adventurous 5-4-3-2-1	Resolute 5-4-3-2-1	Focused 5-4-3-2-1	Fervent 5-4-3-2-1	Dutiful 5-4-3-2-1
Gutsy 5-4-3-2-1	Secure 5-4-3-2-1	Absorbed 5-4-3-2-1	Inspired 5-4-3-2-1	Conscientious 5-4-3-2-1
Risk-Taker 5-4-3-2-1	Confident 5-4-3-2-1	Targeted 5-4-3-2-1	Spirited 5-4-3-2-1	Orderly 5-4-3-2-1
Courageous 5-4-3-2-1	Assured 5-4-3-2-1	Applied 5-4-3-2-1	Tireless 5-4-3-2-1	Compliant 5-4-3-2-1
Col. A TOTAL	**Col. B TOTAL**	**Col. C TOTAL**	**Col. D TOTAL**	**Col. E TOTAL**

Figure 4.3

Column A Total:		Courage
Column B Total:		Confidence
Column C Total:		Concentration
Column D Total:		Passion
Column E Total:		Values
LMI Chart Total:	150	

Figure 4.4

Now enter the data into the appropriate box in Figure 4.5 on page 76.

You can already sense how nervous all of this makes Org. Just knowing what you know at this early stage in the process is enough to help you

Name:	Leadership Style:	Control	Compliance	Social	Stability	Courage	Confidence	Concentration	Passion	Values

Figure 4.5

start looking differently at the people in your organization and how to improve getting things done vs. just doing things. Even if you had much of this knowledge before, and we're merely bringing it back to the surface, this new way to operationalize it will inevitably cause some changes to happen around the old place. Be prepared, Org will resist any changes to his diet. But using the ComposiTeam Leadership System *will* make things happen.

Analyzing the Data

Based on the data you've gathered, it's time to begin analyzing what it all means. The more knowledge you can glean from the LSI and LMI, the more confident you will become with yourself as a leader. A similar process, which will come later, will increase the confidence you have in your team members, not because they will change, but because you will know and understand them better and how their composite personality functions. In Chapter 5 we'll introduce the profiling process for jobs, tasks, objectives, projects, and initiatives. The ultimate benefit of determining your leadership style and motivation, as well as the composite personality of your team, is to compare with the appropriate and relevant profile. You will immediately see where you and/or your team resonate with the profile, and, just as important, what the variances are.

More than anything else, you will better understand your team in the context of your own personal leadership style. You will gain a greater appreciation for the importance of leading them the way you like to be led. You will also become more aware of the strengths each person brings to a team leadership scenario. Increased knowledge about your own thinking and behavior, combined with increased knowledge of *their* thinking and behavior, will push back boundaries and shrink barriers you never knew existed.

Before moving on, it's important to make sure the LMI and LSI are read properly. If your highest score was in the control column, you're predominantly a control specialist. If your highest score was in the compliance column, you're predominantly a compliance specialist. If your highest score was in the social column, you're predominantly a social specialist. If your highest score was in the stability column, you're predominantly a stability specialist. A chapter is devoted to each of these four leadership styles in Part III of this book. For now, the charts that follow show examples of what the LSI specializations look like, including hypothetical LMI rankings. We've included brief highlights of each one's essential leadership style and leadership motivation data.

Leadership style and motivation rankings

The leadership profiles that follow are not necessarily typical of control, compliance, social, or stability specialists, in our experience. None of the leadership profiles we're using for this demonstration are exactly common. As we already mentioned, different folks can be all over the map on these characteristics. The leadership styles, described in Part III of this book, contain detailed descriptions of every possible sequence of styles. The degree to which the styles contrast is a numbers game. The elusive *perfectly balanced* person would average 25 on control, compliance, social, and stability specializations, as well as 30 on courage, confidence, concentration, passion, and values. The reality, of course, is usually very different as we all reveal our uniqueness.

"The only real answer to frustration is to concern
myself with the drawing forth of what is uniquely me."

—Robert K. Greenleaf,
father of the servant-leader concept

Control Specialist		Leadership Styles				Leadership Motivations				
Name:	Leadership Style:	Control	Compliance	Social	Stability	Courage	Confidence	Concentration	Passion	Values
Fred	Control Specialist	40	30	20	10	30	10	40	50	20

Figure 4.6

Fred is a control specialist, as you can plainly see by his numbers. We've intentionally peaked each example's dominant style to illustrate how the specialization is determined. With the average for leadership styles at 25, control specialist Fred (40 is maximum on the LSI) is 15 points above average. We suspect Fred is characteristically impatient to make things happen. He likes action and doesn't like waiting around. He's much more willing to take charge than a backseat.

This impatience can be a positive driving force in the organization. Fred's desire to move things along is tempered by his secondary desire to be accurate and correct with what's done. We know this because of his secondary ranking of compliance (30) issues, which is five points above average. The below-average rankings on social (20) and stability (10) specializations indicate that he de-emphasizes social relationships compared to control and compliance, but more than balance and stability. Stability is occupying the backseat; a full 30 points below control.

Ranking high on passion (50 is maximum on the LMI), Fred is likely to get downright excited, even evangelical, when it comes to the importance and urgency of whatever he's doing. He'll probably invest lots of energy to moving the initiative forward. His 15-points-higher-than-average ranking on concentration (40) means he likes to think things through. Given his impatience, it's even more likely that his higher-than-average concentration ranking indicates that Fred is intensely *focused,* along with being passionate.

His LMI average ranking on courage (30) suggests he will make a reasonable effort to fight any opposition to these principles, but nothing over the top. Fred's below average dominance in values (20) can mean that he's not emotionally invested in any particular set of guiding principles. Fred could very well say, "Whatever works." His lowest ranking on confidence (10) can mean that experience has taught him that things aren't likely to move all that fast, despite his enthusiasm. If they do move quickly, he'll likely feel it's due to influences beyond his own.

Compliance Specialist		Leadership Styles				Leadership Motivations				
Name:	Leadership Style:	Control	Compliance	Social	Stability	Courage	Confidence	Concentration	Passion	Values
Fred	Control Specialist	40	30	20	10	30	10	40	50	20
Beth	Compliance Specialist	10	40	30	20	20	50	30	10	40

Figure 4.7

Beth is a compliance (40) specialist. She is a person who is most comfortable when every *t* is crossed and every *i* is dotted. She wants the columns to add up and reconcile. Her secondary leadership concern is with human relationships (social 30), probably beginning with her own. Her third-level ranking of stability (20), five points below LSI average, indicates that she's only moderately concerned with balance in the organization, which could take the form of equitable distribution of workload. The last-place ranking on control specialization (10) suggests that she is happy to leave the driving to someone else.

Beth has confidence (50) that when every *t* is crossed, every *i* is dotted, and all the columns reconcile, all will be right with the world. In *her* world, anyway. We expect this attitude because of the dominance of confidence in her LMI rankings. We can reason that numbers either add up or they don't. If they do, why *wouldn't* the outcome be predictable and consistent enough to produce confidence over time?

It should come as no surprise that a person devoted to accuracy and correctness, as Beth is, will highly value rules, policies, and procedures as evidenced by her secondary ranking in values (40). An average ranking on concentration (30) could indicate that she is just as likely to follow rules and procedures than to reason something out. Her courage factor (20), like the low control ranking on her LSI, indicates that she'll leave the risk-taking to somebody else. Finally, a low ranking (10) on passion can mean that Beth does not find crossing *t*'s, dotting *i*'s, and reconciling columns of numbers a passionate endeavor; something with which we can agree.

Social Specialist		Leadership Styles				Leadership Motivations				
Name:	Leadership Style:	Control	Compliance	Social	Stability	Courage	Confidence	Concentration	Passion	Values
Fred	Control Specialist	40	30	20	10	30	10	40	50	20
Beth	Compliance Specialist	10	40	30	20	20	50	30	10	40
Reba	Social Specialist	20	10	40	30	20	20	40	40	30

Figure 4.8

Reba is a social (40) specialist. Her leadership style rankings suggest that human relationships are her first priority, with social specialization being 15 points above the LSI average. She is secondarily concerned with stability (30), which is five points above average. The fact that social and stability specializations rank one and two can mean that workload distribution, equitable contributions of effort, and stability of the organization are more important than merely having friends around. Reba could be a candidate for customer service rep of the year with her emphasis on internal relationships within the organization and, quite possibly, between the organization and the community. The third-level ranking on control (20), five points *below* the LSI average, indicates that she'll take a driving role if pressed to do so, but she doesn't have a great deal of confidence in her ability to make things happen. Finally, compliance (10) is not something Reba loses much sleep over.

The dominance of concentration (40) on Reba's leadership motivation inventory can mean that she is a very thoughtful person who doesn't fly off half-cocked. She is just as passionately (40) driven to uphold her values (30), once she's thought them through. But she's likely to pursue these priorities in a quiet and determined manner, as suggested by her 10-points-below-LMI-average rankings on courage (20) and confidence (20). Overall, Reba is a people person. However, she's not a super-confident party-starter. Don't look for her to act spontaneously. She might organize the office bowling team, but probably not round people up for happy hour.

Stability Specialist		Leadership Styles				Leadership Motivations				
Name:	Leadership Style:	Control	Compliance	Social	Stability	Courage	Confidence	Concentration	Passion	Values
Fred	Control Specialist	40	30	20	10	30	10	40	50	20
Beth	Compliance Specialist	10	40	30	20	20	50	30	10	40
Reba	Social Specialist	20	10	40	30	20	20	40	40	30
Mark	Stability Specialist	30	20	10	40	50	40	10	20	30

Figure 4.9

Mark is a stability (40) specialist. Having a secondary emphasis on control (30), which is five points above LSI average, it could be that he is willing to take charge, if it's to establish and/or maintain balance in the organization, or between internal and external organizational factors. He's less worried about compliance (20), and least concerned with human relationships (social 10).

Like everyone else, Mark's LMI can be considered the second tier of his overall leadership profile. If the ranking of his leadership styles (stability, control, compliance, and social) considered along with the degrees of separation, are the first and second dimensions of analysis, then his LMI rankings and their degrees of separation are the third and fourth dimensions. There's a lot of data to consider. The LMI data definitely deepens and enriches our understanding of his leadership style inventory rankings.

Ranking high on courage (50 is maximum on the LMI), Mark is likely to take risks when solving problems or responding to emergencies. His secondary ranking on confidence (40) indicates he is reasonably sure that what he expects to happen *will* happen. His average dominance on values (30) indicates he moderately appreciates the need for policies and procedures, and the value of rules and guiding principles.

His 10-points-below-LMI-average dominance in passion (20) could indicate that he, like Beth, is not emotionally invested in any particular set of guiding principles; although he's slightly less likely to say, "Whatever works," Than Fred is. Mark ranks lowest on concentration (10). Consistent with his high courage ranking (50), he doesn't much like to sit around and ponder his options. He's much more likely to draw fast and shoot from the hip.

Peer-reporting inventories

Depending on the importance of the position, gathering increased data from multiple sources isn't so much about avoiding misrepresentation of information as it is about enriching the database. The more data you can collect, the more reliable the assessment. Peer-reporting inventories enrich the database. They also demonstrate the variance, if any, between an individual's self-perception and the more objective perceptions of others. Gathering 360-degree feedback is always a more reliable indicator than individual self-reporting.

We remind you again, as we constantly remind ourselves, that human behavior is more art than science. Despite all we have learned and know

about the human condition, as much, if not more, remains to be discovered and explained. Knowing who you are as an individual, and how you fit in your organization helps you to leap over many potential stumbling blocks, such as misalignment of your responsibilities with your essential nature. Regardless of the tremendous benefits that come from assessments, such as the LSI and LMI, it's best to remain flexible to variations in mood and adaptation to dynamic circumstances.

Having said that, the richer the data, the more reliable the results, which makes the process *more* scientific than mere guesswork. You could call it *educated art*. Even when working strictly with self-reporting inventories, the information is extremely valuable in the assessment of individual leadership strengths and the alignment of people with tasks and responsibilities.

It's your call whether to combine the self-reporting inventory with the peer-reporting inventories for a cumulative total. If the variance between self-reporting and the peer-reporting averages are five points or less in the various categories, we combine them all together and use that average. If the variances are five points or more in at least one leadership style (control, compliance, social, and stability) and one leadership motivation category (courage, confidence, concentration, passion, and values), we tend to rely on the peer-reporting inventories alone.

The peer-reporting inventories (see pages 83-85) are the strongest representation of how the individual is perceived in the organization. Depending on how important a spot on any particular team is, or how high-profile the initiative, the added value of peer-reporting inventories is, again, your call. In execution, a peer-reporting inventory is exactly the same process as the self-reporting inventory, except that you purposefully invite four or more people to rank terms for an identified individual. The column totals for each invited set of inventories will be entered on the chart in Figure 4.12 and then on the database chart, which you'll see in Chapter 5 (Figure 5.6).

Releasing Fred, Beth, Reba, and Mark

There is leadership potential in all four of these people that is either afraid to come out, or nothing in the way your organization currently operates encourages it to come out. We don't mean that every one of these people is willing or able to take up a sword and shield to lead the charge into the breach. Perhaps none of them will. That's why we're so relentless in preaching the gospel of the new *new* leadership school.

ComposiTeam Peer-Reporting Leadership Style Inventory for [*Name*]			
	Column A	**Column B**	**Column C**	**Column D**
Row 01►	Powerful 4-3-2-1	Analytical 4-3-2-1	Helpful 4-3-2-1	Capable 4-3-2-1
Row 02►	Fearless 4-3-2-1	Detailed 4-3-2-1	Friendly 4-3-2-1	Balanced 4-3-2-1
Row 03►	Controlling 4-3-2-1	Mathematical 4-3-2-1	Upbeat 4-3-2-1	Steady 4-3-2-1
Row 04►	Commanding 4-3-2-1	Accurate 4-3-2-1	Welcoming 4-3-2-1	Strategic 4-3-2-1
Row 05►	Impatient 4-3-2-1	Factual 4-3-2-1	Spontaneous 4-3-2-1	Patient 4-3-2-1
Row 06►	Determined 4-3-2-1	Careful 4-3-2-1	Caring 4-3-2-1	Reliable 4-3-2-1
Row 07►	Dominant 4-3-2-1	Precise 4-3-2-1	Agreeable 4-3-2-1	Rational 4-3-2-1
Row 08►	Competitive 4-3-2-1	Correct 4-3-2-1	Peaceful 4-3-2-1	Evaluative 4-3-2-1
Row 09►	Take Charge 4-3-2-1	Methodical 4-3-2-1	Social 4-3-2-1	Responsible 4-3-2-1
Row 10►	Vigorous 4-3-2-1	Systematic 4-3-2-1	Personable 4-3-2-1	Dependable 4-3-2-1
	Col. A TOTAL	**Col. B TOTAL**	**Col. C TOTAL**	**Col. D TOTAL**

Figure 4.10

Column A Total:		Control Specialist	
Column B Total:		Compliance Specialist	
Column C Total:		Social Specialist	
Column D Total:		Stability Specialist	
LSI Chart Total:	100		

Figure 4.11

ComposiTeam Peer-Reporting Leadership Motivation Inventory for [*Name*]				
Column A	**Column B**	**Column C**	**Column D**	**Column E**
Bold 5-4-3-2-1	Tenacious 5-4-3-2-1	Contemplative 5-4-3-2-1	Passionate 5-4-3-2-1	Honest 5-4-3-2-1
Backbone 5-4-3-2-1	Certain 5-4-3-2-1	Determined 5-4-3-2-1	Driven 5-4-3-2-1	Strong Beliefs 5-4-3-2-1
Brave 5-4-3-2-1	Cool 5-4-3-2-1	Logical 5-4-3-2-1	Eager 5-4-3-2-1	Fair & Just 5-4-3-2-1
Daring 5-4-3-2-1	Composed 5-4-3-2-1	Centered 5-4-3-2-1	Energetic 5-4-3-2-1	Principled 5-4-3-2-1
Defiant 5-4-3-2-1	Sure 5-4-3-2-1	A Finisher 5-4-3-2-1	Enthusiastic 5-4-3-2-1	Purposeful 5-4-3-2-1
Headstrong 5-4-3-2-1	Poised 5-4-3-2-1	Persistent 5-4-3-2-1	Excitable 5-4-3-2-1	Controlled 5-4-3-2-1
Adventurous 5-4-3-2-1	Resolute 5-4-3-2-1	Focused 5-4-3-2-1	Fervent 5-4-3-2-1	Dutiful 5-4-3-2-1
Gutsy 5-4-3-2-1	Secure 5-4-3-2-1	Absorbed 5-4-3-2-1	Inspired 5-4-3-2-1	Conscientious 5-4-3-2-1
Risk-Taker 5-4-3-2-1	Confident 5-4-3-2-1	Targeted 5-4-3-2-1	Spirited 5-4-3-2-1	Orderly 5-4-3-2-1
Courageous 5-4-3-2-1	Assured 5-4-3-2-1	Applied 5-4-3-2-1	Tireless 5-4-3-2-1	Compliant 5-4-3-2-1
Col. A **TOTAL**	**Col. B** **TOTAL**	**Col. C** **TOTAL**	**Col. D** **TOTAL**	**Col. E** **TOTAL**

Figure 4.12

Column A Total:		Courage
Column B Total:		Confidence
Column C Total:		Concentration
Column D Total:		Passion
Column E Total:		Values
LMI Chart Total:	150	

Figure 4.13

Peer-Reporting Leadership Style & Motivation Inventories		Leadership Styles				Leadership Motivations				
Peer-Reporting Inventory for:	Peer-Reporting Inventory filled out by:	Control	Compliance	Social	Stability	Courage	Confidence	Concentration	Passion	Values
Fred	Andy									
Fred	Amy									
Fred	Arnold									
Fred	Beth									
Fred	Donna									
Fred	Mark									
Fred	Reba									
Fred	Sally									
Category Column Totals:										
Divide by # of Inventories:		8	8	8	8	8	8	8	8	8
Peer-reporting Inventory Totals for Fred:										
Fred's Self-reporting Inventory Totals:										
*Variance:										

*Variance = Peer-reporting – Self-reporting

Figure 4.14

We've seen it happen time and time again: Fred, Beth, Reba, Mark, or any of millions like them, are encouraged, acknowledged, and/or rewarded to take greater ownership of the things they are most comfortable and best suited to do. They're not dragged kicking and screaming out of their comfort zones in order to justify paying them more, or to clone others to perform like they do, which is impossible. When their uniquenesses are honored and used to the organization's advantage, people stop merely doing things and things start getting done.

Any of these people could be you. They could be team members in your ring of responsibility. They might be the group or area leaders responsible for the work cell you belong to. As you consider Fred, Beth, Reba, and

Mark's essential leadership styles and motivation data, the best way to tame Org and thereby make the organization begin behaving as you want, is to align the *responsibilities* you ask them to accept, either individually or corporately, with their *leadership profiles.*

If you ask Fred to do something different than what he is most predisposed to do, you're inviting push back, and possibly a complete disconnect. When we begin to profile jobs, tasks, objectives, projects, and initiatives in Chapter 5, you'll see more clearly how the alignment is achieved. It will also become more apparent how far off your present alignment of individuals and teams to tasks, objectives, projects, and initiatives might be, which can explain a great deal in sluggish individual and organization performance.

Calculating Composite Personality

You now know how filling out the leadership style and motivation inventories, either as a self-reporting instrument or a peer review, builds a database of individual information. Self-reporting instruments provide good information to work with. And 360-degree, or peer-reporting, instruments provide richer, more reliable information to work with. It all depends on the relative value of the assignments being made and the responsibilities associated with the job, task, objective, and/or initiative.

Importance is relative, of course, but certain things are just common sense. A team planning the softball banquet is important, but not as important as a senior executive team determining how to restructure the organization's compensation and benefits packages. Decisions made by teams designing new product lines and competitive pricing schemes can affect lots of people inside and outside of the organization, on many levels. The richer the data upon which to make team selections, the better.

Whether the data is self-reported or peer-reported, you can now tell, with a quick glance at the numbers, if a person is a control, compliance, social, or stability specialist. Once each individual's data is on file, you're only a few calculations away from the composite personality of a team. Although team selection is premature before the job, task, objective and/or initiative profiling exercise in Chapter 5 is completed, the calculation is so simple and straightforward that we've chosen to tag it onto the inventories discussion.

Fred's, Beth's, Reba's, and Mark's Composite Personality

There should not be any more people on a team than there are functions to be carried out. We find that when eight to 12 people are arbitrarily placed together to "study" something, and come back with "recommendations," Vilfredo Pareto's 80/20 law kicks in. Invariably, a few team members actually wind up doing something meaningful, and the rest just show up—if that. Part of the team formation process, based on the task, objective, project, or initiative profiling you're learn about in Chapter 5, needs to consider the optimal number of people it will take to execute the task, reach the objective, or complete the initiative.

For the moment, we have Fred, Beth, Reba, and Mark. We don't know what they'll be asked to do as a team, if anything. But they're our guinea pigs to calculate composite personality. Remember that we don't know how much of any character component is above or beneath the surface. The LSI and LMI merely told us what is there.

Calculating composite personality is like putting on a pair of infrared night-vision goggles in the dark and seeing the shape of a dragon appear before you. Prior to that, you might not have ever seen him, although you saw the aftermath of his nightly foraging, and could occasionally hear snoring coming from the custodial closet. Once again, measuring leadership style and motivation makes the invisible *visible*. Start with Fred's, Beth's, Reba's, and Mark's LSI and LMI numbers:

Database Numbers		Leadership Styles				Leadership Motivations				
Name:	Leadership Style:	Control	Compliance	Social	Stability	Courage	Confidence	Concentration	Passion	Values
Fred	Control Specialist	40	30	20	10	30	10	40	50	20
Beth	Compliance Specialist	10	40	30	20	20	50	30	10	40
Reba	Social Specialist	20	10	40	30	20	20	40	40	30
Mark	Stability Specialist	30	20	10	40	50	40	10	20	30

Figure 4.15

Add up each column of column totals and divide by the number of team members as shown in Figure 4.16.

Calculating Composite Personality		Leadership Styles				Leadership Motivations				
Name:	Leadership Style:	Control	Compliance	Social	Stability	Courage	Confidence	Concentration	Passion	Values
Fred	Control Specialist	40	30	20	10	30	10	40	50	20
Beth	Compliance Specialist	10	40	30	20	20	50	30	10	40
Reba	Social Specialist	20	10	40	30	20	20	40	40	30
Mark	Stability Specialist	30	20	10	40	50	40	10	20	30
	Column Totals:	100	100	100	100	120	120	120	120	120
Divide by # of Inventories:		4	4	4	4	4	4	4	4	4
Composite Leadership Profile:		25	25	25	25	30	30	30	30	30

Figure 4.16

That's how simple it is to calculate composite personality. Add up the column totals for each of the leadership style inventory and leadership motivation inventory columns and divide by the number of team members. If your database includes LSI and LMI information on every person in your organization, you can look at your corporate culture as easily as reading a blueprint. Using the ComposiTeam Leadership System as a diagnostic tool, you can profile anything from a simple task to a major initiative and calculate the composite personality of the team you've assigned to execute the task or initiative, and see how well aligned they are.

Provided you have your organizational population's leadership profiles in your database, you can even calculate the composite personality of your entire enterprise (your culture) and profile your mission statement, and see if the fingerprints match. As you'll see in Chapter 5, you can calculate the variance between where you want your culture to be, and where it is. Whether the composite personality of your team aligns with your initiative profile or not, you will know the variance, category by category, you need to compensate for. You might not like what you see, but at least you'll be able to see it; perhaps for the first time.

Symmetry

There will be times when leadership style and/or leadership motivation categories will match. We call this symmetry. We always list the categories in the same order in the name of consistency. The leadership style specializations are always in this order: Control, Compliance, Social, Stability.

Unless one ranks higher than control. In that case, the highest column total wins the name game. If *social* specialization has the highest column total in an individual inventory or a composite personality, the leadership style of the individual or the team is *social specialist.* If two categories *tie* for the top spot, as in Figure 4.17, then the team has a *symmetrical control/social specialization.* An individual would be called a "symmetrical control/social specialist."

You probably noticed that our sample team (Fred, Beth, Reba, and Mark) is completely symmetrical in terms of composite leadership style (see the Composite Leadership Profile line in Figure 4.16). Not only is that rare, you probably don't want a completely symmetrical composite personality; unless of course you have a perfectly symmetrical job, task, objective, project, or initiative profile to align them with. In real life, you're more likely to see a team that looks like this:

Calculating Composite Personality		Leadership Styles				Leadership Motivations				
Name:	**Leadership Style:**	Control	Compliance	Social	Stability	Courage	Confidence	Concentration	Passion	Values
Amy	Control Specialist	39	11	38	12	40	32	20	48	10
Andy	Compliance Specialist	21	40	17	22	23	24	45	17	41
Amelia	Social Specialist	37	12	38	13	15	18	27	49	41
Arnold	Stability Specialist	21	25	25	29	23	23	44	13	47
	Column Totals:	118	88	118	76	101	97	136	127	139
	Divide by # of Inventories:	4	4	4	4	4	4	4	4	4
	Composite Leadership Profile:	29.5	22	29.5	19	25.25	24.25	34	31.75	34.75

Figure 4.17

Yep, a symmetrical "control/social" composite leadership profile (29.5/ 29.5). The leadership style inventory has a marginally high variance of 10.5 between control/social (29.5) at the high end, and stability (19) at the low end. Not an earth-shattering variance, but many composite leadership profiles have less overall variance. In Figure 4.17, no LSI category varies more than 4.5 above or 6 below the LSI average of 25.

The composite leadership motivation inventory is not as symmetrical. Reading the LMI side, Amy, Andy, Amelia, and Arnold's composite personality appears to follow the rules and value procedures and order in things (values = 34.75; 4.75 above the LMI average of 30). They're also a thinking bunch, as evidenced by their high concentration ranking (34; 4 above the LMI average). The LMI in Figure 4.17 is *fairly* well balanced, with a maximum variance of 10.5 between values and confidence, and no single category varying from the average of 30 by more than 4.75 above or 5.75 below.

In the examples we've been using, we have four team members. Unless someone can make a case for more, Fred, Beth, Reba, and Mark, or Amy, Andy, Amelia, and Arnold, should be able to get the job done. We'll delve more into the size of teams in Chapter 6. But, for now, we have yet to profile the job. How do you know which team members to bring together to execute a task, project, objective, or initiative if you haven't profiled the task, project, objective, or initiative…much less know how many should be *on the team*? A crusty newspaper editor once told his reporters to never use the word "very" in an article unless they were willing to substitute the word "damn." We'll go on record saying that the step of profiling the job, task, project, objective, or initiative in Chapter 5 is *very* important.

It's a system

It's critical to point out that your organization is a *system*. When one thing changes, everything is altered. If, for example, the initiative you profile in Chapter 5 calls for a strong control specialization, with a sense of urgency and a need for boldness, you might decide to add Amy to the team of Fred, Beth, Reba, and Mark; thereby altering the system. If five team members will make the team more effective, then adding Amy will move you in the direction you want to go. Working strictly with the potential team members we have in front of us at this moment, and wanting to strengthen control specialization, we suggest adding Amy to create a five-member team with Fred, Beth, Reba, and Mark.

Adding Amy		Leadership Styles				Leadership Motivations				
Name:	Leadership Style:	Control	Compliance	Social	Stability	Courage	Confidence	Concentration	Passion	Values
Amy	Control Specialist	39	11	38	12	40	32	20	48	10
Fred	Control Specialist	40	30	20	10	30	10	40	50	20
Beth	Compliance Specialist	10	40	30	20	20	50	30	10	40
Reba	Social Specialist	20	10	40	30	20	20	40	40	30
Mark	Stability Specialist	30	20	10	40	50	40	10	20	30
	Column Totals:	139	111	138	112	160	152	140	168	130
Divide by # of Inventories:		5	5	5	5	5	5	5	5	5
Composite Leadership Profile:		27.8	22.2	27.6	22.4	32	30.4	28	33.6	26

Figure 4.18

Without Beth		Leadership Styles				Leadership Motivations				
Name:	Leadership Style:	Control	Compliance	Social	Stability	Courage	Confidence	Concentration	Passion	Values
Fred	Control Specialist	40	30	20	10	30	10	40	50	20
Reba	Social Specialist	20	10	40	30	20	20	40	40	30
Mark	Stability Specialist	30	20	10	40	50	40	10	20	30
	Column Totals:	90	60	70	80	100	70	90	110	80
Divide by # of Inventories:		3	3	3	3	3	3	3	3	3
Composite Leadership Profile:		30	20	23.33	26.67	33.33	23.33	30	36.67	26.67

Figure 4.19

Substituting Amy for Beth		Leadership Styles				Leadership Motivations				
Name:	Leadership Style:	Control	Compliance	Social	Stability	Courage	Confidence	Concentration	Passion	Values
Amy	Control Specialist	39	11	38	12	40	32	20	48	10
Fred	Compliance Specialist	40	30	20	10	30	10	40	50	20
Reba	Social Specialist	20	10	40	30	20	20	40	40	30
Mark	Stability Specialist	30	20	10	40	50	40	10	20	30
	Column Totals:	129	71	108	92	140	102	110	158	90
Divide by # of Inventories:		4	4	4	4	4	4	4	4	4
Composite Leadership Profile:		32.25	17.75	27	23	35	25.5	27.5	39.5	22.5

Figure 4.20

Add Yourself		Leadership Styles				Leadership Motivations				
Name:	Leadership Style:	Control	Compliance	Social	Stability	Courage	Confidence	Concentration	Passion	Values
Fred	Compliance Specialist	40	30	20	10	30	10	40	50	20
Reba	Social Specialist	20	10	40	30	20	20	40	40	30
Mark	Stability Specialist	30	20	10	40	50	40	10	20	30
	Column Totals:									
Divide by # of Inventories:		4	4	4	4	4	4	4	4	4
Composite Leadership Profile:										

Figure 4.21

The five-member team of Amy, Fred, Beth, Reba, and Mark produced a control specialist composite leadership profile, but not much of one, with only a 0.2 margin between control and social. Although we haven't profiled our initiative yet, we assume a more dominant control specialization is in order. If the initiative can be handled effectively by three people, you might choose *not* to add Beth in the first place.

The composite leadership profile of Fred, Reba, and Mark (in Figure 4.19) is that of a control specialist. We just don't know if it's *enough* of a control specialist. We won't know that until we profile the initiative. We won't even know if we *want* a composite control specialist until we profile the initiative. You can see, however, that mixing and matching leadership style and motivation inventories in your data will eventually produce the right mix, or as close as possible, given who is available to you.

By not selecting Beth for the team, and letting Fred, Reba, and Mark handle things, you produced a composite personality with a control specialization, just as you did by adding Amy. By adding Amy to make a five-member team, the composite control specialization wasn't as strong. A 3.33 margin in favor of control over the next highest category, stability, was created by not selecting Beth in the first place vs. a mere 0.2 variance in favor of control by adding Amy to the existing team. The ComposiTeam Leadership System is extremely flexible. Another alternative is to create a four-member team with Amy *instead of* Beth (Figure 4.20).

Choosing Amy for this particular team instead of Beth increased the margin between control specialization and social specialization in the composite leadership profile to 5.25, up from 3.33 in the previous best-case scenario. Now that you know your self-reporting LSI and LMI column totals, plug your own personal data into this scenario (Figure 4.21) and see how your presence in the number four spot alters the system.

Chapter 4 Summary:
Keys to Unleashing Leadership

↝ **Love those inventories:** The leadership style inventory reveals the essential leadership style embedded in an individual's personality. The leadership motivation inventory ranks the most likely behavioral response to a dynamic and changing environment. The LMI tends to vary from test to retest much more than the LSI, due to the LMI's adaptive nature. Together, the LSI and LMI information for each individual in your organization forms a database from which you'll be able to align individuals and teams to jobs, tasks, projects, objectives, and initiatives.

- **Peer-reporting vs. self-reporting:** The more data you collect, the higher the reliability. LSI and LMI data that you solicit from a range of peers provides you with several helpful options. Comparing peer-reporting data to self-reporting data is an eye-opener as far as the self-reporting individual's self-awareness. The comparison can confirm the self-reporting data, which indicates the individual has a good grasp on reality. Or it can vary widely, indicating the individual has a distorted self-image, or there is major conspiracy to undermine him or her. Either way, you have a situation to deal with.

- **Honesty is the best policy:** Attempting to fudge the rankings on the ComposiTeam LSI and LMI is a short-sighted, not to mention *unethical,* ploy. No one who fills out the inventories knows how often or in how many ways they'll be used to align unique leadership profiles to various jobs, tasks, projects, objectives, and initiatives. If a person tries to present him- or herself in a particularly favorable manner, we scratch our heads and ask, favorable to what? Some of the best professional opportunities might present themselves to people with just your profile, and you won't know when they're coming. You also want to avoid living a life of make-believe, pretending to be someone you're not. It's not good for your blood pressure.

- **Calculating composite personality:** What you see before you might not be what you're dealing with. Most of what drives human behavior is beneath the surface in the unconscious. The difference when it comes to group behavior is the increased amount of unaccounted for style and motivation data. Team performance and productivity are driven more by the composite personality of team members than by visible individual personalities. That's why the ComposiTeam Leadership System helps to make the invisible *visible.*

- **Org sweating bullets:** As you begin to collect LSI and LMI data on members of your organizational population, you're already changing your culture. If only for paying attention to your people and what makes them tick. Like the Western Electric Hawthorne studies of the 1920s, performance will improve simply by virtue of the fact you're paying attention. You, of course, are not going to stop there. You're on your way to installing a leadership system throughout your organization that will build on the foundation of your previous leadership development activities and personality typology work, with particular emphasis on best fit between jobs, tasks, projects, objectives, initiatives, and the people best suited to shoulder the responsibility with a confident, leadership attitude.

As you move on to Chapter 5, rest assured that you arc already on your way to mastering two pieces of the three-piece CompositeTeam Leadership System. Aligning what people do best with what organizations need most begins with determining what people do best. You now know how to do that. We're not talking about competencies; we're referring to essential leadership styles and motivations. Competencies are important, but they're part of another discussion.

We have always held that, if you're forced to choose, willingness to do the work trumps competency. Willingness to be a team player beats raw talent. Just look at the United States 2004 men's Olympic basketball team—individually: phenomenal, as a team: questionable. If a person is eager, willing, and able to perform a role in an organization, and has sufficient intelligence and aptitude, we'll recommend hiring or promoting that person over an incredibly competent but cynical person every time.

Of course there are effective ways of turning cynical people into highly motivated people. But, out of the blocks, bad apples will do more harm to the bushel than all their competency and talent will contribute. If you consciously or unconsciously hire, or promote, negativity in your organization, guess what you will be spending your time and energy undoing from now until the cows come home?

Don't blame Org for underutilized team member potential. He's just following the trail of crumbs you created. You're close to cleaning up the crumbs. You now know how to assemble leadership style and motivation data. Next, we'll show you exactly how to use it to align what your people do best with what your organization needs most.

Chapter 5

The Initiative Profile

The best preparation for good work tomorrow is to do good work today.

—Elbert Hubbard,
American editor, author, and publisher

Teams, just like individual members of your organizational population, are being paid to perform a function, which is to say, to get specific things done. Before you will know if a person is right for a particular function, or a place on a leadership team, the function needs to be profiled. Otherwise, what is your criteria for selecting the individual to begin with? Profiling a job, task, objective, project, or initiative means *identifying the ideal behavioral characteristics to execute that function.* Unless your team will be made up of robots, the function must be defined in terms of human behavior. Before you assemble a team, you must have a profile of what the team is expected to accomplish—in human terms. It's the old *form follows function* imperative.

Used properly, the CompositTeam Leadership System is a strategic, tactical tool; not an activity to amuse boredom. *Not* aligning what your people do best with what your organization needs most will waste time, energy, and resources. The same old, same old, as familiar as it is, will doom your supervisors, managers, and executives to continue pounding square pegs through round holes. They'll come in every day and start pushing the boulder up the steep hill—*again.*

Org likes organizations that have become so preoccupied with doing things that they rarely get anything done. There's a lot of waste in organizations like that. Just as one person's ceiling is another person's floor, wasted organizational growth and development efforts are a dragon's abundance. Once you begin to collect leadership style and motivation information in your human resources or departmental database, however, Org will begin sniffing the air, not sure what's going on. He won't know what to make of it at first, but he'll suspect that what you're about to do is not a rerun of the same old training and development stuff. He won't know whether to be curious or angry.

All of your leadership style and motivation data could eventually end up in Org's stomach if you don't complete the final two steps in the CompositTeam three-step process:

1. Create a database of leadership styles and motivations for everyone you want in your pool of potential leadership team members.

2. Profile every initiative, objective, project, and/or task you want to form leadership teams to address.

3. Match the initiative profile to the composite leadership profile of the team that best fits.

Because you don't know which individuals will contribute most to the composite leadership style profiles that will best align with the initiative profiles you'll create, we recommend that your database contain as many people as possible; *especially* people you might not initially consider selecting for a leadership team. To us, everybody's a leader. Not a *potential* leader, but a *leader*.

This applies even to organizations that have done extensive typology assessment work in the past. Org has eaten quite a few personality and aptitude assessments over the years, because nothing was ever done with them. They gathered dust in personnel files, or became part of the discarded stack of stuff that was originally intended to improve something, got used once or twice, and left out for the dragon like cookies for Santa on Christmas Eve.

If you use the CompositTeam Leadership System, Org will have to shape up or ship out. The LSI and LMI information you gather and store in your database will be in play as long as you have jobs and tasks to be done, objectives to reach, projects to be finished, and initiatives to be carried out. You'll see momentarily how quickly you can profile jobs, tasks, projects, objectives, and initiatives. Once that's done, you begin alignment, using the leadership profiles in your database.

Speed Is on Your Side

When you sit down with your team, department, or any group of potential team members, and have them fill out the LSI and LMI, you should have completed inventories in hand within 15 minutes, sometimes less. Profiling the job, task, objective, or initiative will take another 15 to 30 minutes, depending on whether or not you make it a group exercise and how much discussion you allow. Spend another 15 minutes aligning composite personalities of teams to the initiative profile and, *in one hour*, you will have a more scientifically selected, higher-performing team, and better alignment between essential leadership styles and motivations and initiative requirements than you've ever had before.

It's a good idea to have people fill out their self-reporting and peer-reporting inventories in advance of an initiative profiling and alignment session. Have them use the forms provided online at *www.compositeam.com*. Once the individual leadership style and motivation inventories are stored in your database, profiling initiatives and aligning best-fit teams will be a much faster process. Isn't that what we all like to hear? Faster, cheaper, better!

The Second Step Becomes the First

Technically speaking, gathering leadership style and motivation information to populate your database of self-reporting and/or peer-reporting inventories is the first thing you'll do, like registering to vote. However, once you've completed the three-step process—completing inventories, profiling the initiative, and aligning the team's composite leadership profile with the initiative profile—each subsequent time you go back to profile another initiative and assemble another team, you begin with step two: you just go vote. Most organizations we work with continuously expand their databases with new people and their LSI and LMI information. The process of building a database of potential team members is only limited by the pool of potential team members available to you.

Leaders with the broadest responsibilities identify initiatives that need to be carried out to complete the overall organizational agenda and achieve the organization's stated goals and objectives. This means determining what they want the organization to achieve in terms of outcomes. These can be financial outcomes, saving the environment outcomes, converting the nonbelievers outcomes, becoming better corporate citizens outcomes—the stuff mission statements are made of.

Successful achievement of the outcomes becomes more likely with a systematic approach that ties the mission to the jobs, tasks, projects, objectives, and initiatives required to realize the desired outcomes. It's a matter of translating ideas into action. The function determines the form. You'll see momentarily that the initiative profiling process is designed to *operationalize ideas*. It translates concepts into the human behavior (*action*) needed to make them real.

Profiling the Initiative

Once an initiative is identified to fill or repair a gap between where an organization is and where it wants to be, it's time to select a leadership team to go after it, right? *Wrong.* Once an initiative is identified, it's time to *profile it.* As a rule, organizational planners and strategists spend far too little time thinking through the various implications of what they're suggesting be done. Then, without a clear picture of what's involved, they select people to serve on teams to tackle the still-ambiguous initiative. Is it any wonder so many team efforts fall short of their charters? It's not necessarily poor team leadership. It's more likely fuzzy reality.

There will always be a certain amount of, "They'll figure it out," wishful thinking around teamwork. You want teams to be free and unobstructed thinkers who will conceive new and creative ways to do things faster, cheaper, and better. But they will be better equipped to do that if they are clearly directed. To say, "We have a problem. Get some folks together, and tell them to go solve it," is not good leadership.

Great leaders say, "We have a problem. Let's profile it, and then assemble the people who best fit the behavioral requirements to address it." They'll take the lead on suggesting solutions, or, possibly, report back that we misread the problem and need to revise the profile.

Owning the initiative

As much as we like to believe that teams can be self-directed, and as hard as we try to give them total autonomy, there is always the issue of ultimate accountability. The buck has to stop somewhere. Somebody has to be responsible for putting a leadership team together and seeing to it that the results are followed through on. We call this person the *initiative owner*, because the team being assembled is built around an initiative that can be translated into actionable language such as reaching a goal, achieving an objective, or completing a task or project.

The whole point is to get something done, make something better than it was, discover a new way, reach more customers, or anything that will make a lasting and sustainable improvement on behalf of your organization and its many and varied stakeholders. It's certainly important to recognize who *owns the initiative.* By the one "who owns the initiative," we're talking about the leader with the broadest responsibility for seeing to it that the initiative is successfully executed.

Beyond that, we really *are* talking about a self-directed team. How much input will be optimal from the outside vs. how much knowledge acquisition and idea generation will be expected from the inside? All of this is in the context of the team's composite personality or composite leadership profile.

The initiative owner is tasked with distributing responsibility and sharing leadership with the right people. The initiative profile/team composite leadership profile alignment determines who those people are. But the initiative, or need for the initiative, must be formalized first. That means that most initiatives originate in the outermost rings of organizational responsibility. The wider the ring of responsibility, the higher-level the profile. As the high-level initiative profile is considered by teams in smaller rings of responsibility, it becomes more detailed and actionable. The initiative owner is responsible for establishing and maintaining the reporting schedule and communications process to connect the team members' work with the initiators of the initiative.

We also like to see initiatives born in the innermost rings of responsibility, where the screws get turned, the software gets written, the prospecting phone calls are dialed, or any other work cell where rubber is meeting the road. Even if initiatives are begun in the outermost rings of organizational responsibility, the profiling process should include representatives from the innermost rings, where the actual work gets done, as a reality check. It's hard to get a detailed perspective if you are orbiting far away from the flash point. The perspective of those with a closer view will always improve the profile.

Naming the initiative

Naming the initiative is important to ensure that expectations are clear. Initiative initiators and/or initiative owners use the naming process to:

› Refine their thinking about what needs to be accomplished.

› Consider all the implications of the initiative.

› Anticipate intended and unintended consequences and outcomes.

› Work and rework the name of the initiative accordingly.

This naming exercise, in and of itself, will significantly increase the odds that the initiative will be successfully executed. The naming process refines and focuses the job, task, objective, or initiative, and will eventually lead to the selection of the best combination of team members to execute the initiative and achieve the desired outcomes. The initiative must be named with *action terms* and *specific goals* that accurately reflect the nature of and remove all ambiguity about what is expected:

> ›   "Reduce annual employee turnover by 15 percent," is better than, "Reduce annual employee turnover."

> ›   "Reduce annual employee turnover by 15 percent with better Employee Recognition," is better yet.

> ›   "Increase customer retention," is better than, "Do a better job with customers."

> ›   "Increase customer retention by 15 percent," is better yet.

> ›   "Increase sales by 15 percent," is better than, "Increase sales."

> ›   "Increase sales *revenues* by 15 percent," is better yet.

> ›   "Reduce waste by 15 percent," is better than, "Reduce waste."

> ›   "Reduce wasted consumables by 15 percent," is more specific.

> ›   "Increase daily output," is better than, "Increase output."

> ›   "Increase daily output by 15 percent," is better yet.

Change the name until it's right

Reworking the initiative's names several times, before team selection, is not unusual. We suggest giving the initiative a preliminary name and then ranking the terms on the initiative profile. After engaging in the discussion required to rank the terms, some tweaking of the name might be in order. Like we said, the naming and profiling exercises are like action research in that they raise awareness and cause creative juices to flow, even if nothing further is done.

Naming the initiative is important so that expectations are clear. Nothing ensures Org a big, juicy midnight meal more than ambiguous expectations and confusing instructions. When you are comfortable with the name you've assigned the initiative, enter it on the initiative style and motivation profile, and on the Initiative Profile line of Figure 5.5.

Public or private?

The initiative owner must be identified and the initiative must be named in a way that clearly and unambiguously ties the purpose to *action*. The profiling process itself might suggest that the first action is to change the name and owner of the initiative, but that's the nature of learning more about anything. The initiative profile can be filled out in a facilitated face-to-face session, facilitated online session, or filled out by an invited group of participants who receive, fill out, and return the initiative profile by e-mail, in a variation on the Delphi technique.

All of these approaches, used together, give the best results. In a facilitated discussion, open dialogue emerges around what the organization's priorities should be, and what actions best promote those interests. Some people participate fully in open, public discussion and debate. Some people are withdrawn and withholding. Outspoken or underspoken, nobody has a monopoly on the truth or perspective. Therefore it's better to enrich your data and increase the reliability of the outcome by inviting as much public *and* private input as possible.

Initiative Profile Principles

A ComposiTeam initiative profile uses the same terms as the self-reporting and peer-reporting inventories. The idea is to create the ideal personality to execute the initiative, which can be as specific or broad as tasks, jobs, projects, objectives, or even profiling a mission statement to see how the executive team's composite personality lines up to the initiative profile. Think of it as the *bionic team member*. You now have the technology to build him or her better than before.

You're not actually building anyone, but you are identifying the ideal candidate to carry out the initiative. The new technology (that is, the ComposiTeam Leadership System) will empower you to match the composite leadership profile of a leadership team to the ideal personality you identify in the initiative profiling exercise. Don't fill out the initiative profile with your current staff in mind. Fill it out with only the *ideal* personality in mind. The system will reveal the composite leadership profile that best matches the initiative profile. Often, that turns out to be a different group than you might have originally thought. Don't limit your possibilities by prejudging who is best for what.

The initiative profile follows the same nine-category contextual framework as an individual's leadership profile and a team's composite leadership profile. Just as the self-reporting and peer-reporting ComposiTeam inventories document leadership styles and motivations, the initiative profiling process can also translate a job description, task, project, objective, and/or initiative into behavioral, actionable terms. These are the overriding concepts behind the initiative profiling terms you'll be ranking:

1. **Control.** How *urgent* is this initiative in terms of the calendar? Is it more important that something get done, even if it's not done right? Usually not. Yet going off half-cocked is nothing new in organizations. Dwight D. Eisenhower said that truly important things are seldom urgent and what seems urgent is usually not that important (or words to that effect). John Kenneth Galbraith said it like this: "It is almost as important to know what's not serious as it is to know what is." Substitute the word "urgent" for "serious" and we're back on point. In our organizational experience, both men are right more often than not. Too often, too much time is allowed for urgent matters and opportunities are missed. Meanwhile, we can be too impatient to find and apply the best resolution for important issues, and yet more opportunities are missed. It's still important for something or someone to keep things moving forward. When it comes to urgency, assumptions can hurt you. The urgency issue needs to be recognized and thoroughly discussed.

2. **Compliance.** How critical is it that every *t* is crossed and every *i* is dotted? Is it a high priority that the columns reconcile? Is this initiative centered around legal, financial, or regulatory needs for *accuracy* and *correctness*? Is it a matter of risk management? If you take additional time to contemplate the quantitative implications, are you diminishing your chances of achieving the best outcome? Profitability and good stewardship of precious resources are always important. How about engineering the perfect machine before the switch is thrown or the key is turned in the ignition? The design process could go on forever if it is allowed to. The value and priorities of correctness and degree of perfection need to be recognized and thoroughly considered.

3. **Social.** Business is about people—plain and simple. It's ultimately a *human relationships* equation. For-profit organizations and not-for-profit organizations exist to serve the needs of human beings and the environment in which we live. Human resourcefulness designs, develops, and delivers the solutions to human wants and needs. How does the initiative under consideration affect human relationships? Is it likely to build and sustain stronger relationships or fracture existing relationships, even diminishing the potential to build new ones? The human cost of initiatives is sometimes the last to be considered, even though the real cost of alienating individuals and groups can be enormous in the near and far term. What value do you place on relationships both internal and external to the organization? People are not as predictable as financial analysis. But people are the source of

all revenues as well as the most sophisticated data-processing tools in generating it. The quality and sustainability of human relationships needs to be factored into the initiative profile.

4. **Stability.** Although organizations have obligations to both their internal and external customers, they also have an obligation to preserve themselves and provide the most *balanced* platform for employment and performance possible. The populations both internal and external to organizations must have their needs met and their health and well-beings provided for if an organization can truly consider itself successful. How can the organization meet such obligations if it is not successful? In terms of balanced planning and execution, what about the urgency issues? What about the use of resources and accountability to governing authority? What about fairness to all involved with and affected by the initiative? Issues of internal and external organizational stability must be addressed in the initiative map.

5. **Courage.** Will the execution of this initiative require an immense sense of personal *power*? Is it the type of courage that is based mostly on a devil-may-care attitude, more than on a proven track record? Does this initiative call for recklessness or merely thinking outside the box? Should caution be thrown to the wind? Will it require boldly going where no one has ever gone before? Will the successful planning and execution of this initiative rely a great deal on self-generated power? Will it matter who is in charge? Does there need to be a dominant personality who's not afraid to take risks and live dangerously?

6. **Confidence.** Confidence, as we use the term, is a form of courage, based on *knowledge* and *experience.* How much does the planning and execution of this initiative depend on solid knowledge of the subject? Is hands-on experience valuable in this initiative, or is theoretical knowledge sufficient? How well grounded does the thinking need to be? How solidly grounded does the team need to be? To what degree is there latitude for discovery? How important is it that what's predicted to happen actually happens? To what degree does the outcome need to be assured?

7. **Concentration.** Sometimes an initiative needs to be well thought out. Deliberate patience to give ideas time to incubate is frequently the best course. The planning and execution of some initiatives need to consider issues such as *persistence* and *focus* on the front end, as well as how they are built into the process. By asking these questions in advance, patience, and the space to let ideas mature, can be protected, if

that's what the originators of the initiative have determined is necessary. Concentrators are not impatient people. They prefer the faint sound of wheels turning inside their heads to noisy distractions.

8. **Passion.** What role will *energy* and *enthusiasm* play in the planning and execution of this initiative? The more linear or data-driven the initiative is, the more likely energy and enthusiasm will be played down in favor of other factors, such as persistence and accuracy. On the other hand, enthusiasm and energy can be very important if the initiative is built around potentially emotional issues like creativity, invention, branding, sales, or marketing. Passion is best represented by an individual's *inability* to keep his or her feelings bottled up inside. When people feel good about something, it's like shaking a soda can and then opening it. That's the kind of stored leadership energy you have everywhere in your organization. All you need to unleash it is an intelligent, systematic way to shake it up.

9. **Values.** How important is it to stay inside the box and follow the *rules*? If the initiative calls for tremendous creativity, excessive rule-following might bind up the process and limit the range of outcomes. Flip that coin over if the initiative is intended to establish limitations that save the organization's resources or help the organization comply with important regulations. Respect for rules might then be in order. You can appreciate how important it is to ask these questions in advance, through the initiative profiling exercise, so the composite profile you select will produce the team best suited to execute the initiative. The highest performing teams are managed by principles just as much as they are driven toward achieving outcomes.

Initiative Profile Instructions

To illustrate, we've filled out an initiative profile we named "Increase sales revenues by 15%." The numbers our clients have come up with in the past might or might not bear any similarity or resemblance to initiative profiles you create for initiatives in your organization. What you will see in this illustration is how the ranking of descriptive terms in the initiative style and motivation profiles produces a distinct fingerprint that can be matched to the fingerprint of a composite leadership profile.

The most defining step in aligning an organizational initiative with the optimal combination of team members (that is, those *collectively* best suited to execute the initiative, vis-à-vis their composite leadership profile) is to profile the initiative. As you did on the self-reporting and/or peer-reporting leadership *style* inventory, rank terms in each row in Figure 5.1 with 4, 3, 2, or 1 next to each of the words in each row. No two terms in the same row (across) can have the same number. The sum of each row across will always be 10.

Once you finish ranking the terms in a single row across, drop down to the next row and repeat the process for each of the 10 rows on the grid. Each of the four *columns* will add up to no more than 40 and no less than 10.

ComposiTeam Initiative Style Profile: Increase Sales Revenues by 15%			
	Column A	**Column B**	**Column C**	**Column D**
Row 01 ▶	Powerful **4**-3-2-1	Analytical 4-3-2-**1**	Helpful 4-**3**-2-1	Capable 4-3-**2**-1
Row 02 ▶	Fearless **4**-3-2-1	Detailed 4-3-2-**1**	Friendly 4-**3**-2-1	Balanced 4-3-**2**-1
Row 03 ▶	Controlling 4-**3**-2-1	Mathematical 4-3-2-**1**	Upbeat **4**-3-2-1	Steady 4-3-**2**-1
Row 04 ▶	Commanding **4**-3-2-1	Accurate 4-3-2-**1**	Welcoming 4-3-**2**-1	Strategic 4-**3**-2-1
Row 05 ▶	Impatient **4**-3-2-1	Factual 4-3-**2**-1	Spontaneous 4-**3**-2-1	Patient 4-3-2-**1**
Row 06 ▶	Determined **4**-3-2-1	Careful 4-3-2-**1**	Caring 4-**3**-2-1	Reliable 4-3-**2**-1
Row 07 ▶	Dominant **4**-3-2-1	Precise 4-3-2-**1**	Agreeable 4-**3**-2-1	Rational 4-3-**2**-1
Row 08 ▶	Competitive **4**-3-2-1	Correct 4-3-**2**-1	Peaceful 4-3-2-**1**	Evaluative 4-**3**-2-1
Row 09 ▶	Take Charge **4**-3-2-1	Methodical 4-**3**-2-1	Social 4-3-**2**-1	Responsible 4-3-2-**1**
Row 10 ▶	Vigorous **4**-3-2-1	Systematic 4-**3**-2-1	Personable 4-3-**2**-1	Dependable 4-3-2-**1**
	Col. A TOTAL 39	**Col. B TOTAL** 16	**Col. C TOTAL** 26	**Col. D TOTAL** 19

Figure 5.1

Column A Total:	39	Control Specialist
Column B Total:	16	Compliance Specialist
Column C Total:	26	Social Specialist
Column D Total:	19	Stability Specialist
Initiative Style Chart Total:	100	

Figure 5.2

The sum of the four columns must be exactly 100. Transfer the column totals to the corresponding control, compliance, social, and stability spots on the initiative line on Figure 5.2.

Just like the leadership motivation inventory, the grid for the initiative motivation profile is similar to the initiative style profile, and serves a similar purpose. Like the initiative style profile, you are again describing the ideal, *bionic,* team member (as in *composite personality*) as honestly and accurately as possible, in the context of leadership. Note that there are now five columns instead of four, but there are still 10 rows. Beside each of the terms *in each row across*, circle or highlight a number from 5 to 1, with 5 beside the term that *best describes* the ideal team member, and 1 beside the term that *least* describes the ideal composite personality for the named initiative.

ComposiTeam Initiative Motivation Profile: Increase Sales Revenues by 15%				
Column A	**Column B**	**Column C**	**Column D**	**Column E**
Bold **5**-4-3-2-1	Tenacious 5-**4**-3-2-1	Contemplative 5-4-3-**2**-1	Passionate 5-4-**3**-2-1	Honest 5-4-3-2-**1**
Backbone 5-**4**-3-2-1	Certain 5-4-3-2-**1**	Determined 5-4-**3**-2-1	Driven **5**-4-3-2-1	Strong Beliefs 5-4-3-**2**-1
Brave 5-**4**-3-2-1	Cool 5-4-**3**-2-1	Logical 5-4-3-2-**1**	Eager **5**-4-3-2-1	Fair & Just 5-4-3-**2**-1
Daring 5-**4**-3-2-1	Composed 5-4-3-**2**-1	Centered 5-4-**3**-2-1	Energetic **5**-4-3-2-1	Principled 5-4-3-2-**1**
Defiant 5-4-3-**2**-1	Sure 5-4-**3**-2-1	A Finisher 5-**4**-3-2-1	Enthusiastic **5**-4-3-2-1	Purposeful 5-4-3-2-**1**
Headstrong 5-**4**-3-2-1	Poised 5-4-3-2-**1**	Persistent **5**-4-3-2-1	Excitable 5-4-**3**-2-1	Controlled 5-4-3-**2**-1
Adventurous 5-4-**3**-2-1	Resolute 5-**4**-3-2-1	Focused 5-4-3-**2**-1	Fervent **5**-4-3-2-1	Dutiful 5-4-3-2-**1**
Gutsy 5-**4**-3-2-1	Secure 5-4-**3**-2-1	Absorbed 5-4-3-2-**1**	Inspired **5**-4-3-2-1	Conscientious 5-4-3-**2**-1
Risk-Taker 5-4-3-**2**-1	Confident 5-4-**3**-2-1	Targeted 5-**4**-3-2-1	Spirited **5**-4-3-2-1	Orderly 5-4-3-2-**1**
Courageous 5-4-**3**-2-1	Assured 5-4-3-**2**-1	Applied 5-**4**-3-2-1	Tireless **5**-4-3-2-1	Compliant 5-4-3-2-**1**
Col. A TOTAL 35	Col. B TOTAL 26	Col. C TOTAL 29	Col. D TOTAL 46	Col. E TOTAL 14

Figure 5.3

Add up the total for each column and enter that total at the base of each column and on the following chart. It's possible that one column could total 50. It is also possible that one column could total as few as 10. As before, the totals are most important in relation to one another, showing which motivational characteristics are most dominant to the least dominant. The sum of all five columns must equal 150.

Column A Total:	35	Courage
Column B Total:	26	Confidence
Column C Total:	29	Concentration
Column D Total:	46	Passion
Column E Total:	14	Values
Initiative Motivation Chart Total:	150	

Figure 5.4

Composite Leadership Profile/Initiative Profile Alignment

Initiative Profile/Composite Personality Alignment									
		Leadership Styles				**Leadership Motivations**			
Name:	**Leadership Style:**	Control	Compliance	Social	Stability	Courage	Confidence	Concentration	Passion	Values
Team Column Totals:										
Divided by:										
Team Composite Leadership Profile:										
Initiative Profile: Increase sales revenues by 15%:		39	16	26	19	35	26	29	46	14
*Variance:										

*Variance = Composite Personality – Initiative

Figure 5.5

Initiative style profile

Although the statistical average style score is 25, we ultimately pay more attention to the variance between the initiative profile and the team's composite leadership profile. Nevertheless, as with the LSI and LMI, knowing what the average is can help put the initiative profile numbers in perspective. For example, our ideal, bionic, composite personality to "Increase sales revenues by 15%," as identified on our initiative profile, turned out to be a control specialist (39), a full 14 points above average, with a secondary dominance in social specialization (26), which is only one above the average style score of 25. The third-ranking specialization is stability (19), with compliance last (16), which are both below average. Obviously our initiative profiling exercise led to the conclusion that there is a certain sense of urgency about getting sales revenues up and, to make this kind of increase happen, we need some impatience, which many control specialists tend to have. As you see as we go along, control specialists are also not typically bound up by rules or convention.

The secondary strength of the social specialization (26) came about because this organization values long-term relationships with customers. Therefore, building and sustaining human relationships must be part of this composite leadership profile. If we go totally with shoot-from-the-hip, charge into the breach, gung-ho control specialists, important human relations factors might get ignored and/or trampled underfoot.

However, some control specialists have strong secondary dominance in, of all things, social specialization. This will balance out what we've asked for. Without acknowledging the human relations component, the sales increases we're after might be realized initially, but won't be maintained over time. Eventually, Org will eat the whole initiative as people lose confidence.

We decided that stability (19) and compliance (16) issues are minor in this scenario, when compared to the needs that control and social specialists fill. Stability and compliance are represented in the initiative profile, but not likely to be championed to the tune of control and human relationship issues. If you and your associates named and profiled this initiative, your numbers might come out differently, depending on your sense of urgency, human factors, organizational balance, and compliance.

Different factions within your organization will profile the initiative differently, so gather lots of rich data from face-to-face and online facilitated discussions, as well as e-mailed initiative profiles in order to heighten reliability. The more data you have to work with, the more objective and reliable your analysis will be. Limiting sources heightens the likelihood of contamination and bias. Nothing disconnects worker bees faster then elitist edicts from out-of-touch executives.

Initiative motivation profile

Although the statistical average motivation score is 30, we again ultimately pay more attention to the variance between the initiative profile and the team's composite leadership profile. As for motivation, our ideal, bionic, composite personality, as documented by the initiative profile, was first and foremost passionate (46). In our most technical manner, we describe 16 points over the average of 30 as "big-time passionate." We felt that the ideal composite personality would adapt to its mission and environment with enthusiasm and high energy. This issue is important enough to the health and well-being of our organization that it warrants stomping on the gas, stoking the fires in the boilers, and lighting the afterburners.

The secondary dominance of courage (35), still five points above average, shows that we also want our ideal, bionic, composite personality to not be intimidated by the competition, obstacles thrown in its path, or excessive internal regulation. Where others might become faint, we want our ideal composite personality to be reasonably bold and unflinching. But we don't want the members of the composite personality *so* bold and courageous as to spend their free time bungee jumping.

We felt that the ability to stay on task, as in concentration (29), being nearly average, was also important. Time, energy, and resources spent getting back on track after losing focus can delay the initiative, waste energy, and be expensive. Confidence (26) is less important. We wanted our ideal composite personality to be reasonably assured that what they were doing will work, but not hesitate to take risks. Finally, the values ranking (14) is low because we weren't worried about how faithfully this particular group of people follows rules. We'd rather see the group thinking outside the bun than bound up by regulation. Principles are important, though, and that means the initiative owner needs to pay attention.

The Wrong Team for the Wrong Reasons

You'll notice there are no team members listed in Figure 5.5. That's because, ideally, the initiative profile comes *before* team member selection. If you select team members before you examine and measure the initiative, how can you know if you have the right people on Jim Collins's bus?

In the database of leadership style profiles we've assembled for demonstration purposes, the self-reporting and peer-reporting inventories miraculously match (See pages 112–114).

As we covered in Chapter 4, the peer-reporting inventories are a more reliable source of data. We've included both here to preserve the integrity of the database chart. By keeping the self-reporting inventory data above the peer-reporting data on the chart, the comparison we talked about is always instantly available.

To keep up with our examples, we've divided our database into control specialists, compliance specialists, social specialists, and stability specialists. You may want to simply keep the people in your database in alphabetical order, regardless of their leadership style profiles. Again, these charts and all the charts in this book are available at *www.compositeam.com*.

We calculated Fred, Beth, Reba, and Mark's composite leadership profile by adding up the category columns for the leadership styles—control, compliance, social, and stability—and the leadership motivation categories—courage, confidence, concentration, passion, and values—then dividing by the number of members on the team. The *variance*, which is how far out of alignment the composite leadership profile is from the initiative profile, is fairly dramatic in the control and compliance categories, as well as in passion, and values.

The control specialization of this group is 14 points below what the initiative profile calls for. Compliance is nine points higher, social is one point less, and stability is six points higher than called for. Courage on this team's composite leadership profile is five points low, confidence is four points more than the initiative profile, concentration is one point higher. Passion is 16 points behind, and values is 16 points ahead.

This doesn't mean that Fred, Beth, Reba, and Mark can't execute this initiative, but they're not likely to do it the way the initiative profile calls for. They're fighting against their essential natures by large margins in a number of critical categories. As they gravitate, consciously or unconsciously, toward their natural leadership styles of control, compliance, social, or stability, they're likely to leave important issues uncovered and, possibly, unattended. When faced with challenges and threats, they'll instinctively retreat to their motivational comfort zones, which is not where you want the team members executing this particular initiative to be.

Control Specialists

Name: Amy

Leadership Style: Control Specialist

Self-reporting Inventory

Control	Compliance	Social	Stability	Courage	Confidence	Concentration	Passion	Values
39	11	38	12	40	32	20	48	10

Peer-reporting Inventories

Control	Compliance	Social	Stability	Courage	Confidence	Concentration	Passion	Values
39	11	38	12	40	32	20	48	10

Variance (Self Report – Peer Report = Variance)

Control	Compliance	Social	Stability	Courage	Confidence	Concentration	Passion	Values
0	0	0	0	0	0	0	0	0

Name: Donna

Leadership Style: Control Specialist

Self-reporting Inventory

Control	Compliance	Social	Stability	Courage	Confidence	Concentration	Passion	Values
38	13	32	17	38	32	20	46	14

Peer-reporting Inventories

Control	Compliance	Social	Stability	Courage	Confidence	Concentration	Passion	Values
38	13	32	17	38	32	20	46	14

Variance (Self Report – Peer Report = Variance)

Control	Compliance	Social	Stability	Courage	Confidence	Concentration	Passion	Values
0	0	0	0	0	0	0	0	0

Name: Fred

Leadership Style: Control Specialist

Self-reporting Inventory

Control	Compliance	Social	Stability	Courage	Confidence	Concentration	Passion	Values
40	30	20	10	30	10	40	50	20

Peer-reporting Inventories

Control	Compliance	Social	Stability	Courage	Confidence	Concentration	Passion	Values
40	30	20	10	30	10	40	50	20

Variance (Self Report – Peer Report = Variance)

Control	Compliance	Social	Stability	Courage	Confidence	Concentration	Passion	Values
0	0	0	0	0	0	0	0	0

Name: Sally

Leadership Style: Control Specialist

Self-reporting Inventory

Control	Compliance	Social	Stability	Courage	Confidence	Concentration	Passion	Values
39	10	14	37	32	30	36	40	12

Peer-reporting Inventories

Control	Compliance	Social	Stability	Courage	Confidence	Concentration	Passion	Values
39	10	14	37	32	30	36	40	12

Variance (Self Report – Peer Report = Variance)

Control	Compliance	Social	Stability	Courage	Confidence	Concentration	Passion	Values
0	0	0	0	0	0	0	0	0

Figure 5.6

Compliance Specialists

Name: Andy

Leadership Style: Compliance Specialist

Self-reporting Inventory

Control	Compliance	Social	Stability	Courage	Confidence	Concentration	Passion	Values
21	25	26	29	33	23	44	13	37

Peer-reporting Inventories

Control	Compliance	Social	Stability	Courage	Confidence	Concentration	Passion	Values
21	25	26	29	33	23	44	13	37

Variance (Self Report – Peer Report = Variance)

Control	Compliance	Social	Stability	Courage	Confidence	Concentration	Passion	Values
0	0	0	0	0	0	0	0	0

Name: Beth

Leadership Style: Compliance Specialist

Self-reporting Inventory

Control	Compliance	Social	Stability	Courage	Confidence	Concentration	Passion	Values
10	40	30	20	10	50	40	30	20

Peer-reporting Inventories

Control	Compliance	Social	Stability	Courage	Confidence	Concentration	Passion	Values
10	40	30	20	10	50	40	30	20

Variance (Self Report – Peer Report = Variance)

Control	Compliance	Social	Stability	Courage	Confidence	Concentration	Passion	Values
0	0	0	0	0	0	0	0	0

Figure 5.7

Social Specialists

Name: Amelia

Leadership Style: Social Specialist

Self-reporting Inventory

Control	Compliance	Social	Stability	Courage	Confidence	Concentration	Passion	Values
37	12	38	13	15	18	27	49	41

Peer-reporting Inventories

Control	Compliance	Social	Stability	Courage	Confidence	Concentration	Passion	Values
37	12	38	13	15	18	27	49	41

Variance (Self Report – Peer Report = Variance)

Control	Compliance	Social	Stability	Courage	Confidence	Concentration	Passion	Values
0	0	0	0	0	0	0	0	0

Name: Reba

Leadership Style: Social Specialist

Self-reporting Inventory

Control	Compliance	Social	Stability	Courage	Confidence	Concentration	Passion	Values
20	10	40	30	20	20	40	40	30

Peer-reporting Inventories

Control	Compliance	Social	Stability	Courage	Confidence	Concentration	Passion	Values
20	10	40	30	20	20	40	40	30

Variance (Self Report – Peer Report = Variance)

Control	Compliance	Social	Stability	Courage	Confidence	Concentration	Passion	Values
0	0	0	0	0	0	0	0	0

Figure 5.8

Stability Specialists								
Name: Arnold								
Leadership Style: Stability Specialist								
Self-reporting Inventory								
Control	Compliance	Social	Stability	Courage	Confidence	Concentration	Passion	Values
21	25	25	29	23	23	44	13	47
Peer-reporting Inventories								
Control	Compliance	Social	Stability	Courage	Confidence	Concentration	Passion	Values
21	25	25	29	23	23	44	13	47
Variance (Self Report – Peer Report = Variance)								
Control	Compliance	Social	Stability	Courage	Confidence	Concentration	Passion	Values
0	0	0	0	0	0	0	0	0
Name: Reba								
Leadership Style: Stability Specialist								
Self-reporting Inventory								
Control	Compliance	Social	Stability	Courage	Confidence	Concentration	Passion	Values
30	20	10	40	50	40	10	20	30
Peer-reporting Inventories								
Control	Compliance	Social	Stability	Courage	Confidence	Concentration	Passion	Values
30	20	10	40	50	40	10	20	30
Variance (Self Report – Peer Report = Variance)								
Control	Compliance	Social	Stability	Courage	Confidence	Concentration	Passion	Values
0	0	0	0	0	0	0	0	0

Figure 5.9

Initiative Profile Database								
Name of Initiative:								
Leadership Style called for:								
Profile Owner:								
Facilitated Face-to-Face Discussion Initiative Profile:								
Control	Compliance	Social	Stability	Courage	Confidence	Concentration	Passion	Values
Facilitated Online Discussion Profile:								
Control	Compliance	Social	Stability	Courage	Confidence	Concentration	Passion	Values
Variance: Facilitated Face-to-Face vs. Facilitated Online (Face-to-Face – Online = Variance)								
Control	Compliance	Social	Stability	Courage	Confidence	Concentration	Passion	Values
E-mailed Initiative Profiles:								
Control	Compliance	Social	Stability	Courage	Confidence	Concentration	Passion	Values
Variance: Facilitated Face-to-Face vs. E-mailed (Face-to-Face – E-mail = Variance)								
Control	Compliance	Social	Stability	Courage	Confidence	Concentration	Passion	Values
Composite Initiative Profile from all or Selected Sources:								
Control	Compliance	Social	Stability	Courage	Confidence	Concentration	Passion	Values

Figure 5.10

"Fred, Beth, Reba, and Mark have always been a good team in the past," you say. "Why not put them on this assignment?"

"Okay," we agree quickly, as only someone with an ace in the hole will do. "But tell us one thing first: What, exactly, do you mean when you say, 'good team'?"

"I mean they get along and don't cause any trouble," you assure us. "Besides, they're usually the ones not doing anything else."

"And that's good for exactly what reason...?" It's a leading question, but we couldn't resist.

"When people get along, I have no problems," you reason. We admit to ourselves that it's an appealing reason. A trap we could easily fall into.

"How do you know the work is getting done as efficiently, effectively, or as quickly as it might otherwise be?"

"How otherwise?" you ask, looking at us slightly askance.

"If you had a team whose composite leadership profile was aligned with the initiative profile. *That's* how otherwise."

"That sounds logical," you say in your best Vulcan accent. "But would they get along with each other?"

"That's up to you," we say. "You'll need to stay on top of what each team member's leadership profile looks like and what he or she is bringing to the effort. You'll need to manage the creative tension in the team."

"How do I do that?"

"By being damn clear about your expectations from each individual in terms of his or her identified strengths, and the team, based on the composite personality."

"Where can I get my hands on this kind of information?" you inquire incredulously.

"By studying Chapters 6 through 14," we assure you. "Each style and motivation is explained, along with how they combine, what kind of language resonates with each one, and how you can best support their efforts vis-à-vis their composite leadership style."

"As in their composite personality," you say with growing confidence.

"Same thing," we assure you.

"I can actually manage the below-the-surface, and otherwise invisible, aspects of his or her leadership styles and motivations," you say, stroking your chin contemplatively.

"Correct-o-mundo," say we.

"It sounds doable," you say. "But, if we align the composite leadership profile with the initiative profile, and it works as well as you say it does, Org's not going to like it."

"Let us worry about Org," we say.

"With Fred, Beth, Reba, and Mark, he always gets plenty to eat," you reflect.

"Do you want to see why?" we tease.

We can tell by the look in your eyes that you can't resist a demonstration. So we snatch Fred, Beth, Reba, and Mark's leadership profile information from your departmental database and enter it in Figure 5.11, which happens to be the composite leadership profile/initiative profile alignment chart compiled to "Increase sales revenues by 15%."

If team members are courageous, they're likely to attack. If they're confident, they're likely to stare the problem down, or move steadily ahead as the bombs burst around them. If they're concentrators, they're likely to withdraw and ponder the situation and its various possibilities. If they're passionate, they're likely to leap off the wall into a sea of enemy

Composite Leadership Profile/Initiative Profile Alignment Chart									
		Leadership Styles				**Leadership Motivations**			
Name:	**Leadership Style:**	Control	Compliance	Social	Stability	Courage	Confidence	Concentration	Passion	Values
Fred	Control Specialist	40	30	20	10	30	10	40	50	20
Beth	Compliance Specialist	10	40	30	20	20	50	30	10	40
Reba	Social Specialist	20	10	40	30	20	20	40	40	30
Mark	Stability Specialist	30	20	10	40	50	40	10	20	30
Team Column Totals:		100	100	100	100	120	120	120	120	120
Divided by:		4	4	4	4	4	4	4	4	4
Team Composite Leadership Profile:		25	25	25	25	30	30	30	30	30
Initiative Profile: Increase sales revenues by 15%:		39	16	26	19	35	26	29	46	14
*Variance:		−14	+9	−1	+6	−5	+4	+1	−16	+16

*Variance = Composite Leadership Profile − Initiative Profile

Figure 5.11

troops, or go after a fire-breathing dragon armed with only their bare hands. If they hold values dear, they're likely to hold fast to the rules of engagement, even as the enemy twists, distorts, and breaks the rules.

The whole point of identifying the natural strengths and essential nature of your organizational population is to align their natural energy flow to the needs of the organization. That's how you get the greatest results for the least effort. That's how you get maximum return for minimum investment. Making your people swim upstream, against the current, in addition to meeting their assigned responsibilities is inexcusable, especially now that you know there's a better way to get them moving with the current to make all that natural motion work for you. The ComposiTeam Leadership System is not a cure-all panacea magic-bullet solution to everything that ails an organization. But the difference in efficiency and results can be as profound as hauling goods in oxcarts along muddy roads vs. flying Boeing 747 cargo jets. That's what unleashing leadership will do for you.

Ah, the Perfect World

Composite Leadership Profile/Initiative Profile Alignment Chart									
		Leadership Styles				Leadership Motivations			
Name:	Leadership Style:	Control	Compliance	Social	Stability	Courage	Confidence	Concentration	Passion	Values
Amy	Control Specialist	39	11	38	12	40	32	20	48	10
Donna	Control Specialist	38	13	32	17	38	32	20	46	14
Fred	Control Specialist	40	30	20	10	30	10	40	50	20
Sally	Control Specialist	39	10	14	37	32	30	36	40	12
Team Column Totals:		156	64	104	76	140	104	116	184	56
Divided by:		4	4	4	4	4	4	4	4	4
Team Composite Leadership Profile:		39	16	26	19	35	26	29	46	14
Initiative Profile: Increase sales revenues by 15%:		39	16	26	19	35	26	29	46	14
*Variance:		0	0	0	0	0	0	0	0	0

*Variance = Composite Leadership Profile – Initiative Profile

Figure 5.12

No *i* in t-e-a-m

Note that Fred is the only original left on this team. Donna and Sally had to be recruited. You hadn't even considered them before, and, voilà, there they are: the bionic women. If we lived in a perfect world, the composite leadership profile of all teams would align perfectly with the initiative profile you create. Take a last, longing look at Figure 5.12, because it's rare that a team's composite personality so perfectly matches the profile of the initiative they're being asked to execute. As you wipe the admiring tear from your eye, marveling at the beauty of perfect team/ initiative alignment, with a perfect set of zeros on the variance line, don't miss the obvious benefit of the leadership *team approach*.

No one's individual leadership profile in our database aligns perfectly with the initiative profile. The composite leadership profile of a group of people gives you a much better shot at covering the initiative profile bases you identified. Shared leadership responsibility is how you build your ideal, bionic leader. It's a matter of employing the right process; not achieving perfection. Using the ComposiTeam process, you can get into the perfection ball park.

Alignment Priorities

If the world were perfect, Org would be eating perfectly balanced dragon food and he'd be as buff and ripped as a male swimsuit model. But dragons tend to carry a few extra tons around the middle. So it is in real life. Dieting, exercise, and weight loss are easier for some than for others, and achieving good results is easier for everybody when the conditions are right. Achieving the perfect alignment between the team composite leadership profile and your initiative profile is easier when there are lots of potential team members in your database. The larger your organizational population, the more likely you can approach perfection in alignment. The smaller your database, the more compensation for variance is called for. We'll talk more about managing that variance in Chapter 6.

At this point, it's important to ask, "What happens when the alignment has variance, no matter how you try to mix and match team member candidates from your database?" Don't despair. If your pool of team member candidates is limited and you will need to manage a certain amount of variance, no matter what, follow the priority rankings you established in your initiative profile. If the initiative profile ranks control specialization highest, then make sure you assemble a team with a control specialist composite personality—with team control specialization numbers that match the initiative profile as closely as possible. If you're going to attempt perfection in alignment, that's where to do it.

If you have a 39 for control specialization on your initiative profile, try to assemble a team with a 39 for control specialization in their composite leadership profile. If social specialization is ranked second, your next order of business is to try and match those numbers. If social specialization has a number of 26 on your initiative profile, try to get as close to 26 as possible on your team's composite leadership profile.

Work hardest at aligning the *highest numbers* on your initiative profile. Those are the categories that you've identified as most important. If you need to wrestle with variances, make them on the least important categories. If you can get your variance down to zero, do it where your highest priorities are. Between leadership style and motivation, align your leadership style numbers first. Control, compliance, social, and stability are your highest priorities in whatever order their numbers dictate.

Profiles Will Differ

As you profile different initiatives, different composite leadership profiles will be called for to execute the initiative, or any component task, project, or objective you identify. If you apply the ComposiTeam Leadership System consistently, you should see improved results across the board. Here are several initiative profiles that call for diverse composite leadership profiles. As we mentioned in Chapter 4, this is why attempting to fudge the inventories is silly. You never know how you or others whom you're evaluating in peer inventories will fit into the alignment process. We've left our ideal, bionic, team for "Increasing Sales Revenues by 15%" in place to see how quickly any given team, regardless of how perfect for one assignment, can fall out of alignment.

The initiative profile "Reduce Annual Employee Turnover by 15% With Better Employee Recognition" calls for a social specialist composite leadership profile (Figure 5.13). The variations are most pronounced in excessive control and courage, and the most profound deficiency in values. Our ideal, bionic team for "Increasing Sales Revenues by 15%" would struggle to pull this initiative off well.

Composite Leadership Profile/Initiative Profile Alignment Chart										
		Leadership Styles				Leadership Motivations				
Name:	Leadership Style:	Control	Compliance	Social	Stability	Courage	Confidence	Concentration	Passion	Values
Amy	Control Specialist	39	11	38	12	40	32	20	48	10
Donna	Control Specialist	38	13	32	17	38	32	20	46	14
Fred	Control Specialist	40	30	20	10	30	10	40	50	20
Sally	Control Specialist	39	10	14	37	32	30	36	40	12
Team Column Totals:		156	64	104	76	140	104	116	184	56
Divided by:		4	4	4	4	4	4	4	4	4
Team Composite Leadership Profile for Increasing Sales Revenues by 15%:		39	16	26	19	35	26	29	46	14
Initiative Profile: Increase sales revenues by 15% With Better Employee Recognition:		12	20	40	28	18	20	25	48	39
*Variance:		+27	–4	–14	–9	+17	+6	+4	–2	–25

*Variance = Composite Leadership Profile – Initiative Profile

Figure 5.13

The initiative profile "Reduce Wasted Consumables by 15%" is similar to that of an internal audit or compliance review (Figure 5.14). You definitely want someone committed to meticulous record-keeping and monitoring. Nothing like those linear bean counters for a job like this. As unglamorous as it might sound, this kind of initiative saves organizations enormous amounts of money each year. With luck, it will help the environment, too.

Composite Leadership Profile/Initiative Profile Alignment Chart									
		Leadership Styles				Leadership Motivations			
Name:	Leadership Style:	Control	Compliance	Social	Stability	Courage	Confidence	Concentration	Passion	Values
Amy	Control Specialist	39	11	38	12	40	32	20	48	10
Donna	Control Specialist	38	13	32	17	38	32	20	46	14
Fred	Control Specialist	40	30	20	10	30	10	40	50	20
Sally	Control Specialist	39	10	14	37	32	30	36	40	12
Team Column Totals:		156	64	104	76	140	104	116	184	56
Divided by:		4	4	4	4	4	4	4	4	4
Team Composite Leadership Profile (for Increasing Sales Revenues by 15%:		39	16	26	19	35	26	29	46	14
Initiative Profile: Reduce Wasted Consumables by 15%		16	38	12	34	13	18	42	37	40
*Variance:		+23	−22	+14	−15	+22	+8	−13	+9	−26

*Variance = Composite Leadership Profile − Initiative Profile
Figure 5.14

Once again, our ideal, bionic team created for "Increasing Sales Revenues by 15%" would probably boot this initiative with large variances in nearly every category, except perhaps confidence and passion. But who wants to be passionate about bean counting? Bean counters, of course. But who else?

The initiative profile for "Increasing Daily Output by 15%" calls for a stability specialist composite leadership profile (Figure 5.15). Stability specialists are concerned with fair and equitable distribution of workload. More than that, they're committed to maximizing productivity and organizational performance. They are often experts in work-process redesign. If you want your organization to fire on all cylinders, look to your stability specialists.

Composite Leadership Profile/Initiative Profile Alignment Chart										
		Leadership Styles				Leadership Motivations				
Name:	Leadership Style:	Control	Compliance	Social	Stability	Courage	Confidence	Concentration	Passion	Values
Amy	Control Specialist	39	11	38	12	40	32	20	48	10
Donna	Control Specialist	38	13	32	17	38	32	20	46	14
Fred	Control Specialist	40	30	20	10	30	10	40	50	20
Sally	Control Specialist	39	10	14	37	32	30	36	40	12
Team Column Totals:		156	64	104	76	140	104	116	184	56
Divided by:		4	4	4	4	4	4	4	4	4
Team Composite Leadership Profile (for Increasing Sales Revenues by 15%:		39	16	26	19	35	26	29	46	14
Initiative Profile: Increase Daily Output by 15%		15	20	25	40	22	24	36	26	42
*Variance:		+24	–4	+1	–21	+13	+2	–7	+20	–28

*Variance = Composite Leadership Profile – Initiative Profile

Figure 5.15

Our ideal, bionic team for "Increasing Sales Revenues by 15%" brings too much impatience and urgency to get the organization humming like a well-oiled machine. The team has much more courage and passion than are called for, in our opinion; so much so that the desired outcome could be jeopardized. With little or no respect for rules, policies, and procedures, the highly control-oriented team disqualifies itself. With this team in charge of this stability-oriented initiative, Org would feast on discarded TQM, Six-Sigma, and ISO paraphernalia.

Chapter 5 Summary:
Keys to Unleashing Leadership

↦ **Follow the steps, then don't:** Remember the three steps to the Composi-Team Leadership System:

1. Create a database of leadership styles and motivations for everyone you want in your pool of potential leadership team members.

2. Profile every initiative, objective, project, and/or task you want to form leadership teams to address.

3. Match the initiative profile to the composite leadership profile of the team that best fits.

After you've run through the process once, you'll continuously gather new leadership profile data on members of your organizational population. However, where the steps are concerned, you'll begin the initiative profile/composite leadership profile two-step. Initiative profile/composite leadership profile, initiative profile/composite leadership profile, over and over again. Repeat application as needed.

↦ **Name it right:** Make sure that you remain flexible to adjust the name of the initiative until you have action words that truly reflect the do-ability of the initiative and can be translated into human behavior. Unless you have robots to execute the initiative, you had best deal in human-speak. The name should not only adequately describe the initiative in actionable terms, it should be visual language that will resonate with as many people as possible, particularly the people most directly related to its execution.

↦ **Gather information far and wide:** Facilitated face-to-face and online discussions about the initiative and what type of ideal personality will best execute it help the prospective team hit the ground running when they're put in place. Facilitated discussions provide forums and opportunities for many people to participate in what historically have been closed-door meetings on mahogany row. In addition to face-to-face and online facilitated discussions, initiative profiles can be sent to people online who will fill them out and return them by a designated deadline, again expanding your data pool and increasing the objectivity and reliability of your profile.

- **Initiative profile/composite leadership profile alignment:** This is the payoff. You wouldn't attempt to loosen a bolt with your bare hands. The ComposiTeam Leadership System is like the wrench you'd grab for the bolt. It gives you leverage that you otherwise wouldn't have to get the job done faster and more efficiently than you can without it. In a relatively short period of time, in the sanctity of your office, the conference room, or the break area, you can run through this process quickly, coming out of the experience with much more productive and efficient human alignment than ever before.

- **Keep an open mind:** The system is going to potentially recommend some people for teams that you might not have thought of before. That's because it's seeing a lot of what you don't see with the naked eye. As the initiative profiles change, so will the ideal, bionic composite leadership profiles to match them. Focus on aligning the initiative profile numbers and composite leadership profile numbers for the most critical categories first, and work down from there. Avoid falling back on gut-level team-member selection, because you're probably scratching the wrong itch.

Looking ahead to Chapter 6, there are several additional issues to consider when managing composite leadership teams. Team size is a consideration, as well as managing variances, and progress reporting from specialization categories. Stay tuned.

Chapter 6

Managing the Team

Most men would feel insulted if it were proposed to
employ them in throwing stones over a wall, and then in
throwing them back, merely that they might earn their
wages. But many are no more worthily employed now.

—Henry David Thoreau

Adopting the ComposiTeam Leadership System, or even your own variation on the concept, is going to start affecting your organizational dragon. Not only will the increased efficiency and improved morale change Org's diet, he'll become a restless sleeper as he senses things are changing around the workplace. He might start having nightmares (daymares?) such as this one:

Imagine yourself pacing back and forth in front of an enormous flag, stretched to cover the entire wall behind you. This is your great moment in history. You are an initiative owner, and you're briefing your newly selected composite leadership team. You point with your riding crop and slap it in the palm of your hand now and then for emphasis. If a riding crop is not your style, point with a doughnut.

"Every one of you has been selected to participate on this team because you bring unique talents and abilities to the effort. Some are obvious, such as expertise in accounting or engineering; others are more subtle, such as a predisposition to consider human relationships and the balance of interests between internal and external organizational issues. Although some of you are here because of specific competencies, and others because of the specific leadership styles you contribute, every one of you has been selected because *together* you form a composite leadership profile that best matches the profile for this initiative.

"The initiative we're going to execute together has been thought through and talked through by ringleaders at and beyond my ring of responsibility. As you work to execute this initiative, you might find that there are aspects we didn't consider. We want you to report that at your earliest opportunity, even if it means adjusting the initiative profile or the composition of the team. There are no boundaries to the thinking in this group, as long as we stay on task.

"You haven't been selected because you think and act alike. It's likely some of you haven't served on a team together before. Some of you might disagree on what's most important regarding this initiative. You might sense creative tension among you. When and if you do, consider other points of view. We're not here to prove one another right or wrong. We expect that you'll sharpen each other's thinking and make the execution of this initiative more efficient, effective, and profitable for everyone.

"My job is to support your activities by providing whatever you require to execute this initiative, guide the effort as necessary, and keep others in the organization informed of the progress and other issues you report. Your job is to take leadership responsibility for your role in this effort. You need to function at your best without carrying a cumbersome organization on your shoulders. I'll do my best to keep administration out of your way. If I'm not doing my job, it's your responsibility to report that in a constructive way. Likewise, I'll be constructive in the guidance and support I provide.

"In the interest of this team and the organization that pays each of us, we owe this initiative our best effort. As I said before, you're different from one another in a variety of ways. On the other hand, you're alike in many ways. The one place where all of our paths cross is our loyalty to this organization and the effort we're putting forth. When the organization wins, we all win; our families win, our customers win, and our community wins. It's that simple. Now good luck, and *get back to work*."

Valuing People Is Serious Business

We're just kidding about the "…*get back to work*," bit. The riding crop is up to you. Although we've never worked with a riding-crop-carrying client, we have worked with clients who, just to be funny, like to tell their team members, "Get back to work." It's not funny. It's not the end of the world, either. But, sending a message that essentially means, "I'm the superior, you're the subordinate," "I'm powerful, you're not," or "I yell, you listen," even behind the veil of humor is still the wrong message.

If your team members are not important, why are they on the payroll? Just because they're not earning what you earn, does that mean you want to get rid of them and do their work? None of us are beyond expendability. On the other hand, we all have a great deal to contribute, as long as we're aligned properly with what we're expected to accomplish, regardless of where we are in the organization. The issue isn't: "Is this person important?" It's: "Is this person aligned properly with what we're asking him or her to do?" This is never more important than when you're facilitating people working together, whether on a formally selected team, or at a department or organizational level.

Not Reinventing the Team

The concept of "team" has been studied inside-out and all the way around by many people over many years. We're not here to reinvent that wheel. Whatever you do to build up morale on teams and improve their efficiency and/or effectiveness is probably helping. But whatever you're doing is going to produce better results if you have the right people, working on the right initiative. That's what's most important.

If you play team-building games, they'll be better games with the right people. If you go on retreats and navigate rope courses, the navigation will mean much more with the right people. If you take your teams out to shoot each other with paint balls, they'll be better shots if they're shooting at the right people. Ask yourself: "If my team members are not selected based on how well their composite leadership profile is aligned with an initiative profile, what's the point of paint balls?" You might wonder that last thing anyway, unless your people are bored.

We don't want to pop anybody's team-development balloons. There is much literature and expertise around to help your teams bond better, improve internal and external communications, and/or stay focused. None of those efforts are wasted. We're saying that *the first and most important element of any team-building endeavor is to make sure you've aligned what people do best with what the organization needs most.* Beyond that, choose teams and fire away.

Size of the team

There is a great deal of literature and thought on team size. As we briefly touched on earlier, we think the size of the team should not be arbitrary. It makes no sense to us that a team should be formed for the sake of forming a team. Neither does it make sense to have someone on a team for no reason. We've established how prospective team members should be evaluated in terms of how their individual leadership profiles contribute to the team's composite leadership profile.

The team composite leadership profile that aligns best with the initiative profile should be assembled with the fewest people possible. If four will do it, then four it is. The only reason to vary from this minimalist approach is because there are more chores than four people can do.

The initiative profiling exercise should include discussion of how many people this job, task, objective, project, or initiative will require to execute. If it calls for someone who lives in every state in the Union, that's a whopper of a team. You're already half the size of the United States Senate right out of the box. One person per continent will at least cut it down to seven.

During the profiling exercise, determining the optimal size of the leadership team will reveal if the scope of the initiative is too broadly defined from the start. Beyond combining individual leadership profiles to create the optimal composite leadership profile, people need to have specific roles to play, depending on what the team is expected to do. But adding a team member based on a specific competency will change the composite leadership profile.

Assembling leadership teams is like three-dimensional chess. When you add someone to the system to create a horizontal effect, you create a vertical effect at the same time, and vice versa. These are the factors you need to contend with when selecting leadership team members from your database. It can get complicated, but that's why you're paid the big bucks. We admit that it's easier to just walk around the office and see who's not doing anything at the moment or who's out of the office at the moment, stick them on a team, and say, "You guys figure it out."

To do it right, your first priority in team selection is to get the leadership style dimension (control, compliance, social, and stability) of the initiative profile aligned as best you can with the leadership style dimension of the team's composite leadership profile. Aligning the most dominant leadership style on the initiative profile, then the second, third, and so on will immediately begin to identify the number of team members required.

If there is no clearly articulateable reason for someone to be on a leadership team, then someone strayed from the initiative profiling or team member selection process. Reevaluate. Golf and bowling handicaps, softball batting averages, chili recipes, and fashion choices aren't good criteria for team selection, unless you're assembling a golf, bowling, softball, bake-off, or fashion team. Even then, there are parameters on the number of team members.

Dealing with limitations

Issues such as size of team and three-dimensional team member selection raise some important questions for initiative owners:

➤ What if Fred, Beth, Reba, and Mark are the only people I have available?

› You can still assign them the responsibility of executing the initiative, but the variances show you the weaknesses, so to speak, in how their composite leadership profile aligns with the initiative profile. You can anticipate where the system is bound to experience the most stress. If it breaks, you know where it most likely needs repair.

› Reduce the likelihood of their effort failing by anticipating where they might *disconnect*, based on the variances. Don't wait for them to start blaming one another for gaps in the process when it's a variance item, not a personal shortcoming. Fill the gap with expertise from the outside, with your own expertise, or with additional information you're able to squirrel up for the team. Hire additional people, if possible, or outsource the initiative. Consider your options and compensate.

› By knowing what the variances between your team's composite leadership profile and your initiative profile, you know where attention is required most. You no longer need to scratch your head and wonder why it's not coming together the way you want. Study your options and discuss the variances openly with your team. Don't let them twist in the wind wondering what's wrong.

➤ What if certain competencies must be represented on this team?

› Go to your database and find the person(s) with those competencies who *also* bring the composite leadership profile of the team into the best alignment with the initiative profile. If the competency representative doesn't contribute much in the way of personality/profile alignment, select additional team members to bring the composite personality and initiative profile into better alignment.

> › Remember to explain to everyone why they're there, the way you did in Org's daymare. If people are on the team primarily because they represent core competencies, point that out. If they're there because they bring balancing leadership profiles to achieve alignment with the initiative profile, explain that, too. Everybody plays a role and is on the team for a reason. All team members must be reassured as to the precise contribution they're expected to make.

➤ What difference does the variance make?

> › The initiative owner can immediately track activity based on contributing strengths. This is particularly important for tracking *composite performance.* If expectations, based on the team's composite personality, are not being realized, the initiative owner can identify where the low-performing specializations are being overpowered.

> › Assuming there is little or no variance, if "Increase Sales Revenues by 15%" is performing weakly on building and sustaining human relationships as a secondary specialization, social specialization is probably being overpowered by control and needs to be propped up or championed.

> › If there is a pronounced variance between the social specialization in the initiative profile and the team's composite leadership profile, the initiative owner, as well as all team members, should anticipate the shortfall and take steps to compensate for it, as we described in the bullet points under the first question, study the alignment, and make the necessary compensation.

Reporting

A key factor in the success of any team effort, especially the ComposiTeam Leadership System, is regularly planned progress reporting. The initiative owner must agree, in consultation with his or her team members, how often to report on progress. When using the ComposiTeam Leadership System, leadership style categories are critical. When the team members report on progress, each should report from within his or her dominant leadership style.

Through the alignment of an initiative profile and a composite leadership profile, the initiative owner, and the team member, knows what leadership style and motivation category the team member is expected to report on. A control specialist is expected to report on his or her control specialization; not compliance, social, or stability. The exception to this occurs when there is no specialization on the team to cover a category. If the initiative profile calls for a diminished priority on stability, for example, and the composite personality is comprised of two control specialists and two social specialists, the team member with the strongest stability ranking can report on stability issues.

If, as in our example in Chapter 5, all four team members are control specialists, the team member assigned to report on compliance, social, and stability issues will be the team members with the greatest dominance in that category. If the initiative profile is that of a control specialist, as in "Increase Sales Revenues by 15%," the strongest control specialist on the team reports on control. If the initiative profile is that of a compliance specialist, the strongest compliance specialist on the team reports on compliance. The same goes for social and stability. Again, the farther you get away from the dominant leadership style category, the lower the need to align perfectly. The leadership motivation categories (courage, confidence, concentration, passion, and values) are secondary in alignment priority to the leadership style categories (control, compliance, social, and stability).

We suggest using a uniform reporting chart such as the one in Figure 6.1 on pages 132–133. You might want to adapt yours to the specifics of your organization and initiative. However, don't lose sight of how important it is for the team members to report from their areas of specialization as much as possible.

Contamination vs. Enrichment

You've probably noticed by now that every person is likely to address these issues according to his or her competency discipline or leadership profile. The vice president of sales will say, "Let's get our hands on the money now and work out the bugs later." The vice president of finance will say, "We need to run the numbers on this before we do anything." The vice president of human resources will say, "Are we sure this is the best thing for our people?" The chief operating officer will say, "We need to make sure we have a balanced workload to maximize productivity."

Some might say that the organization is starting to sound like the Tower of Babble. Indeed, Org likes to hear babbling around the office whenever he wakes up and rolls over during the day. He smiles because

Progress Report for: [*Name of Initiative*]									
Report's Leadership Style Perspective: [Choose *Control, Compliance, Social, Stability, Courage, Confidence, Concentration, Passion,* or *Values*]									
Name of Team Member:									
Individual Leadership Style:									
Individual Leadership Profile:									
Control	Compliance	Social	Stability	Courage	Confidence	Concentration	Passion	Values	
Initiative Owner:									
Initiative Start Date:									
Report Copied To:									
Date of Report:									
Date of Last Report:									
Description of Actual Progress Between Reports:									
Issues of Urgency:									
Competitive Issues:									
Delays or Roadblocks:									
Other Issues to Note:									

Date of Next Report:								
Description of Anticipated Progress Between Reports:								
Issues of Urgency:								
Competitive Issues:								
Delays or Roadblocks:								
Other Issues to Note:								
Team Composite Leadership Profile:								
Control	Compliance	Social	Stability	Courage	Confidence	Concentration	Passion	Values
Initiative Profile:								
Control	Compliance	Social	Stability	Courage	Confidence	Concentration	Passion	Values
Variance: (Composite Leadership Profile – Initiative Profile = Variance)								
Control	Compliance	Social	Stability	Courage	Confidence	Concentration	Passion	Values

Figure 6.1

he knows there will be a lot to eat that night. But will there be? What might sound like conflicting, contradictory babble to some may sound like a richly diverse organization to the trained ear.

The rich diversity of leadership styles and motivations on a leadership team produces that creative tension of which we're so fond. Properly managed and supported by the initiative owner, those diverse points of view will pull the crosshairs of the initiative profile directly over the target. Creative tension can help the leadership team execute the initiative with surgical precision.

Weighting

Not only do issues of diverse opinion and leadership profile orientation need to be recognized and managed properly, disparity of power must be recognized. Ideally, every member of the team has the same institutional authority. If some members of the team have more institutional power over other team members, the stronger members are likely to exert themselves, while the weaker members withdraw. Neither party might be consciously aware of exerting or withdrawing if it's become second nature, which, in hierarchical organizations, is a distinct probability.

We have elected not to attempt power weightings for leadership teams because the varying degrees of power and authority, along with the ways they are manifest, produce too many variables. If you *must* compose teams with members at varying levels of institutional power, that disparity must be managed similarly to the way that divergence in individual personality traits is managed. Differences in leadership style and motivation are embraced and used to the team's advantage rather than allowing the creative tension to impede progress and cause disconnects between team members.

As we said early on, it's easiest to manage a team with similar souls and like minds. They'll probably get along great. But you're most likely to lose enormous amounts of potential creativity and productivity in exchange for your little peace of mind.

In the same way that disparity in institutional authority can disrupt and imbalance a leadership team, popular authority can do the same. *Leaders in name* can be undermined by *leaders in fact* at any time. If you're relying on your institutional authority to encourage participation and compliance from your leadership team, you'll be lucky to get it. The resonance that comes from aligning what your people do best with what the organization needs most is the most powerful motivator you can hope for. Achieving that resonance will put your institutional authority in harmony with popular authority. Or, better yet, the two might merge and become one.

Because popular authority can't be accurately measured any more than the precise influence of institutional power, it can't be consistently weighted as part of the ComposiTeam Leadership System. However, if you study the cow paths in the carpet, the way we discussed in Chapter 2, you'll be able to factor it into your management craft.

Chapter 6 Summary: Keys to Unleashing Leadership

- **People are money:** Make sure you value your people. Sure, they cost you money in direct and indirect compensation, taxes, and other costs, hidden and visible. But, theoretically, they generate more revenue than they cost you. If you make a concerted, conscious, methodical effort to maximize their leadership potential and productivity, you're going to realize a lot more revenue from their efforts.

- **Right-size your team:** Don't put people on a leadership team who don't need to be there. Who *does* need to be there? The people who, together, produce the composite leadership profile that will align best with your initiative profile. You definitely need those guys on your team. Ideally, if special competencies are called for, the composite leadership profile will still align. Mixing and matching potential team members from your database will ultimately reveal the ideal size of your ideal team roster.

- **Manage your variances:** There will sometimes be limitations. Your choice of team members might be limited or restricted. You can always put a team together with a composite leadership profile that's as close to your initiative profile as you can get, and then compensate in whatever way you can. Not knowing how much, or in which categories, your team varies from your initiative profile is like working blind. Not knowing what your initiative calls for in terms of human behavior is like working *double-blind*.

- **Specialized reporting:** Regularly scheduled progress reporting is important to the success of any initiative. Intra-team, inter-team, and extra-team (with the rest of the world) communications are essential.

When, how, and to whom reports should be submitted are as important as any other aspect of team work. Make sure that all leadership style and motivation issues are addressed in every report. Choose who is most appropriate to report on each category and then follow through to make sure they do. Reporting on all leadership style and motivation categories will ensure an even flow of balanced information.

☛ **Vive la différence!** The diverse opinions, backgrounds, leadership styles, and motivations are the rich fuel that your organization runs on. But you need to tune the engine. If the mixture is too rich, you could stall out. If the mixture is too lean, the engine starves. Mixing and matching, aligning and assigning are all part of brilliantly managing the diverse resources available to you. Do everything within your power to increase the desire to participate among your team members. Use every trick up your sleeve to reduce the desire to disconnect among your team members.

Who is that standing over at the water cooler? It looks like a dragon, but he's dressed in business casual. It's Org alright. Your consistent and systematic approach to aligning what your people do best with what your organization needs most has made a believer out of him.

We told you it was possible. We told you, if he found it more fun to be part of the team than to forage behind it, he'd change his attitude. He is, after all, the composite culture of your organization. When people put innovative and creative new ways of doing things to use, change is sustained, things improve, and Org is happy to scarf on the remnants of old initiatives and programs cast off as your organization moves boldly into the future. To keep Org from backsliding and losing your team composite leadership profile/initiative profile alignment advantages, you must sooner or later deal with the one factor that can unhinge everything: *fear.*

Chapter 7

The Fear Factor

Knowledge is the antidote to fear.

—Ralph Waldo Emerson

Before you can release the stored, pent-up leadership potential in your organization, you must deal with fear. Fear is the one thing that can unhinge *everything*. The ComposiTeam Leadership System provides the framework to master individual and organizational fear, and maximize individual and organizational performance. If leadership is going to become an expectation at all levels, you will expect nothing less.

When we study the gap between organizational expectations and actual performance, there's usually no ambiguity whatsoever as to who is in charge. That would be too easy. If confusion about who's in charge isn't the problem, then what is? Usually, it is *fear*. Fear is the number-one cause of people running around organizations acting like idiots. We've all been there and done that. There have been times when we've all engaged in idiotic and counterproductive behavior as we tried to compensate for our feelings of uncertainty, self-doubt, incompetence, and general anxiety.

Fear is the chief cause of irresponsible behavior in for-profit and not-for-profit businesses, education, and government. There are probably fewer snowflakes in a blizzard than there are examples of persons in positions of leadership responsibility making the wrong choices or avoiding important decisions because they're consciously or unconsciously paralyzed by fear.

Who among us hasn't looked back at moments of compromise and/or indecision and wished we had acted more boldly? Some people live their entire lives that way. It reminds us once again of Thoreau, who said, "The mass of men lead lives of quiet desperation." Nothing blocks the thoughts and actions necessary for leadership success more than fear. All of the leadership skill-building in the world won't produce a truly effective leader until he or she has mastered fear. The last thing you want people bringing to a leadership team is fear. It's contagious.

You could say that Org feeds on fear, especially the fear that comes from people being assigned to positions of responsibility outside of their areas of natural talent and expertise. More accurately, the misalignment of people's essential natures, emotional purposes, and organizational roles generates a lot of dragon food in the form of discarded training and motivational stuff intended to compensate for the misalignment and the sense of trepidation that comes with it.

With proper alignment between what people do best and what organizations need most, the compensatory training and motivational stuff wouldn't have been necessary in the first place. The team members could have engaged in training and mastery activities to build up what they're already best suited for, and they would have internalized the learning as a result. Both the resonant training and its internalization would have kept the stuff out of Org's reach.

Mastering fear through recognition of unique strengths and essential natures will set the stage for everyone in your organization to become a leader in name *and* in fact. We've taken some time to establish the pivotal role that Org (your organizational culture) as well as old, new, and *new* new school concepts of leadership set the stage to adopt a new leadership philosophy and implement a systemic approach to team leadership. Now, it's important to understand the debilitating role fear plays in undoing all of your best organizational design, development, training, and motivational efforts. It's time for you to become a *fear-buster* in your organization.

The Myth of Fearlessness

There is no such thing as a truly fearless leader. A literal interpretation implies that effective leaders have no fear—not true. Leaders are people, and people experience fear. Anyone who believes that she or he is truly without fear should not be trusted as a leader of human beings. Such a person would not possess the empathy or the genuine regard that responsible leadership calls for. It's one thing to toy with your own reality, but it's something else to take liberties with the reality of others. Everyone experiences fear.

The best way to conquer or at least diminish fear in organizational life is to avoid placing people in its path. Fear occurs when individuals face the potential loss of something they consider valuable. The more valuable something is to someone's health and well-being, even if the person's very health and well-being are what's at stake, the greater the fear of losing it. Dignity, self-respect, and the respect of others are all on the list, too. Becoming aware of individuals' strengths and comfort zones is the first step to engaging them in activities and initiatives that resonate with their essential natures. The more a person's professional responsibilities resonate with who he or she is, the less likely it is that fear will be a negative factor.

Promoting fear

Pulling people out of the ranks and appointing them as leaders can lead to a host of potential problems. Militaristic hierarchical organizations with clearly defined leader vs. subordinate models make it impossible for peers to remain peers after a promotion has been made. Fred has worked alongside Joe and Jennifer for years. They have much in common, including a vested interest in gaining recognition at their level. Once Joe is promoted, he is no longer vested in the same objectives. As much as bosses like to pretend that they are still *buddies* with their former peers, the relationship changes—and it's largely fear that changes it.

The more that former peers—now bosses—attempt to ignore the organizational differences between leaders and subordinates in hierarchical organizations, the greater the opportunity for fear and loathing to creep in. Misunderstandings, dishonesty, abuse of power, and other relational malfunctions are common when working people try to pretend that nothing has changed after a peer becomes a boss. New bosses are *fearful* of losing their newly acquired power, and former peers become equally *fearful* that the newly acquired power will be used against them.

When leadership is made an expectation for everyone, this problem is greatly diminished and, hopefully, eliminated. Instead of emphasizing power over one another, the issue becomes power over your job. Instead of equating responsibility for the performance of others with higher pay (and the fear of losing it), compensation should be tied to direct contributions to the company's stated goals and objectives. We don't know of any companies that presently name *managing a bunch of people* as an organizational objective.

In hierarchical organizations, fear of losing position, power, money, and benefits is always influencing your thoughts and contaminating your ability to do good work. If whatever you were good at has been replaced, and higher pay is predicated upon managing a bunch of people, we don't blame you for being scared. People who are not well-suited to leading and inspiring others, yet are compensated to do exactly that, must eventually lay awake at night wondering, "If they ever find out how bad I am at this, I'll get canned. Why didn't I keep doing what I knew how to do and was comfortable with?"

Consider the molecular model as an antidote for fear. At least when work cells are developed around specific jobs, tasks, objectives, projects, or initiatives, ringleaders know why they're supporting, encouraging, and sustaining the best alignment of people's essential natures with specific responsibilities. That's 90 percent of the leader's job. Instead of making people's needs a distraction from the organization's needs, alignment of composite leadership profiles and initiative profiles wrap the needs of both into one neat package. That takes the fear out of leadership.

Fear can be a friend

Fear is neutral. In itself, it is neither good nor bad. It's how you respond to fear that counts. On the good side, fear can be a great early warning system, and can serve to heighten your senses and keep you alert when danger is near. Ignoring fear can be deadly, as in pretending you're not afraid of the giant black bear charging at you in the woods.

In the true-life story of The Great Santini, captured in the 1979 movie of the same name, the adolescent son of a Marine supersonic fighter pilot asks his seemingly fearless and invincible father, "Dad, are you ever afraid when you fly?"

"Hell, yes," the straight-talking Lieutenant Colonel "Bull" Meecham responds. "That's what makes me good."

No one thinks any less of the Colonel for being so blunt and honest. People tend to think highly of those who are courageous enough to be self-disclosing. Denying being afraid can lead to many dangers, not the least of which is being exposed as a fraud. Learning to deal with the reality of fear brings hope and opens up endless possibilities.

On the other hand, allowing fear to limit your senses to mere survival can have a long-term debilitating effect on your personal and professional lives. Org, if not successfully dealt with, can bring down a whole organization. Yet, some continue to pretend (a) that he doesn't exist, or (b) he's nothing to be afraid of. That kind of denial can be dangerous. People are least affected by organizational fear (or Org) when they are operating from within their natural strengths and abilities—that is, their comfort zones.

Unleashing leadership is about ordinary people being asked to take leadership responsibility for things they know and understand, not simply conforming to a predetermined concept of leadership and taking on responsibility for unfamiliar things in uncomfortable circumstances. We believe in basing the expectation of leadership on individual and composite strengths and abilities, not transplanting the individual into that fearful place called the unknown.

Fighting Fear

The greatest common fear among persons in positions of responsibility for the performance of others is dealing with the problems those human beings always seem to have. Persons in positions of responsibility for the performance of others fear the problems others bring because they might not be able to solve or even neutralize them. Knowing how to orchestrate strengths diminishes that fear. Much as a symphony conductor understands how to blend the very different instruments in an orchestra into a harmonious whole, policy-makers that understand the human dynamics they're working with can anticipate attitudes and behaviors.

Effective leaders don't waste time or energy pretending that fear doesn't exist. Even though there is no such thing as a fearless leader, you can achieve the next best thing. Aligning what people do best with what organizations need most is the best way to keep people functioning in their comfort zones, where they experience maximum confidence. With such alignment, commitment soars and the debilitating effect of fear diminishes. Effective leaders also develop new skills to conquer fear whenever it comes and wherever it comes from.

Persons in positions of leadership responsibility who attempt to hide their fear and/or pretend that fear has no effect on their thoughts or actions are not being honest with themselves or the people for whom they are responsible. Individuals who engage in such deceit are far from ideal leadership candidates. Even though they might put on a good show and give the outward appearance of being confident leadership material (in the traditional sense), when push comes to shove, only those with the right perspective on fear will be able to bring out the very best in their team members, and only then after they have learned to bring out the best in themselves.

Attempting to hide or deny fear only means that fear is that much more in control. Danny Cox, coauthor of *Leadership When the Heat's On* (McGraw-Hill, 2002), maintains that if we don't actively take charge of fear, fear will take charge of us. A core issue and primary promise of *Unleashing Leadership* is to help master fear by aligning individual and team composite leadership profiles with the needs of the organization. In this way, fear no longer blocks the thoughts and actions that will help propel you and your enterprise to greater success.

Loss vs. Gain

Different people have different economies—financial and emotional. Some fear being embarrassed and losing pride more than losing money. Others fear losing a relationship. For some it's control. For yet others it is status. When money is the main issue, the actual fear might be about losing security, status, and other things that money can buy. An individual's economic comfort zone is mostly determined by what she or he values most. Engaging in any activity that puts the valued commodity at risk will push most people outside of their comfort zones, and into the grip of fear.

Proper alignment of people's essential natures with their organization's needs shifts focus from fear of loss to anticipation of increasing competency. Most people tend to be comfortable doing things that come naturally to them. Bold behavior and risk-taking come more easily when you feel reasonably confident about what you're doing.

Competency is something that is developed and/or proven over time, and usually both. When your natural talents and abilities are identified, and you focus on developing them, competency is truly maximized. The first step is to identify your essential nature. The next step is to align your essential nature with the tasks you set out to perform and responsibilities you agree to accept. That's what the CompositTeam Leadership System does. No matter how skilled you are across different competencies, you will always be most competent at those things that are consistent with your natural talents and abilities. That alignment will release the boldest and most creative forces available within you.

This doesn't mean that you subordinate the mission of your company to the essential nature of the staff. The mission comes first. To best fulfill the mission you must align your human resources with your organizational opportunities. The highest stakeholders in the company establish the mission. Operational stakeholders make it so.

The hurricane drill

Fear that is fueled by operating outside one's comfort zone is not overcome by venturing farther into uncharted waters. However, it is true that systematic desensitization will diminish fear because taking low-threat baby steps will gradually reduce the tension of entering unfamiliar and anxiety-provoking territory. The difference is, the baby steps will be a thoughtful and intentional decision, not a blind charge at full speed. The charge could be costly and irresponsible. Is the gamble worth it?

It makes much more sense, from a productivity, efficiency, and team loyalty perspective, to align the individual's natural strengths and abilities with his or her role in the organization. Operating in unfamiliar and/ or anxiety-provoking territory tends to bring on the hurricane drill. As the hurricane approaches, people act defensively. They run for cover, board up the windows, lock their doors, and pile the sand bags high.

People are also savvy enough to realize that, even after the initial trauma has subsided, they might be sitting in the peaceful eye of the storm and a repeat performance can blow through at any time. Very few people can stay entirely out of harm's way from cradle to grave, and we're not suggesting that living defensively is a good technique for personal or professional growth and development. We think that accepting the inevitability of defensive behavior is enough for organizational designers to adopt a leadership system that will serve as a solid, storm-proof foundation, whether the wind is blowing or not.

Avoidance vs. Intention

Fear opposes attraction, even though the two often seem to dance together when you least expect it. All of us tend to act for one of two purposes: to keep something bad from happening or to cause something good to happen. That's the difference between avoidance and intention. Do you make decisions because you're fearful of losing something you consider personally valuable, or is the decision based on your intention to cause something good to happen?

Fear is a driving force in avoidant behavior. In the chess match of life, avoidant behavior can range from calculated maneuvers to sheer survival. It's easy to spot the avoidant element in obsessive/compulsive behavior. Someone that takes ritualistic behavior to an extreme, such as excessive hand washing to avoid germs, is avoiding the negative consequences of germs, whatever those exaggerated consequences seem to be in that person's imagination. In the workplace, excessive attention to numbers, projections, and reports can serve the same avoidant purpose as hand washing.

Corporate executives or politicians that surround themselves with puppets are most likely insulating themselves from the possibility of being seriously challenged by ideas that might result in their embarrassment. In more extreme cases, they might be engaging in unethical or illegal behavior that their loyal operatives will help to hide or take the fall for, if necessary. In these and far less extreme cases, avoidant behavior usually results in the expenditure of energy and resources to avoid something negative instead of spending those same energies and resources in the pursuit of something positive.

Although preventing something negative from happening or engaging in damage control can be interpreted as a positive act, as in the hurricane drill, we think that positive behavior, especially in organizational life, is a result of thoughtful planning and assessment of all possible outcomes. In other words, it is *intentional.* The intention of positive behavior is to bring about an outcome that is good for as many people as possible while costing as little as possible. In any discussion of leadership, you can appreciate how important it is to determine if behavior is avoidant or intentional.

Avoidant behavior causes people to withdraw and build protective barriers. Other than intentionally deceiving or neglecting internal and external stakeholders, we can't think of anything more damaging and demoralizing to organizational health than placing people in positions of responsibility that cause them to withdraw and spend their energy building protective barriers.

Inside/Outside

Fear causes people to focus internally. Reducing fear through alignment with their essential natures and natural abilities will shift their focus to external, organizational issues. Survival is internally focused. Creativity is externally focused. The kind of collaborative leadership that you want practiced throughout your organization is impossible in an environment of fear, avoidance, defensiveness, and internal focus.

Only when people can think outside of themselves and beyond their personal circumstances can they see the big picture. Only when people can balance concern for their own well-being and success with the well-being and success of others will they adopt the behaviors that lead to higher productivity and sustained growth. The seemingly elusive organizational behaviors that organizational designers, top executives, and stakeholders dream about will come naturally once the natural talents and abilities of the organizational population have been identified and properly aligned.

Fear vs. Anxiety

Fear and anxiety are two different things, although both are hazardous to organizational health. Fear is caused by an identifiable object. Anxiety is a generalized discomfort and uneasiness for which there doesn't seem to be a specific or single cause. Fear is caused by the anticipation of danger, most often manifested in the form of emotional or physical pain.

If a big office safe is being lowered to the sidewalk from several stories up, most people will not walk directly under it. The reason is obvious: They're afraid it will come loose and crash down on top of them. The object of fear is the safe and the dent it could leave in the cranium. Is it a reasonable fear? Sure. The safe coming down on top of your head, no matter how unlikely or improbable, could nevertheless ruin your day.

As the object of fear, the iron safe is real and tangible. The potential physical pain and harm it represents is real enough to motivate folks to walk around rather than underneath it. Fear expectedly diminishes once the safe and the danger it poses are behind us. Walking beside tall buildings with the perpetual fear that, without warning, something might come crashing down to the sidewalk is an anxiety issue. Could something fall from a tall building without warning? Yes. Can a mugger appear nearly anywhere at any time of day? Sure. Can hijacked airliners crash into buildings when least expected? Are there reasons to be anxious? You betcha. But what has worry ever done for you or the organization for which you work?

Without a specific object, anxiety is more of a state of being and affects people differently and more continuously than fear, which approaches and retreats with the proximity of the object. In most cases, anxiety is more unreasonable than fear, even though many fears are themselves unreasonable. Either way, people often hesitate to move boldly ahead with decisions they know in their hearts they should make. Sometimes they make decisions to act based on fear and/or anxiety when the more prudent course is to hold fast. In other words, they bolt when they should be bold.

Life is enough of a guessing game without allowing fear and/or anxiety to dictate policy. The last thing you want policy-makers to do is make decisions based on anxiety and/or fear. The old Org used to love that, of course. Many policy-makers avoid taking risks, *or* leap without looking, because fear and anxiety have allowed their judgment to become clouded. An anti-organization dragon wins either way. The organization is not going to grow and prosper when it's either bound up by fear or raging out of control, running as fast as it can from its own anxiety. In the chaos, there will be lots of refuse laying around for Org to eat. Fortunately, you now know a better way to feed and care for Org.

Pleasure vs. Pain

The two most fundamental ways to motivate human beings and their pets are the promise of pleasure and the threat of pain. Of the two, the threat of pain is the most powerful motivator and tends to produce the most immediate, if only short-term, results. Consider the dog that will do tricks for a doggie treat, even for the *possibility* of receiving a treat. If the same dog is familiar with the discomfort of crossing an electronic fence, the offer of a doggie treat is not likely to induce the pup to cross.

The threat of pain produces avoidant behavior. In the opposite case, intentional behavior moves you toward pleasure. When pain becomes the price for pleasure, the issue becomes sacrifice, and the internal struggle begins. The example of classically conditioned animals might seem inappropriate in a book primarily about people functioning in organizations. Yet, all too often, leaders *in name* attempt to manage by intimidation and threats. It's surprising how many executives will openly brag about keeping their people in line by threatening discipline or termination. Pitting team members against one another is another all-too-common tactic to keep people in constant fear of losing their jobs.

For most working people, the loss of a job poses a serious threat to their personal well-being and the well-being of their families. For most people, lifestyle is directly tied to compensation for work. Loss of these resources can, and often does, mean losing the comforts and, worse yet, the security that people have come to depend upon. Loss of a job can result in everything from a diminished social status in the community to the danger of no longer being able to provide basic needs for yourself and your family.

The promise of pleasure is not as powerful as the threat of pain. Doing what's necessary to achieve more and improve your lifestyle seems to be a less powerful motivator than fighting like mad not to lose what you already have. Avoiding pain is usually an immediate consideration. Working toward pleasure is a longer-term issue. The longer the pleasure, the greater the effort and attention span required.

Pain and pleasure can be better sized up when set side-by-side on the table. Here's a dollar. You can purchase the pleasure with it, as long as you're willing to accept the pain as well. In other words, buying the pleasure means buying the pain that goes with it. Or you can use your dollar to forgo both. The average person, given that choice, will invest in avoiding pain before she or he will accept the pain for the sake of the pleasure. Garth Brooks sings, "…if I'd missed the pain, I'd have had to miss the dance." Noble words in retrospect. But few folks would have opted for the dance up front if they had known, at the time, that pain was part of the deal.

Pleasure is still the motivator of choice for highly effective, and visionary, leaders. Pain remains the primary motivational tool for ineffective (short-sighted) managers, especially when it is used as a weapon to produce rapid results. But pain will not positively shape behavior over the long haul. Using pain as a motivator creates a number of problems: squelching creativity, strangling enthusiasm, smothering excitement, and choking the life out of loyalty are just a few. Motivating with pain creates paranoid people and a plump organizational dragon.

Leadership, Vision, and Fear

When we say that leaders need to act on the truth of the past, the irreplaceability of the present, and the inevitability of the future, we are describing someone with vision. Saying that a leadership attitude is expected from everyone in the organization is to say that you want everyone on your payroll to act with vision. Add patience and persistence to vision and you're fast approaching the ideal leadership attitude.

Vision requires an outward view. A visionary must be able to lift his or her gaze outside of him- or herself, look beyond issues of self, and see beyond the moment. We believe that humans have a transcendent capacity to get outside of ourselves and consider the situation with all of its moral and ethical, past, present, and future implications. Fear puts blinders on the vision necessary to effectively lead ourselves and/or be an effective leader for others.

Laying out a plan that includes short-, mid-, and long-term pleasure as rewards for positive behavior will produce the greatest creativity, enthusiasm, and loyalty possible. This requires patience and courage on the part of leaders. If they're afraid of not showing immediate, short-term, financial results, and cave in to pressure tactics as a result, they won't protect the time necessary to produce long-term results based on the promise of pleasure. In the typical organization, it takes a courageous leader to defend the concepts of time and patience in the face of impatient, short-sighted thinking.

On tour to promote his leadership book, former New York mayor, Rudolph Giuliani, said, "Knowing who you are and what you're about is critical to effective leadership." He went on to say that knowing your strengths means little unless you're willing to accept the areas in which you need help. He added *planning* to the list of leadership qualities. Part of being a well-prepared leader is self-awareness and awareness of others and their strengths and weaknesses. Finally, he talked about courage as the overriding factor in effective leadership. Echoing what many others consider true courage, he defined it as being afraid, knowing you're afraid, and moving ahead in spite of it.

Great leaders are not strangers to pain. They have experienced it. They understand it. They don't like it. But they don't shy away from doing what is right because of it. For the person who has a tremendous fear of being wrong, admitting a mistake is a painful step to becoming right. Some will say that pain is a constant companion and serves as a good adviser and counsel.

A Self-Fulfilling Prophecy

Fear feeds on its own fat. People that operate from a place of fear will most likely see their fears realized. It's not hard to see why. Fear will block the creative and possibly risky behaviors necessary to produce positive outcomes. Without creativity and risk, the results will most likely be negative. The cycle of fear, feeding on itself, repeats itself endlessly.

Negative thinking begets negative thinking. People who predict, "It won't work," later, when their half-hearted efforts fail, say smugly, "I told you it wouldn't work." If they start with, "It probably won't work," and then it *does work*, they won't be forced to admit that they were wrong on the front end. It's almost as if they are more afraid of being wrong than achieving a positive outcome.

Not being wrong is more important to many people than being right. If people are truly concerned with doing the right thing, they will admit when they're wrong if it helps the right thing get done. But, to many, the fear of being wrong blocks any possibility of ever getting it right. They will go to ridiculous lengths to defend the wrong position or point of view to avoid facing their worst fears. It is the fear that guarantees failure. If this strong-willed individual is in a position of leadership responsibility, the damage can be catastrophic.

Standard Operating Procedures

In most organizations, policies lead to paralysis. A policy, by nature, is an attempt to regulate problems or conflicts out of a process. Bureaucrats are infamous for ignoring the inevitability of human error and/or flexibility as they attempt to design policies and processes that, although executed by human beings, will produce the desired result as reliably and repetitively as a punch press. Get over it. People make mistakes. Even when they don't, it's human nature to repeat tasks with slight variation depending on mood, energy level, distractions, and so on.

Most policies are fear-based: fear of causing injury, fear of inconsistency, and fear of litigation. As a litigious society, we are our own worst enemies. Even before trial lawyers, policy-makers were engaged in the practice of writing policies and procedures, many of which have brought entire organizations down to the level of their lowest common denominator. So powerful was the fear that someone might take advantage of the situation, or make an honest mistake, that all of the creativity and potential above the line was sacrificed.

Damn the torpedoes

Effective leaders take risks and don't allow fear to stifle the best potential in themselves or their organizations. This doesn't mean they're daredevils. That would be irresponsible. Just being willing to act in a well-reasoned manner, and accept and deal with human inconsistencies and idiosyncrasies for the sake of high achievement is enough to get a leader in trouble with the CPP (Company Policy Police).

Many organizations will sacrifice their best and brightest people on an altar to maintaining policy. The fact is that, especially in larger bureaucracies, the person who retires after a long tenure is probably the person who never made any waves. People who demonstrate what we could loosely refer to as fearless qualities, that is, risk-taking, advocating change, and encouraging creativity and innovation, are often hunted down and dealt with harshly. They are judged and often expelled by the unwritten and unspoken rules that subordinate positive potential to the avoidance of pain.

Chapter 7 Summary:
Keys to Unleashing Leadership

The myth of the fearless leader: We could have called it the "legend of the fearless leader." That might have been more accurate. People tend to believe in legends because they want to. Organizational executives want to believe that there is a person out there who will ride herd on their employees and whip them into shape, at the same time leading a charge against the competition and making them run for the hills. All the time spent trying to locate the legendary leader is spent ignoring the leadership potential right under their noses.

Fear can be a friend: Fear isn't always to be feared. There are good reasons to be afraid sometimes. There are always internal and external threats to your enterprise to which you need to respond. To remain oblivious, or pretend they don't cause you alarm, is to set yourself up for disaster. The key is not to be driven by fear and anxiety. It's good radar, though, an early warning system that can help keep you, and your team members, on your toes.

Comfort zones: People don't like to spend much time outside of them. That wouldn't be important to a supervisor, manager, or an organizational executive such as you, except for the behavior it causes. When people are outside of their comfort zones, they begin to act defensively. They often focus more on not losing what they have than on becoming more productive. The energy and resources they could be spending on proactively contributing to the achievement of personal and organizational goals and objectives is spent building walls instead.

Displacement: Two opposite things can't occupy the same space at the same time. That's why acting with intention is important if you're trying to dislodge another situation or behavior. If you don't act, inertia sets in and unwanted behaviors and attitudes malinger. Making a decision to be more proactive and concentrate on promoting specific attitudes and behaviors, and then *doing something*, displaces the inertia. The same applies to motivating with attraction rather than fear, and pleasure vs. pain. They can't occupy the same space, and it's within your control to use one to displace the other.

➡ **Standard operating procedures:** Flexibility is far more important to overcoming fear than rigidity. It's possible to be so afraid that something bad is going to happen, that you contribute to it happening. If all of your thoughts and energy are focused on avoidance, where are you going? Is your gaze so fixed on the thing you're afraid of that you're backing into the future? Obviously, if you're an organizational decision- and/or policy-maker, that behavior can negatively impact lots of folks. Keep your SOP flexible by basing it on positive principles you're trying to promote rather than on strictly forbidding behavior you're trying to eliminate.

To move beyond the paralyzing effects of fear to function more productively, with increased loyalty, participation, and enthusiasm from everyone, you must begin with understanding the essential elements of human behavior in organizations. By committing to align organizational behavior with organizational needs, you won over Org. He joined the good guys. Now, to keep it that way, you need to make these new practices a way of organizational life. You need to become a tireless advocate for the essence of individual and composite personality, and how that knowledge can help unleash the stored or pent-up leadership potential in your organization.

Let these new thoughts about organization, leadership, and fear into the mull around in your head. You're getting ready to move into Part III of this book, where you'll read detailed descriptions of each leadership style: control, compliance, social, and stability. This is yet more foundation and background for aligning what your people do best with what your organization needs most.

Leadership Styles

Chapter 8

The Control Specialist

Who, with a natural instinct to discern
What knowledge can perform, is diligent to learn;
Abides by this resolve, and stops not there,
But makes his moral being his prime care;
Who, doomed to go in company with Pain,

Turns his necessity to glorious gain;
In face of these doth exercise a power
Which is our human nature's highest dower;
Controls them and subdues, transmutes, bereaves
Of their bad influence, and their good receives.

—William Wordsworth,
"Character of a Happy Warrior"

Leader to Leader

As much as we'd like to see collaborative leadership and shared responsibility become the rule and not the exception in organizations, leading is most often still an individual responsibility. Yes, the composite leadership profile will dominate the leadership team's performance. But leadership is two-dimensional in that leadership functions aren't performed in a vacuum. Yet each individual faces his or her leadership challenges, at some level, *as an individual.* Leadership is ultimately a process that affects many people.

This chapter deals with the leadership style we call the *control specialist.* An essential element of leadership development where control specialists are concerned is to reinforce positive uses of their impulse to control. We urge you to visualize the control specialist in either individual or collaborative leadership roles, depending on your situation and/or application. When considering the control specialist as a leader with institutional authority, you can cast the other three basic styles—compliance, social, and stability—in subordinate roles.

You can also consider the control specialist as part of a leadership team or working in isolation, although the latter is rarely the case. Ideally, all members of your organizational population will face each other as leader to leader. Large ringleader to smaller ringleader, large initiative owner to larger initiative owner, it doesn't matter; just because one fish is larger than another doesn't make either one stop being a fish.

Strength or weakness

Each leadership style is defined by its weaknesses as well as its strengths, even though a name such as *control* might sound like pure strength. Fear is a primary and powerful behavioral determinant in every human being. People often develop what appear to be the strongest characteristics of their personalities as weapons against the debilitating effects of fear and anxiety.

Combining styles and discussing how each can contribute to the success of the other is one way of studying how diverse styles can serve to strengthen, and be strengthened by, the others. When considered in isolation, an individual's compensatory characteristics can provide a vital road map to personal growth and development. What causes fear to one individual might not cause fear in another. Regardless of how a person came about his or her dominant leadership style, it's safe to assume that others can play important and complementary roles.

As we've emphasized throughout this book, everyone is in a position of leadership, even if she or he works in relative isolation, as what leadership author and speaker, Danny Cox, calls an "Island of Excellence." Even though a position might be subordinate in terms of the organizational food chain, we'll never look upon any organizational position as subordinate in importance. The collaborative approach to leadership that we recommend is based on looking at each team member as a potential contributor, with the result being a much more comprehensive and effective leadership system. Knowing how each individual's leadership profile helps shape the composite profile of whatever group they belong to, from a two-person dyad, to the entire organization, you can appreciate why more knowledge of each style and motivation empowers you as a leader.

Control Issues

Control, in the context used by William Wordsworth in the quote that opens the chapter, is virtuous in that it helps subdue the less desirable aspects of our human nature. We don't look upon control over others as a virtue in and of itself. We know there are times when it seems like life would be easier if we could snap our fingers and get everyone's immediate attention. But that would also rob us of much of the richness that comes from the input of others. At best, we might want to regard the exercise of control over others as a sometimes necessary evil.

If an individual is intent on maintaining control over others for the sake of control, the motivation is likely to be fear-based and intended to avoid some undesirable outcome (undesirable to the controller). Such a person does not trust others with his or her well-being. Such people might have good reason not to trust, perhaps beginning in early childhood. Whatever the cause, mistrust can be extremely toxic to collaborative work environments and, as professional adults, it's our obligation to one another to find a way past these fears.

Gaining and maintaining *self*-control is usually considered a good thing. Gaining and maintaining control over others is desirable only in limited circumstances. Law enforcement professionals are trained to establish and maintain control in crisis situations, such as when making an arrest or deescalating a violent situation. We hope that leadership challenges for our average readers don't include bringing down violent criminals in their offices and workspaces.

Having said that, we've observed how many managers, and others in leadership positions, establish and maintain control over others almost as if they *are* maintaining order on a cellblock; assuming that their subordinates will riot and cause havoc at the slightest opportunity. Control seems to be at the very top of many a leader's agenda. In the absence of more enlightened and effective methods of interacting with others and influencing human behavior, exercising some sort of control over others seems to be the first choice in management style.

Not everyone comes from a place of mistrust. Sometimes a control approach to leadership is taught by mentors and senior executives to up-and-coming leaders, because that's what they were taught. Either way, exercising control over others *for the sake of control* is lazy leadership at best and defensive leadership at worst.

Whether or not we agree with those who seek to control others, there are too many people doing it to ignore. Control-oriented people, whatever their motivations, are extremely common in organizational life. In our experience, control is the most common style among people who have been appointed to positions of leadership. True to our positive natures, we will examine the many ways that a control specialist can, and often does, make good leader.

In the military hierarchy model of leadership and organization, control is expected from leaders rather than leadership being expected from everyone. When team members appear to be off-the-wall or seem disorganized, a manager's superiors are likely to ask the rhetorical question, "Why can't you control your people?" As much as Tom Peters and others have preached the virtues and benefits of occasional chaos and creative disorder in organizational life, the dominant management attitude is to maintain order, even at the cost of creativity and innovation. Why else are workers referred to as the "rank and file"?

When business experts, consultants, and authors, such as Donald Kurako and Richard Hodgetts (*Entrepreneurship: A Contemporary Approach*, 5th ed, South-Western, 2000) say things such as, "Authoritarian management is being replaced by a networking, people-style of management, characterized by horizontal coordination and support," the evidence indicates they are being more optimistic than realistic. There are more examples of people-centered management practices now than ever before. But to say that a major paradigm shift has taken place is a stretch.

We are strong proponents of people-centered, collaborative leadership, and provide teaching, consulting, and coaching in how to engender it. People-centered management approaches have been *proven* to increase innovation, productivity, and profits. But that's not the reason why the evolution of organization management from hierarchical to horizontal seems to be moving at the speed of molasses. The nail in the foot that keeps the momentum toward progressive leadership techniques walking in circles is the basic nature of the leaders themselves, as well as the skill sets and organizational parameters they've inherited.

Control and power

The first word on the LSI is "powerful," because many people believe that power is synonymous with controlling others. Those who feel it's important to be in control of others have a corresponding need to feel powerful. Many of these people have trust issues, complicated by impatience. The *truly* powerful person is patient and quietly self-assured. Those exercising *self*-control and personal discipline won't necessarily experience a rush of power as much as a sense of satisfaction when everyone on their team pulls his or her oar a little more enthusiastically and in synchronous motion with the rest.

Those who are comforted in the sense of power based on control over others are not likely to experience much in the way of inner peace, serenity, or long-term satisfaction from their leadership style. A power rush can increase feelings of security and create the illusion of satisfaction, but real and lasting satisfaction will only result from a relationship with team members based on trust and mutual respect. The higher a ringleader's popular authority index, the more secure he or she can feel.

Power vs. influence

Having power is a lot like having money. It's good to have it available to you when you need it. However, most leaders who think they need power to get people to do what they're supposed to do actually need *influence*, which is a different concept. Nevertheless, someone without that knowledge, or lacking the patience to motivate people in ways other than exercising institutional control, will readily fall back on power. Because power is the fuel for a control specialist, she or he is vulnerable to shifting his or her attention away from accomplishment of organizational tasks, objectives, projects, and initiatives to preserving and protecting his or her own power.

Power has a practical purpose in organizational leadership. But it can also be very seductive. When the control specialist is in a position of leadership, there is always a potential for abuse of power. An abuse of power is not necessarily intentional. Power is sometimes a zero-sum commodity, especially in hierarchical organizations. For the control specialist to have enough power to influence the behavior of others, the others must have less power. When power is used to control the behavior of others, it's the *disparity* that modifies the behavior of the weaker. When power is equally distributed, as in the collaborative leadership model, people rely on other leadership skills to get things done. New and improved leadership skills must be supported by the leadership system within the organization. A control-based leader can't be expected to relinquish his or her power without new skills to take its place and principles that reinforce the new paradigm.

Control and fearlessness

Many control specialists might buy into the myth of fearlessness on the outside, but have a much more difficult time convincing themselves. Giving the appearance of having no fear seems to strengthen the outward perception of power, and vice versa. Some control specialists are tempted to demonstrate their courage and fearlessness as a means of proving that they deserve the power bestowed upon them by their superiors. Boards are notorious for wanting CEOs to be powerful, *take charge* types. Unfortunately, the focus that *should be* on the pursuit of organizational priorities is too often misdirected by demonstrations of control meant to impress and intimidate.

Control itself is not a sound basis for leadership performance. If a control specialist has no challenge requiring a powerful-looking response, she or he might spend otherwise productive time and resources creating one. Add to that the need to create the *perception* of power and fearlessness, and the control specialist can wind up leading the whole organization off track just to keep up the charade.

It is important to focus on organizational goals and keep them in perspective, which can make positive use of the control specialist's desire to lead the way. Simple preservation of control demands attention and resources better spent elsewhere. If a leader attends to those things that help focus organizational energies on attainment of organizational goals, she or he will be exercising *authentic* control.

Control and controlling

Confidence is a byproduct of successful experience. The control specialist, like anyone else, can develop confidence and a desire to control around those things she or he is good at. Control specialists in leadership positions will develop enhanced leadership skills as they have more success leading their team members in the achievement of personal and organizational goals. Wanting to be in charge because you're genuinely good at it is far different than wanting to be in charge because you're insecure in any other capacity. There are good reasons and ways to exercise control. There are also some not so good ways.

A certain amount of transient confidence can come from getting good at controlling others. But controlling others purely through disparity of power is only as reliable as the subordinates' willingness to put up with it. In an employers' market, control specialists can control others with impunity. In an employees' market, the control specialist's power is watered down. Control specialists who base their relationships with team members on earned respect, trust, and goal-focus will be effective leaders in any kind of market. People in positions of leadership who can earn popular authority to complement their institutional authority, are the least vulnerable to the changing fortunes of the marketplace.

Control and commanding

> "There is nothing more difficult to take in hand, more perilous to conduct, than to take a lead in the introduction of a new order of things, because the innovation has for enemies all who have done well under the old conditions and lukewarm defenders in those who may do well under the new."

> —Machiavelli

Effective leadership, in teams or individually, always means leading change. In order to overcome the fear and uncertainty that many people associate with change, a leader must be able to transcend the moment and reflect on the new moment that lies ahead. In a word, there are times when someone needs to assume *command*. This, along with accepting and acting on the lessons of the past and respecting the irreplaceability of the present, is an act of maturity, which is one of the many types of intelligence in which leaders should excel. Like controlling, taking command as a defensive compensation for insecurity is a scary proposition.

One would hope someone in command, even temporarily, would be intelligent enough to keep the big picture in mind. The term *intelligence* can mean different things to different people. Intelligence, in the conventional sense, is not usually the number-one criteria for placing people in positions of leadership, despite the fact that many leaders (control specialists at the front of the line), think that their intelligence was the number-one criterion for selection. As we pointed out earlier, power-orientation does not necessarily lead to the shrewdest or most intelligent leadership techniques. However, many people in positions of leadership consider themselves exceedingly smart for no other reason than they have the corner office, their name on the door, the reserved parking space, and so on.

Control specialists with a good handle on how their leadership style affects other people will recognize various kinds of intelligence throughout the organization and work to channel them into a sort of organizational super-intelligence. Understanding the principles behind the concept of composite personality is the mark of a truly intelligent, mature control specialist.

On the other side of that coin is the control specialist who seeks control, at least in part, because of the doubts she or he has in his or her own intellectual capacity and capability. Effective leaders, regardless of their leadership styles, know that whatever they lack, they can more than make up for by means of the talents and abilities of others on their teams. It's one thing to say, "None of us are as smart as all of us." It's another thing to have an effective leadership system to make productive use of collective creativity and capabilities.

Control and impatience

Control specialists tend to be impatient people. They are inclined toward action over reflection and get nervous when things aren't happening fast enough for them. Because they are quick to make up their minds, whether or not they have fully considered all of the ramifications of their actions, control specialists often exercise their power and control to compel others to act before the less impetuous folks are comfortable to move. Control specialists ask power and authority questions such as, "How far can we go with this before they clip our wings?"

It's common for subordinates to catch the flack when something screws up due to poor planning. This is an exceptionally bitter pill to swallow when the subordinate didn't want to go off half-cocked in the first place, but was given no choice by the control specialist for whom she or he works. Impatience is a good thing when people are dragging their feet and need to be prodded.

Impatience is a bad thing when it moves things along faster than they should be moved. Impatience can be expensive because, as the old saying goes, "There never seems to be enough time to do it right the first time, but there is always enough time to do it over again." What productive activity could people be engaged in today if they weren't tied up redoing what we paid them to do yesterday?

On the positive side, a control specialist's impatience can keep the team from procrastinating, overthinking, over-engineering, or overanalyzing something. It's a hedge against paralysis by analysis. One of the biggest problems Walt Disney had with the immensely creative Imagineers was getting them to a stopping point when designing rides and attractions for the theme parks. They could go on creating forever, but there had to be a time to stop designing and start building.

There is always an optimum balance between planning and doing. Control specialists have a tendency to keep things moving, which can be a positive pressure. As always, the more control specialists know, understand, and accept about their unique leadership styles, the more effective and useful their impatience can, and will, be.

Control and determination

As with their impatience, control specialists often possess a determination that will keep projects and initiatives moving when less resolute players are ready to throw in the towel. Determination can be fueled by pride, fear of failure, stubbornness, or numerous other factors, individually or in combination with one another. Regardless of its origin, determination can produce either positive or negative results.

There are times when throwing in the towel is the best solution and can prevent further embarrassment, continued economic losses, or long-term damage to morale and effectiveness inside and outside of the organization. At other times, quitting too soon can waste time and resources that have been invested in development of a new product, service, or work process. An enlightened control specialist can put his or her determination to good use keeping projects alive and on track. Somewhere in the mix is the wisdom of W.C. Fields who said:

> "If at first you don't succeed, try again. Then quit.
> There's no use being a damn fool about it."

Control and dominance

Sometimes it's good to know who is in charge. This is especially true if team members trust and respect the person in charge; whether it be a ringleader in a molecular organization, or a department head in a hierarchy. Under normal circumstances, in an organization with well-distributed power, it is not all that important to know who is in charge of others as long as everyone takes leadership responsibility for him- or herself. Of course it should always be clear where the responsibility rests.

Control specialists who demonstrate domination over others to illustrate the disparity of power they thrive on almost certainly damage their team's ability to function independently with confidence. We mentioned executives or supervisors who "joke" with their subordinates saying things such as, "Get back to work," and "How you doin', easy money?" even with a wink and a chuckle, are subtly saying, "I'm in control here, not you."

It might sound thin-skinned to even bring up such subtle comments. But the emotional odor left in the air after such statements, even when "just teasing," is hard to ignore. Subordinates know they are subordinate. When someone, even jokingly, feels a need to remind them, they have to wonder why. Obviously, practicing what Ken Blanchard calls

"Sea Gull Management" is not at all subtle. Flying into the office, flapping your wings loudly, and crapping on everybody's heads before flying out again leaves the unmistakable message that somebody is in control, and it's not the people with sea gull droppings on their heads.

Control and competitiveness

Control specialists tend to be competitive people, which is another way of saying they like to *win*. Unlike the win/win scenarios that you might expect from social or stability specialists, control specialists want someone to lose—as long as it's not them. To most control specialists, the existence of a loser heightens the cache of the winner. In competitive sports, that's great. In an organization, where everyone is supposed to be pulling their oars in the same direction, it can be disruptive and counterproductive.

If you want to control a control specialist, put them in a contest. The competitive nature that many control specialists possess can be focused and applied with great success to competitive situations in the marketplace. Competition is a fundamental component of a free market economy. Competition helps to breed excellence as providers of services and manufacturers of products compete for your money and ongoing patronage.

Friendly competitions among individuals and factions within an organization can be fun and productive, as long as the competition does not serve to de-motivate the majority of competitors. As a general rule, control specialists can make best use of their competitive spirits by finding competitive challenges outside of the organization. That's why *competitive issues* are reported on by control specialists in our ComposiTeam progress reporting format.

Control and taking charge

Control specialists can be quick to explore options and alternatives, often as a direct result of their low threshold for boredom. Sometimes being the only people who want to go where no person has gone before means taking charge of the team's adventure operations. However, impatience often gets the most of control specialists, and they have been known to change horses long before prudence calls for a change. If control specialists get too impatient, they might get off the horse they're riding before the next one comes alongside.

On the other hand, a control specialist's desire to see rapid and tangible results, even from unorthodox methods, can sometimes keep the door open to new ideas and concepts. Control specialists can be champions of exploration and innovation if they feel there is a possibility of shortening the distance between the beginning and the end of a process or project. Control specialists that know and accept their tendencies can become encouragers and supporters of creative and investigative activities in their organizations.

Control and vigor

Most control specialists operate at a high energy level. Call it their impatience, sense of power, or competitiveness, something seems to turn up their volume and constantly keep their batteries charged. They can be an effective driving force in the organization, or drive everyone in the organization nuts. Sometimes, control specialists alternate from one extreme to the other.

As a positive feature of the control specialist, vigor can be infectious and help keep things hopping when the overall energy level in the organization drops. It's not enough to initiate change in an enterprise; the hardest part is sustaining it through doubting, debating, and outright resistance. A vigorous control specialist can help keep change initiatives alive, not to mention keeping others alert—others that might otherwise doze off and/or give up.

Relationships: Internal and External

Knowledge of one's own leadership style is only the beginning. Leadership is about relationships—individual and collective. As a leader, you have as many relationships as you have contact with other people. At the same time, some relationships can be lumped together in groupings, such as customer relationships. Unless you are a salesperson, customer service representative, or other individual that has face-to-face contact with external customers, it's likely that customers are a group with which you have a particular and, possibly, a somewhat distant relationship.

Even though distance between you and your customers doesn't sound very desirable, it is reality for many leaders—especially those in larger organizations. That is why your relationships with individual team members and teams are extremely important. When you have limited exposure to the people that pay good money for your products or services, your team members that do have face-to-face (or telephone-to-ear) contact are your personal representatives. As your external customers experience your team members, they are experiencing *you*. How important does that make your relationship with your internal customers?

The control specialist and the compliance specialist

Perhaps the ultimate contrast to the control specialist is the compliance specialist. It is common for compliance and control to be the top two leadership styles, even though they can represent diverse characteristics. When this happens, it is more likely that a compliance specialist is masking as a control specialist than vice versa. The calculating nature of the compliance specialist means his or her goal in life is to make things add up correctly. If he or she is sufficiently passionate about that, he or she might exercise some measure of control to ensure it happens.

Compliance specialists have been known to fantasize that, if they were in charge, everyone would be forced into compliance, and all would be right with the world. As such, the compliance specialist can be either an asset or an annoyance to the control specialist. Compliance specialists hesitate rather than charge ahead, preferring to take the time to predict whether or not the numbers will add up. Most thoroughbred control specialists will worry about the numbers later, if at all.

When the stakeholders demand to see the numbers, the compliance specialist can be the control specialist's best friend. Control specialists often make elaborate presentations of financial and production figures authored by diligent compliance specialists. For the most part, compliance specialists, like their stability counterparts, don't challenge control specialists for the limelight. They are rational people who don't feel much need for the irrational world of popularity and power.

Compliance specialists enjoy analyzing things. Alert control specialists see that compliance specialists are ready, willing, and able to do all of the analysis necessary on a project while they themselves prefer to take a more aggressive and active role. There's a hang-up if, for any reason, the control specialist is forced to wait for the compliance specialist's analysis before taking action. Then the control specialist begins complaining about paralysis by analysis, and she or he sometimes has a good point.

The compliance specialist's strong desire to be accurate and exact can be a blessing or curse as far as the control specialist is concerned. The compliance specialist's accuracy can be applauded as the control specialist's accuracy by those farther up the organizational food chain. If the truth be known, the control specialist is not concerned with accuracy and doesn't have the patience to achieve it. It's only the weight of reporting to higher powers that makes the compliance specialist's penchant for accuracy tolerable to the control specialist. When presenting a medium-range plan, control specialists truly appreciate compliance specialists' work.

The compliance specialist's natural skepticism is frequently perceived by the control specialist as a burr under his or her saddle. When control specialists want to charge ahead, they don't want to hear about the possibility of failure or disappointing results. The compliance specialist's skepticism might be well founded, and the smart control specialist in a leadership position will pay attention to the compliance specialist's predictive track record.

Compliance specialists are inquisitive, but not for the same reasons that control specialists are. Control specialists are curious in most cases because they're looking to be entertained. Compliance specialists are inquisitive because they're looking for flaws or inaccuracies. Compliance specialists can do a great service for control specialists by warning them of possible snags before a project bombs. Of course, control specialists don't want wet blankets thrown over their pet projects. Control specialists need to curb their insatiable appetites for adventure if they are to derive maximum benefit from compliance specialists.

Compliance specialists look for things to do more than just add up; things should also match. An inventory of 10 pairs of shoes is not good enough. Ten pairs of *black* shoes, with *two-inch heels*. That's better. Order is a big thing to compliance specialists, which can drive an impatient control specialist out of his or her mind. As always, the control specialist can always take credit for a well-ordered presentation of the compliance specialist's devising.

A control specialist's inconsistency and unpredictability can be offset by the compliance specialist's consistency and predictability. This might not be important to the control specialist, but she or he is probably intelligent enough to realize that those who are rating his or her leadership performance are probably looking for those qualities, as well as consistency. Like the social and stability specialists, the compliance specialist can provide qualities that the control specialist is lacking, but show up to others as well rounded leadership.

The control specialist and the social specialist

If the leader is a control specialist, there are some tremendous opportunities for synergy with social specialists. Where control specialists have a tendency to concern themselves with power issues, social specialists are eager to please. Social specialists will not overtly challenge control specialists for power. Because of their intense desire for everyone to get along with one another, social specialists will actually use their influence to block insurrections by other control specialists intent on forcing a power struggle. That is, unless the insurgents can convince the social specialist that the coup will be bloodless and friendly, although we've never seen that case successfully argued. Social specialists are friendly, not dumb.

Control specialists are not instinctively drawn to matters of morale. In the extreme, they are the legendary manifestation of, "When I want you to have an opinion, I'll give it to you." The upbeat attitudes and effervescent dispositions of social specialists on their teams can go a long way to keeping attitudes positive, if the control specialist will let the social specialists exert their influence and take charge of the social activities in and related to the workplace. The control specialist can consult with the social specialist to ascertain if there are enough social activities in and related to the workplace to help maintain positive attitudes. The control specialist must accept that social interaction has a positive effect on team members and is more than merely goofing off.

The welcoming nature of social specialists can also benefit a control specialist in a leadership position by balancing the more matter-of-fact approach characteristic of control specialists. It is common for social specialists to take new team members or others who have just been singed by a fiery control specialist aside and attempt to smooth things over. The issue, if there was one, or the disparity of power between the control specialist and the injured party are of little concern to the social specialist, who merely wants to make the unfriendly vibes go away.

Social specialists are spontaneous in that they remain agile enough to quickly pursue the course of least conflict. Control specialists, more than any other single leadership style, can cause conflict in any number of ways. Conflict is often of little consequence to control specialists because, in their lofty leadership positions, real or imagined, they are usually above the fray. The rapid response to conflict on the part of social specialists on the team also helps to extinguish flames before the control specialist feels the heat. If there is a strong social influence on the team, a controlling leader might think that she or he is running a smoother operation than she or he really is.

Social specialists will get excited at the prospect of doing something fun. Simply being surrounded by happy people is fun to a social specialist. When a control specialist stumbles across an opportunity for his or her team to do something enjoyable, the social specialist will want to take charge or, at the very least, champion the activity. Because promoting good times is not a control specialist's number-one priority, the social specialist can assume the responsibilities that control specialists don't really want anyway. In the end, and if there is no immediate, looming threat, the control specialist enjoys the atmosphere created by the social specialist.

Whereas control specialists expect their team members and others to accept their points of view because of who it's coming from, social specialists need to rely more on being persuasive and convincing. They do this by selling the desirable aspects of an activity or a project. Even without a conscious arrangement between the control specialist and the social specialist, the latter will promote the control specialist's agenda rather than allow it to dampen the team's spirits.

Control specialists are sometimes quiet people. If a control specialist relies heavily on the disparity of power between leader and team members, she or he might not invest much effort in communicating beyond seeing to it that his or her orders are transmitted to the worker bees. Social specialists are generally verbal individuals that speak as they think. Spoken words can come out about as fast as the social specialist can think them. While this can help fill the vacuum if the control specialist on the team withdraws from some reason, it can also drive the control specialist crazy and cause what the social specialist fears most—conflict. Smart control specialists put social specialists in charge of distributing information.

The personable and social nature of social specialists can be a complement to the control specialist. Rarely, if ever, will a social specialist attempt to occupy the same space as the control specialist. They are driven by different desires. Outside of the workplace, in those moments when a control specialist gives into his or her inner desire for temporary companionship, without the threat of obligation, a social specialist might unwittingly become an unconventional companion.

The control specialist and the stability specialist

If the only tool you have is a hammer, every problem looks like a nail. If that is the mantra of the extreme control specialist, the stability specialist carries a toolbox full of tools. If not, she or he knows where to get his or her hands on the correct tool quickly. The stability specialist's instinctive drive for balance and stability means that she or he will concentrate his or her efforts toward eliminating or circumventing situations and issues that will destabilize the team and/or the organization as a whole.

Control specialists who live up to their billing as impulsive and impatient leaders can receive a great deal of assistance from the methodical stability specialist. Because the most stabilizing and unifying factor for the team to center on is the task, the stability specialist will take on the responsibility to see the project through. The control specialist's tendency to zip here and zap there won't distract the stability specialist's step-by-step approach.

While the control specialist and the social specialist are bouncing off the walls, each in their unique way, the stability specialist is calmly going about his or her business and anyone else's business that is slipping. When the control specialist and the social specialist disappear, the stability specialist calmly takes up the slack and keeps the rest of the team on task, as some members of the team tend to disappear right after the initiative owner does.

The same discordant behaviors on the part of the control specialist that trigger the social specialist's frantic attempts to smooth ruffled feathers causes the stability specialist to seek alternative activities and shifts in assignments to get team members' minds and energies refocused on the task ahead of them. If the boat is rocking, the stability specialist will shift the load and ballast to steady it. Shrewd control specialists seek out advice and counsel from their stability specialists to ensure that the team's best efforts are always being applied to accomplishment and achievement and, whenever possible, to avoid instigating disruptive behaviors.

Stability specialists are reliable by nature, which can compensate in many ways for a control specialist's short attention span. It's not that control specialists don't like things to get finished, their impatience often gives way to distractions, and buttoning up tasks is frequently left to others, most often the stability specialist. The stability specialist expects to step in when the control specialist heads off in another direction and does so quietly and, after enough experience, methodically.

The stability specialist's agreeable nature can cause control specialists to assume that they are investing enough time and attention to get things done. The reality is that these complementary characteristics add up to a powerful combination. Control specialists are great at initiating things and leading the exciting and entertaining ramp-up activities. Stability specialists take it from there and see to it that the job gets finished, long after the control specialist has moved on to something else. Being agreeable people and wanting to avoid disruptive disagreements, the stability specialist catches task responsibilities dropped from the control specialist's hands before they hit the ground.

The transition appears seamless to the outsider, if the outsider notices that a transition of responsibility has taken place at all. Stability specialists are generally so unassuming that the contributions they make go unnoticed. A control specialist won't tolerate not being noticed for an accomplishment and the social specialist will be wounded if ignored, but the stability specialist will take anonymity in stride. She or he is not in it for the glory and is not terribly bothered when others receive the applause.

While the social specialist is attempting to convince the control specialist's opponents (and/or victims) that the controlling person is not really that bad, the stability specialist is attempting to refocus team members on the task and away from conflict. The stability specialist is not phobic about conflict the way that the social specialist is. She or he will even tolerate or possibly engage in conflict if it will move the project forward. Those committed to stability will demonstrate faithfulness to their leaders partially out of an empathic capacity to appreciate the weight on the ringleader/initiative owner's shoulders, as well as on his or her fellow team members. The stability specialist knows the weight of the control specialist's responsibilities because so much is transferred to his or her stabilizing shoulders anyway.

While other influences steal the control specialist's attention, seduce him or her with a more attractive activity, or scream louder for his or her attention, the stability specialist will pick up the slack and fill in the gaps as necessary. "Responsibility" is his or her middle name. When a critical challenge faces the team, the stability specialist follows the biblical mandate from the Book of Isaiah: "Send me." If you catch stability specialists off guard and ask why they are doing something, don't be surprised if they say, "Somebody has to."

Stability specialists seem to have an inner peacefulness about them that is a distinct contrast to the control specialist. To the observant control specialist, the presence of a stability specialist will be comforting. The peacefulness that the stability specialist feels comes from the experienced knowledge that things will be done if folks merely spend enough time patiently sticking to their knitting.

Every organization has some folks that are first to arrive in the morning and are frequently found by the custodial crew late at night, still at it. These are not the control specialists. They are the control specialists' guardian angels—stability specialists. In Org's overeating, midnight-snacking days, it was usually the stability specialist hearing those strange, late-night noises.

The Impossible Dream

All people in positions of leadership are potentially subject to unrealistic and unreasonable expectations by those above and below them on the organizational food chain. That's one of the reasons for the maxim "It's lonely at the top." Who in his right mind would volunteer for a leadership position if he knew it was going to be so demanding? Oh, we forgot about the money, benefits, seniority thing. In a molecular organization, people work less in isolation, and are, therefore, less likely to be lonely.

Many people expect their leaders to be control, social, stability, and compliance specialists all rolled into one—with equal aptitudes for all styles. Super-leaders, if you will. By recognizing and embracing the differences between the styles represented among your team members, and actively supplementing your own talents and abilities with theirs, you can provide well-balanced and super productive leadership. Effective leadership, leading the way you like to be led, is never lonely.

**Chapter 8 Summary:
Keys to Unleashing Leadership**

☛ **A fish is still a fish:** Don't be confused by our insistence that everyone is a leader followed by a side dialogue in which we say, "But, if you're a leader with institutional authority in a traditional hierarchy...." Until the day that every organization adopts a molecular operating structure (and we don't see that happening this quarter), most of us will fall somewhere on an organizational food chain; and we'll need to apply these ComposiTeam principles to our individual and team situations. At the end of the day, though, we still insist that everyone is a leader, the fact that you might not have the biggest office doesn't change that.

- **Diversity strengthens:** What causes fear to one individual might not cause fear in another. Regardless of how a person came about his or her dominant leadership style, it's safe to assume that others can play important and complementary roles. Diversity in disciplines, thinking, and competencies will only be a strengthening factor if you manage it correctly, through a well-designed leadership system. Arbitrarily dumping people in the big organizational salad bowl and mixing them up will produce mixed-up people.

- **Good points and bad points:** Every leadership style represented has strengths and weaknesses. The objective of implementing a coordinated, organization-wide leadership system is to position people to support and enhance each other's strengths, and compensate for one another's weaknesses. On the street, they say, "I've got your back." In organizations, we can either expect people to have each other's backs naturally (in which case some will and some won't), or we can make it an expectation. More than an expectation, we can provide the tools and structure to pull it off.

- **Leading is about relationships:** The "It's lonely at the top" thing is misleading. Leadership, at any level, is about relationships. If a person is completely isolated, it becomes about leading oneself. But how often is one completely isolated? Even in the midst of a bustling organization, each person still has the responsibility to lead themselves. The fact that there are others in positions of institutional authority, popular authority—or both—ideally means that you have support for your self-leadership and your leadership responsibility to others.

- **Control specialists enrich the mix:** Control specialists can fill gaps that their peers, compliance, social, and stability specialists leave behind. Compliance, social, and stability specialists can do the same for control specialists. Control specialists, by nature, lead the way. So, it's particularly important that they lead the way they want to be led. If not, then it's important for their fellow team members to step up and supplement control specialists in ways everyone would like to be led.

Control specialists are some of the most colorful people in the organizational portrait. But they are just as interdependent on the skills and essential natures of their team members from other leadership styles as anyone. Success is a team effort. The big difference in approaching team efforts with a well-coordinated, systematic leadership program vs. sending select candidates to leadership school and hoping for the best is in efficiency.

The vast majority of the time, the job gets done. The question is, "Will the job get done in a well-orchestrated, cost-effective, (dare we say) *profitable* manner?" That depends on how much you're leaving to chance. As we said early on, we're all lucky some of the time. But we're not all lucky all of the time. If you want to return Org to his former, gluttonous self, just keep relying on luck. It's during those unlucky times that a conscientious, systematic approach to leadership, based on the composite leadership profile of your people, makes for the best of times— lucky or not.

Chapter 9

The Compliance Specialist

*Anything that can be counted counts, and not everything
that counts can be counted.*

—Albert Einstein

Leader to Leader

Compliance specialists ask policy questions such as, "What is the rule on this?" They are often found in the leadership position and the other three basic styles—control, social, and stability—in subordinate roles. It's common to find engineers or financial types (who are frequently compliance specialists) running organizations. The fictitious notion that you can actually reengineer an organizational population of human beings like rebuilding an engine block in a 1964 Mustang is catnip to a compliance specialist. A strong compliance/control combination is sure to take a mechanistic approach to organizational design and operation.

Compliance specialists make good additions to leadership teams because of their desires for accuracy and attention to detail; qualities that control and social specialists don't usually have much use for. It's also common to see compliance specialists working in isolation, crunching numbers, writing software code, or working with their computer-assisted drawings. Compliance specialists are often placid individuals in search of the sum. They have supreme confidence in the fact that two plus two equals four. It always has and it always will. There is no need to panic or act hysterically, two things you'll rarely see compliance specialists do. They are assured that when the storm has passed, when the dust settles, when all is said and done, the immutable, mathematical truths of the universe will still be intact.

It is when compliance specialists expect their fellow team members to conform to the immutable, mathematical truths of the universe that things start to get dicey. Two plus two equals four, except when it comes to human beings. Since the days of Genesis, the population of the earth has been divided between those who think human behavior should be dictated by hard and fast rules and those who believe people should behave in a manner consistent with their unique personalities. Theological issues aside, the debate continues to this day.

The fact that compliance specialists believe in the rule of absolute law doesn't change the fact that human beings have been unique and complex creatures from day one, with a natural inclination to create rules that suit themselves and ignore those that don't. Before our ancient ancestors realized that there is absolute and predictable mathematical order in the universe, we were already getting to be a little nutty around the edges.

The Compliance Specialist's Perfect World

The compliance specialist's vision for a perfect world, where everybody shows up for work on time, goes to lunch at 12 sharp and is back at their stations by the stroke of 1, where everyone pays their bills on time, and everyone's checkbooks are perfectly balanced...is unrealistic. Yet, everyone needs to have his or her own utopian dream. So, we'll allow compliance specialists their fantasy. We won't argue that many of the world's problems would be resolved if we all acted a little more like compliance specialists.

Compliance specialists tend to be honest folks who are typically rule-bound and high in values. Stealing only messes up the books. Compliance specialists like things to be tidy and orderly. The proof is in their immaculate sock and underwear drawers. When a true compliance specialist has been implicated in unethical or illegal behavior, you can bet that a control specialist has a tight grip on his or her throat—or that romance, love, and/or infatuation has a lot to do with it.

Compliance and analysis

Sitting through a meeting with an overzealous compliance specialist can be like enduring fingernails dragged across a chalkboard, especially if you're a control specialist. Here is an example of when it's helpful to examine the leadership motivation inventory to see what might be driving certain behaviors. If a compliance specialist is low on both courage and confidence, she or he might burrow under statistics and compliance issues to avoid being associated with any sort of risk.

A compliance specialist with a reasonably well-balanced inventory of underlying motivational factors won't unreasonably hold up the show. It is when compliance specialists are well balanced in their motivational inventories that their analysis should be most heeded. Compliance specialists are thinking through details that the other three leadership styles, even the stability specialist, might overlook. The most reliable way to predict future behavior is to analyze past behavior. Few of us have patience for that. We're fortunate that compliance specialists will serve that function and, possibly, keep us from repeating past mistakes and miscalculations.

Compliance and details

When the rest of the team is ready to go out and put the plan into action, the compliance specialist is likely to raise his or her pencil and say, "Not so fast." There is always one more fact to check, one more detail to cover, one more *i* to dot, or one more *t* to cross. Most people are ready to rock and roll the moment a concept begins to formalize in their minds. Most of us are optimistically confident that the details will work themselves out on the fly, and aren't worrisome enough to hold up progress. The compliance specialist doesn't mind postponing progress until a plan is in place to manage all of the details.

Too much attention to readiness can immobilize an organization, so somewhere between the control specialist's Fire-Ready-Aim approach and the compliance specialist's obsession with minutia is the optimal balance of action and caution. Social specialists don't mind delaying a launch if they can socialize in the interim. Stability specialists will not stay at the starting line any longer than absolutely necessary, but they are receptive to the compliance specialists' concerns. Compliance specialists appreciate the stability specialists' patience and belief that taking time to do it right in the beginning will save time and money in the end.

Compliance and mathematics

To compliance specialists, calculating is not an activity reserved for numbers. In the world of a compliance specialist, calculating means sweating over the details, and everything and everyone eventually becomes a detail—or a digit. These people liken everything in the natural universe to numbers. It's a much cleaner and practical approach. To a compliance specialist, a person that is employed full time is a FTE (full-time equivalent). That allows a bean counter to add up the part-time status of several persons and express the number as FTEs. Once people are converted to numbers, it is easier to plug them into equations, algorithms, and calculations.

In leadership positions, compliance specialists aren't known for an empathetic or relationship-driven approach. They are more likely to develop a formula for how the team should perform based on expectations expressed completely in mathematical or engineering terms. There's nothing wrong with accounting for a great deal of business performance in numerical terms. We need metrics. The calculating approach, however, doesn't factor in what happens when a three is not really a three or a seven is more of a seven today than it was yesterday.

To compliance specialists, people and human performance should not change, just as numbers don't change. Compliance specialists are particularly fond of the way numbers interact with other numbers, and wish human behavior would be so fixed, static, and eternally replicable. The bad news, as far as compliance specialists are concerned, is that human beings interact with one another in extremely dynamic ways.

Stability specialists, with their desire to maintain a balanced and efficient operation, are less of an annoyance to compliance specialists than control and social specialists, who tend to color outside of the lines, each for their own reasons. Compliance specialists are generally down to earth, well grounded, predictable, loyal to the rules and policies of the organization, and cause very little disruption to the equilibrium of the office or plant. As a good balancing factor in leadership teams, compliance specialists are often the hardest to locate. There seems to be a greater abundance of control and social specialist.

Compliance and accuracy

More than just wanting to hit the target, compliance specialists want to hit the center of the target—the bull's eye. In thinking of the world in a linear, numerical manner, compliance specialists aren't inclined to fudge, stretch, or bend. Numbers are precise. That's why you won't hear compliance specialists saying that an outcome is "close enough." If the target was five, four is not five, even if the rest of the team thinks that four is close enough. Compliance specialists won't pitch a fit over it, especially if the discrepancy is minor. But, at the very least, they'll sigh and roll their eyes.

This desire for accuracy can work in the other direction. When the team is dancing around the office celebrating that they turned in a seven against a target of five, the compliance specialist, not a dancer to begin with, sits and studies the numbers. When a social specialist pleads with him or her to come out of his or her counting cave and join the merrymaking, the compliance specialist will probably get up, walk to the door, and close it. If the target was missed, in one direction or the other, it troubles the accuracy-minded compliance specialist. She or he feels the process was not methodical enough. If it had been, the target would not have been missed.

Compliance and facts

To the compliance specialist, it is reasonable to be rational. Most people that characterize themselves as rational, as opposed to excitable or spontaneous, find comfort in well-thought-out activities and can scarcely tolerate anything that's sprung on them at the last minute. The compliance specialist's credo is: *"If it's worth doing, it's worth planning."* Past facts should be predictors of future facts. That's rational and sound advice for anyone involved in organizational activities. Even the social specialist's bonding functions will pay bigger dividends if they've been strategically planned and executed based on facts rather than emotions.

The logic behind the compliance specialist's stoicism is sound. Effective execution is a function of good planning. When a pilot is landing an aircraft, the planning process begins long before she or he is anywhere near the airport. Rate of descent, air speed, weight, distance, weather, air-traffic-control instructions, and many other facts must be considered. The more details the pilot attends to in preparation for landing, the shorter the list of potential problems. The shorter the list of potential problems, the faster and more effectively the pilot can deal with one should it arise.

Similar to the stability specialist, the compliance specialist's fore-consciousness can head off potential disasters, save precious resources, and present a more solid and stable image to the marketplace and community. Doesn't that make you want to hug a CPA? There is a lot to recommend by being rational in business and organizational in life. But don't get carried away and put the accounts receivable department in charge of a party. As the 19th century expression says, "Keep Boston in your parlor and Paris in your bedroom, and never mix them up."

Compliance and carefulness

Although an increasing number of compliance specialists were marching to the control specialist's tune when reporting corporate earnings and debt figures, the insatiable inquisitiveness inherent to their breed caught up with them. You can get a few compliance specialists to act against their own natures all of the time, but you can't get all compliance specialists to turn the other way. Cooking the books is so opposite every fiber in the compliance specialist's body that doing it over time, with ever-larger stakes, is impossible to hide. The whistle-blowers weren't control specialists. They were curious, and extremely *careful*, compliance specialist.

Those who work against their own natures will eventually crack, or their kindred spirits will. Trying to hide the corporate and government accounting scandals of the 1990s was like trying to nail a lid over Old Faithful in Yellowstone Park. The pressure will cause leakage at first and, before long, the lid will blow sky high. It's only nature trying to regain equilibrium.

Trying to manage people who are acting against their basic natures is like nailing that lid on top of Old Faithful. Any efficiency and productivity you might have achieved early in the operation will develop leaks and cracks. If you crank up the pressure high enough without aligning what people do best with what the organization needs most, the lid will come off. Nature abhors a vacuum. We believe that nature isn't fond of imbalances, either. The care with which a compliance specialist operates should be matched to the nature of his or her responsibilities. Anything else would be reckless.

Leading in any way other than how you like to be led is a formula for stress and pressure as you try to reconcile the irreconcilable. A compliance specialist likes to be left alone and given time and space to peacefully perform his or her careful calculations. As the head of an organization, a compliance specialist has unruly and over-eager control and social specialists who, if left to their own devices, will turn the place into a zoo. The control specialist in a position of leadership responsibility, however, must lead in a participative and involved manner, unlike his or her first preference. Knowing and accepting this is a great foundation for making necessary adjustments without betraying the compliance specialist's essentially careful nature.

Compliance and precision

Engineers are, by nature, compliance specialists. It could be said that compliance specialists are, by nature, engineers. Physics, like mathematics, is a discipline based on immutable laws. Precision is the name of the game for compliance specialists, and the rest of the team is fortunate to have someone on board that will invest time and energy into making things as precise as possible.

Precision is more critical to some activities than others. Growing produce is not as precise an activity as aircraft manufacturing. Service industries have a slightly different relationship to precision than do manufacturers. Adhering to the simplest and most precise standards results in products that last longer, and need fewer repairs, as we learned from "Ol' Lonely," the Maytag repairman. The compliance specialist's obsession with precision ultimately benefits internal *and* external customers.

Compliance and correctness

Correctness is not synonymous with predictability. Many people can be predictably unpredictable and/or unreliable, and still be correct once in awhile. Compliance specialists bring a predictable dimension to any team they're on in that they attempt to be correct all of the time. Like the stability specialist, this predictability can be a source of comfort and confidence for other team members, even though the things the compliance specialist can be relied upon to do, such as obsess over correctness, are not everybody's favorite activities.

Someone needs to research, analyze, and project with correctness and accuracy, and compliance specialists do those things extremely well. While they might do these things in isolation, they will report their findings, at length, to the team. Compliance specialists can be counted on to deliver detailed written reports, PowerPoint presentations, and lectures as if everyone in the audience were as enchanted by the detail and calculation protocol as the compliance specialist.

It's like the neighbors inviting you over to sit through two hours of their vacation slides. It's entertainment to them and torture to you. Can you imagine two hours of explanation as to why these calculations are correct? Perhaps we could assign the social specialist to present the compliance specialist's findings. That would spice things up. It might also result in a resignation from the compliance specialist.

Compliance and being methodical

In addition to what we've already mentioned about the compliance specialist's reliability, predictability, and precision, this individual is the type you can set your watch by. In a word, methodical. Routine is characteristic of the compliance specialist, for many of the reasons we've mentioned. Routine is the opposite of spontaneity. Social specialists thrive on spontaneity and control specialists bore easily, while compliance specialist avoid spontaneity at all costs and have an unbelievably high threshold for boredom. The compliance specialist's consistency makes a good floor and ceiling between which the social specialist's spontaneity and the control specialist's lack of discipline can operate.

The compliance specialist's methodical consistency will act to calibrate the behavioral extremes characteristic of the other leadership styles. As long as there is a compliance specialist on the team, caution will not be thrown entirely to the wind. The conversation will eventually come back around to consider conventional alternatives. In nature, constant erosion of wind-blown sand and water eventually smoothes the sharp edges off rocks. Consistency's sister, constancy, will help keep corporate creativity channeled toward productivity and profitability.

Compliance and being systematic

Compliance specialists understand that life in the linear world is eminently systemic. Any rule-based culture has distinct boundaries. To compliance specialists, operating within the boundaries is acceptable, and operating outside the boundaries is potentially problematic. Compliance specialists would rather expend energy avoiding problems than solving them. Wherever human beings are involved, however, problems will be unavoidable. Nobody has yet been able to make human beings adhere to a *strict system* of anything. Systems need, by design, to anticipate and accommodate volatility.

Enlightened compliance specialists understand that nonlinear human behavior *is* systemic, albeit in a less predictable manner than linear mathematical systems. In this regard, compliance specialists can be extremely helpful on leadership teams. Some human beings, for whatever reason (and no two reasons seem to be exactly the same), naturally establish boundaries. Others can be relied upon to predictably violate those boundaries. Human behavior is far more complex than simple addition, subtraction, multiplication, and division can account for.

The combination of factors and the varying degrees to which different factors interact to produce human thinking and behavior still defy neat and tidy explanation. Compliance specialists are confounded by the unpredictable and unexplainable part of human nature. To be truly effective, leadership must deal with all of it.

Healthy Skepticism

Compliance specialists rarely ride the bandwagon. For them, it's too noisy, crowded, and chaotic. Historical performance seems to etch itself indelibly in the compliance specialist's mind. They are true students of the natural universe and its cyclical tendencies. If something happened one way in the past, chances are good that, in the absence of a significant intervention, it will happen again. In this way, compliance specialists can be decent predictors of human behavior.

Control specialists are often optimists, if not flat out gifted at denial. Social specialists trumpet their optimism throughout the organization. Stability specialists allow themselves some guarded optimism. Compliance specialists don't buy it for a minute. They look to key performance indicators, based on past performance and, if the projections are out of line, she or he will not hesitate to say so. This is why many compliance specialists developed ulcers and sold, under sufficient pressure, their souls to the devil over the past several decades, as accounting practices increasingly became the domain of compliance specialists.

The compliance specialist and the control specialist

These two have a dynamic relationship that can bounce back and forth between best friend/worst enemy scenarios. When the compliance specialist backs up the control specialist's position on a project, process, or strategic system, the control specialist buys lunch. Control specialists have lucid moments from time to time, especially at the outset of a new initiative, when they get into the playbook and resolve to follow the rules. When they do, compliance specialists are their best friends.

Alas, control specialists are not known for their consistency. The New Year's resolutions they keep reinventing throughout the year are interspersed with tumbles off the regularity wagon. They get excited when they hear new and revolutionary ideas. They are vulnerable to turn-a-fast-buck schemes profligated by slick salespersons. Impatient as they can be, control specialists might even stir the organizational pot just to see if it will speed things up, or at least become more entertaining. At these times, the last person the control specialist wants to see walking down the hall is the compliance specialist with a spreadsheet under his or her arm.

Before the compliance specialist gets a chance to open his or her mouth, the control specialist raises his or her hand as if to stop traffic and says, "I know what you're going to say, *but*...." The control specialist's excuse generator kicks into high gear at the very sight of the compliance specialist because, in many ways, the compliance specialist is the control specialist's conscience. When the control and compliance specialists start doing this little dance, the rest of the team can be comforted in the fact that this particular control specialist *has* a conscience, and he or she might listen to it.

The compliance specialist and the social specialist

These two also have a love/hate merry-go-round. The compliance specialist is a constant thorn in the social specialist's attempts to keep the organization in a perpetual party mode. Celebrating and all around merrymaking are not the compliance specialist's style. Furthermore, she or he sees no inherent value in goofing off. Therefore, the compliance specialist, if in charge of finances, might tend to starve the social specialist's recreation budget, and overall withhold support for social activities.

The social specialist, holding no grudges and repulsed by hostility, figures that the compliance specialist's dreary attitude is in need of just the type of adjustment she or he can provide. The social specialist relentlessly tries to cheer up and generally humor the compliance specialist, aggravating the *i*-dotter/*t*-crosser to no end. On the surface, the compliance specialist protests such treatment.

Beneath the surface, the compliance specialist revels in the social specialist's attention and will not lighten up for fear that she or he will back off. To the social specialist, the compliance specialist is a black hole, with an infinite need for his or her entertainment and attempts at bonding. Such is the timeless dance between the fusing social specialist and the isolating compliance specialist.

The compliance specialist and the stability specialist

These two styles are very similar in a number of ways. The compliance specialist can count on the stability specialist to make nice with the social specialist so the compliance specialist doesn't need to reveal how much she or he truly enjoys the attention. In his or her mediation role, the stability specialist keeps the social and compliance specialists connected, although not as overtly as passing junior high school–style romance notes. The stability specialist's intervention, when a compliance specialist is considering one of the social specialist's schemes, allows the compliance specialist to *withhold objection.*

The stability specialist enables the compliance specialist to hold a hard line on various issues by running interference with the control specialist.

Without the stability specialist's intervention, compliance specialists would have to take on control specialists directly. Compliance specialists tend to be passive fighters and control specialists tend to be attackers. Direct confrontations between the two seldom turn out well for the compliance specialist. This is one reason why whistle-blowing is so difficult for compliance specialists, and has won them the admiration of many when they actually rise to the challenge.

Just as the stability specialist plays a mediating role with the control, social, and compliance specialist, the compliance specialist's analytical nature, desire to be detailed and precise, and do it right the first time, all resonate with the stability specialist's agenda and help achieve organizational balance. The stability specialist can become as impatient with the compliance specialist as anyone else, but she or he is highly appreciative of the compliance specialist's overall contributions to the cost-effective achievement of organizational goals and objectives.

Chapter 9 Summary: Keys to Unleashing Leadership

- **Counted on to count:** If there is anything we can rely on compliance specialists to do, it's to be reliable. Compliance specialists count, and they count. On one hand, they add up columns and perform all kinds of mathematical computations to paint the organization, not *by* the numbers, but in a language *of* numbers. On the other hand, compliance specialists count for a lot in team composition. They bring a realistic grounding in facts and essential truths to counterbalance the impetuousness of control and social specialists. In short, compliance specialists count both ways.

- **The world is perfect in its imperfection:** This might well be your most challenging task when dealing with compliance specialists. The world is not perfect in the compliance specialist's estimation, because there are too many people in it. People are not predictable, are ruled by their emotions more than facts, and are not consistent in their behavior. Newsflash: The world will be what it will be, whether the compliance specialist likes it or not. We might as well consider it perfect, in its own way, and design our leadership systems to be as dynamic as possible.

- **Analysis and inertia:** Compliance specialists can overanalyze any-thing. This is their gift to us and their curse on us, all at once. Overanalysis can bring even a molecular organization to a standstill. Most hierarchical organizations have long ago been stopped in their tracks by compliance specialists, combined with already cynical team members. By balancing compliance specialists with control special-ists whenever possible, the resulting creative tension will make the control specialist more accountable and the control specialist will resist the compliance specialist's efforts to slow things down.

- **Healthy skepticism:** Nothing is right until every *t* is crossed and every *i* is dotted. Until that happens, the compliance specialist is skeptical. The control specialist and social specialist, even the stability special-ist to some degree, might be satisfied that the details will work them-selves out as time goes by. Not the compliance specialist. Even when the columns add up and reconcile, the compliance specialist might show up late for the party because he or she stayed late to go over the numbers "…one last time."

- **A balancing factor:** The stability specialist is probably the most happy to have compliance specialists around. The stability specialist not only appreciates much of the linear perspective compliance special-ists bring to the team, but also the fact that they are such natural counterbalances to the more volatile control and social specialists. If a leadership system is going to be well balanced, it needs balancing factors. Compliance specialists seem to bring that balancing juxtapo-sition to every team relationship they have.

It's hard for control and social specialists to understand why compliance specialists are so linear about the world. The truth is, it doesn't matter whether they understand or not. It will be enough if they just appreciate the positive and balancing influence compliance specialists have. We think the same thing should apply to limiting the amount of influence compliance specialists wield.

Compliance specialists, if given too much unchecked authority to force compliance out of everyone, will probably increase the cynicism index in their organizations, and leave the old, gluttonous Org in charge of the graveyard shift and, ultimately, of the whole enterprise. That's not good. We move next to the social specialist to see one way the compliance specialist's zealous analytical approach can be countered (constructively).

Chapter 10

The Social Specialist

It is one of the beautiful compensations of this life that no one can sincerely try to help another without helping himself.

—Charles Dudley Warren

Leader to Leader

The social specialist asks relationship questions. When the compliance specialist asks, "What's the rule on this?" the social specialist might say, "The first rule is that everybody wins." As we suggested with the control specialist, you need to consider the social specialist in several capacities as you read this chapter. Think of the social specialist in the conventional leadership position and the other three basic styles—control, stability, and compliance—in subordinate or collaborative roles. You might also consider the social specialist working in isolation, although that would be sheer torture to a social specialist and a highly unlikely scenario.

The social specialist is not one to fight to be in charge. However, of all the leadership styles, she or he is most likely to jump at the opportunity to *share* leadership responsibilities. If for no other reason, collaborative leadership requires continuous contact and communication. An individual who thrives on relationships will be all over that. The social specialist might or might not seek as much control as possible. But she or he will always be on the move; visiting others around the workplace or convening impromptu gatherings in his or her office.

Relationships: The Substance of the Social Specialist

Will the social specialist be driven by a pure desire to maximize the leadership potential of a small group or team? Probably not. Perhaps the social specialist has a shortage of meaningful relationships outside of the workplace and seeks to make up for lost time where there is a captive audience. She or he might be motivated to maintain close and constant contact with others by a strong desire to avoid loneliness or to focus on others, thus avoiding self-reflection—or both. Everyone is motivated by some degree of avoidant as well as intentional behavior. The social specialist is no different.

On the surface, who can argue with solid social relationships among coworkers, unless the relationships become in any way unprofessional? As a rule, we enjoy encountering social specialists in organizations because they tend to be effective bonding agents. The relationships that social specialists hold together can be refined, enhanced, and strengthened through learning and improved communication.

Social and being helpful

The social specialist's greatest fear is rejection. Influence is a hedge against that possibility. Social specialists can't successfully butt heads with control specialists, at least not consistently. So, the social specialist develops other means of control, such as being incredibly helpful. Social specialists are relationship designers and brokers. Control is important to them because, without it, the enormously complex and difficult task of keeping people connected would be left to chance. A social specialist can't allow team members to drift apart and isolate themselves. A fractured and hostile organization, filled with friction, is contrary to everything the social specialist holds dear.

Whereas the ability to command is a tool for the control specialist, the ability to be persuasive comes in handy for a social specialist. What better tool is there than helpfulness? Besides, it comes naturally to the social specialist. The most influential social specialists can be helpful enough around control specialists to determine, at least in part, what the control specialist is going to command.

Of course, this is all without the control specialist's knowledge or consent. The social specialist's toolbox of persuasive techniques is potentially larger than that of any other leadership style. A social specialist will pull out whatever it takes to connect folks and keep them hooked up. Excessive bugging is just as possible and probable as excessive begging. Social specialists are shameless (within reason) when attempting to ensure that everyone gets along.

Social and being friendly

The social specialist is genuinely friendly and enjoys the company of other friendly people. When you see the social specialist's smiling face, you're looking at the real deal. Someone that feigns happiness to compensate for a deep unhappiness is a faux social specialist, and won't consistently demonstrate the joy-enhancing behaviors for which social specialists are known.

When there is a darker countenance lurking behind the smile, it won't take very long for other team members to spot it. The net result will be mistrust, which is the opposite reaction one has to a truly relationship-driven individual. Social specialists live to be true-blue friends. Over time, the strength of their convictions reveals their true characters.

Those who appear on the surface to value relationships and collaboration, but have a telltale odor of manipulation, are not social specialists. Control is extremely important to a codependent who must maintain control that appears to be compassionate in order to keep people hooked into feeding his or her neediness. There are still others who are, in reality, users of people in a more sociopathic and/or histrionic fashion. These persons are all smiles on the outside and hidden agenda on the inside. No matter how engaging the smiles, they do not earn the trust of their fellow team members over time and don't have the ongoing positive impact that social specialists can have.

Social and being upbeat

Being upbeat, positive, and helpful can help draw others out of their doldrums and boost them up to a more productive level. Being too upbeat can wear people out. Being upbeat in moderation will always have a positive impact on the organization. An upbeat person will become an anchor of sorts for others who just can't keep their spirits up, no matter what. These chronic mopers can develop reliance on social specialists to lift their spirits, especially in tough times.

When the social specialist sends out a communication, it's likely to be read and accepted, considering its source. The upbeat person is generally considered to be nonthreatening and believed to have the team's best interest at heart. The social specialist wants what is best for everyone. The potential downside is the organization's vulnerability. A social specialist can value what she or he perceives to be the personal relationships between team members over fulfillment of the organization's strategic goals and objectives. A relationship-driven individual will not only tend to go along to get along, but might orchestrate everything within his or her power to make it so.

Social and being welcoming

Conflict is to social specialists what kryptonite is to Superman. The social specialist will jump in and act as peacemaker when needed, but would prefer to head off any unpleasantness before it heats up. Conflict is intolerable to the social specialist, even if it doesn't involve him or her directly. Just being around hostility is enough to bring on a panic attack for the social specialist.

Social specialists use their welcoming, receptive natures to initiate personal interactions; be they with familiar faces or strangers. You might have seen a social specialist greet a frustrated customer or fellow team member warmly only to be rebuffed. Chances are good that the social specialist shook off the unfriendly retort and tried the friendly, welcoming approach again. If the unhappy person seems inconsolable, a true social specialist will probably politely disengage and move on rather than be swept up in the unpleasantness. If the social specialist drops everything to rescue the gloomy person from his or her mood, there could be suspicious boundary issues in other organizational relationships and interactions.

Social and being spontaneous

It is hard to plan for people's moods. More than that, if making people happy and helping them get along is your number-one agenda, there's a time for planning and a time to shoot from the hip. Social specialists will plan in advance to bring the cupcakes and party favors when there is a birthday in the office. However, they will also be the first to cook up an instant celebration for the smallest reason.

What most non-relationship-driven individuals fail to realize is that the social specialist's radar is constantly sweeping the company landscape for any potential moodiness. That's why she or he might appear out of nowhere and invite everyone into the conference room for a "no-reason" party. You might believe him or her when she says that there is no reason for the party, but the *only reason* for the gathering is the blip on the radar that the social specialist detected and interpreted as a possible hint of negativity in the neighborhood.

Social and being caring

Social specialists are not good at hiding their true feelings. The fact is, they can care too much. When a person's emotional barometer is out there for all to see, it's best to keep the mood positive, so that works out in the social specialist's favor. Social specialists often appear excitable because they get so pumped up when good things happen. When a genuinely good cause for celebration pops up, half of the social specialist's job is done for him or her. He or she no longer is faced with getting people to relax and enjoy themselves for no reason. The bottom line is that the social specialist *really does care* that people get along and conflict is minimized or eliminated.

How does a social specialist show she or he cares? By throwing a party. When something worth celebrating occurs, the social specialist can scarcely contain his or her glee. When a party is in order, without any need for coercion on the part of the social specialist, it's almost too good to be true.

When a salesperson or executive on the road scores a home run, she or he usually calls in and asks for the social specialist first, knowing that the social specialist will gush when she or he hears the news. That's a nice stroke for the home-run hitter. She or he is also aware that the social specialist will drop everything and enthusiastically spread the news throughout the organization. Good internal publicity never hurt anyone's vertical mobility.

Social and being agreeable

If you're having a hard time getting your boss's attention or outshining an internal competitor in the organization, the social specialist can be your best friend. Not that we endorse playing office politics, but sometimes you're left no choice. What better campaign to run than a positive one? When the social specialist is your campaign manager, that's exactly what you'll get. The social specialist will do everything in his or her power to facilitate agreement on the issues that otherwise might keep you at odds with others.

True social specialists are as sincere as the day is long, and will work tirelessly to achieve consensus. They also like to talk a great deal. Communication is the wagon that relationships ride on, and social specialists are constantly using communication skills to promote positive relationships. If the social specialist touts you as a dedicated hard worker, she or he will do so with such passion that even your worst skeptics might buy in. The social specialist will usually help you plead your case if it means keeping things warm and fuzzy around the office, factory, or worksite.

Social and being peaceful

We credit *Leadership When the Heat's On* coauthor Danny Cox again, this time with the concept of the "third party compliment." When Party A hears that Party B said something complimentary about him or her, it's hard to remain hostile toward Party B. This is an exceptionally effective leadership technique if Parties A and B are on your team—even if Party A never mentioned Party B. Saying so anyway will smooth things a great deal between the two and produce a more productive atmosphere. If you want to guarantee that Party B will hear any good thing that is said about him or her, make sure the social specialist hears about it. A true social specialist can't resist a relationship-building or peacemaking opportunity.

Much of what we've been saying about the positive impact social specialists can have on their organizations is based on his or her impulse to continuously connect. Intelligent ringleaders recognize and include the social specialist's impulse to communicate in their internal strategies. It's within the social specialist's essential nature to engender communication, so why not put that energy to good use? Communication, especially informal communication, comes naturally to relationship-driven individuals. Effective ringleaders recognize this impulse as a strength that social specialists can contribute to the team.

Social and being sociable

Social interactions, from group activities to individual personal interactions, have a protocol based in the culture of your organization and community. Familiarity with such protocol is another opportunity for social specialists to contribute to the organization's relational needs. Control specialists, with their noses close to the cash register; stability specialists, with their noses on the task trail; and compliance specialists, with their noses in the books, aren't good candidates with which to trust social responsibilities.

Social specialists have natural curiosities and expertise in matters of social interaction. It's wise to trust social specialists' instincts and recommendations about corporate image in the community and activities that bolster your enlightened self-interests. Social manners and customs are the social specialist's cup of tea. Effective leaders know that appearances mean a great deal to the way your organization is perceived, both internally and externally. If it's true that it requires 50 positive experiences to compensate for one negative experience, avoiding the first organizational embarrassment is a significant issue. Social specialists can save you a lot.

Social and being personable

Effective leaders have learned that nobody cares how much you know until they know how much you care about them. If others don't believe that they are cared about, yours will be a lonely voice in the wilderness. Social specialists can teach everyone else a great deal on the topic of being personable. We recommend going so far as to recognize the personable nature of social specialists in your organization as admirable attributes, right up there with technical competencies.

Rewarded behavior is repeated behavior. Social specialists don't need much encouragement, if any, to be personable. It is a good investment to encourage emulation of the social specialist's personable behavior throughout the organization. It will be easier for some than for others, but it won't hurt anyone to become more friendly and accessible. They might enjoy the fresh air.

In the Mix: Social Specialists and Their Peers

Social specialists are often just friendly people that give out good vibes and enjoy getting some in return. Not only does the social specialist thrive on relationships, she or he thinks that everyone else should thrive on relationships, too. This can become annoying to control and compliance specialists. Like anything else, social specialists need to be taken in moderation.

The social specialist and the control specialist

Almost without exception, the social specialist is in a subordinate position to the control specialist. In most organizations, the archetypal social specialist is a female in some type of clerical role. This is not surprising when you consider that the social specialist does not possess the same level of ambition that the control specialist does. In fact, the two bear little resemblance to one another when it comes to office politics.

Social specialists are driven to develop and maintain relationships, even at the expense of organizational performance and productivity. Control specialists are driven to acquire and hold on to power, sometimes at the expense of organizational performance and productivity. The social specialist doesn't envy the control specialist's power or covet the power position. She or he is more likely to bug the control specialist incessantly to use his or her power for generating stronger and more endearing relationships throughout the organization.

It's no wonder that, around the office, the control specialist often ignores the social specialist, except when something the social specialist does proves to be a tremendous benefit or aggravation to the control specialist. Much of the patching up that social specialists do with fractured relationships is a direct result of the control specialist's bruising approach to motivation and discipline. Social specialists spend a great deal of time and energy explaining to team members that the control specialist is really a nice person and she or he doesn't truly mean the harsh and blunt things she or he says with such callousness.

Whether or not the social specialist actually believes the spin she or he gives the control specialist's behavior is immaterial. The social specialist is not above the liberal use of propaganda to keep the niceness flowing. It doesn't matter to a social specialist if people really like each other deep down, as long as they make a convincing appearance of simpatico around the office.

If the control specialist encounters a stealth social specialist who is actually a codependent, fixated on subversive and covert acquisition of power and control, watch out. Feathers will not only be ruffled, they will fly. The codependent will pretend the control specialist is in charge, but the subversive social specialist will thwart the control specialist's attempts to exercise true control at every turn. The control specialist won't have any clue as to what's happening, nor will she or he have a handle on the situation to grasp. Frustration will simmer, then boil, then watch out!

The result will be a control specialist out of control, à la the bull in a china shop. The codependent's logic goes like this: the more frustrated and out of control the control specialist becomes, the more she or he needs the codependent. The fur flies when the control specialist discovers she or he has been had and tries to rid him- or herself of the codependent who, in turn, will bite and hang on like a rabid squirrel. Of course, the social specialist will deny any intentional contribution to the fracas.

True social specialists can spot false social specialists a mile away. The former understands the latter's destructive effect on company morale. Whether she or he is in control or not, in most organizations, control specialists keep social specialists busy smoothing ruffled feathers. Sometimes the feathers that need smoothing belong to the social specialist, which invokes the participation of other social specialists or, in extreme cases, the stability specialist. A social specialist in tears is a codependent's window of opportunity for capture, if only for a short-term relationship.

The social specialist and the stability specialist

With his or her intense focus on maintaining equilibrium, the stability specialist appreciates the social specialist's positive impact on the organization. The stability specialist also understands that the social specialist's warm and fuzzy way of doing business isn't intended to increase productivity or improve efficiency. But that's okay. The stability specialist is a fan of the social specialist's work, in as much as both leadership styles are tireless promoters of a smooth operation.

The issue of conflict that strikes terror into the hearts of social specialists is not as frightening to a stability specialist. Stability specialists are, out of necessity and by virtue of their essential natures, willing to accept and deal with the reality and inevitability of conflict. They'll take the comforting and mediating efforts of the social specialist as far they go and then gently put the social specialist in timeout when and if the level of organizational conflict immobilizes the relationship-aholic.

When things get too hot for the social specialist to handle, as in the case of an inconsolable customer, the stability specialist takes it from there. Stability specialists, appreciating the positive influence social specialists bring to the organization, will protect them as much as possible. This protection is mostly carried out in stability specialist fashion, behind the scenes and often without the social specialist's knowledge.

The social specialist and the compliance specialist

Social specialists like to tease the compliance specialists in accounting and, on occasion, an exceptionally spirited compliance specialist will return the favor. Social specialists know that compliance specialists are harmless. Compliance specialists know that social specialists will not get in the way of their appointed accounting—much. Control specialists get annoyed on the record by the social specialist's occasional impromptu work stoppages, but they secretly appreciate the distraction.

For the most part, social and compliance specialists lead a peaceful coexistence in organizational life. There is little reason for conflict. Compliance specialists seldom draw attention to themselves and scarcely create a blip on the social specialist's radar screen. The most frequent interactions between social and compliance specialists occur when a social specialist approaches a high-ranking compliance specialist, begging funds to underwrite some social event.

If the social specialist's begging is sufficiently intense, the compliance specialist might cut loose some slush funding to get rid of the relentless butterfly. The alternative is to send the social specialist to the control specialist in charge, which will, in turn, get the compliance specialist chewed out. Where the social specialist/compliance specialist combination is concerned, capitulation is common. No wonder there is so little friction in their relationship. Consistent with Carl Jung's comment in Chapter 3, the social specialist tends to transform everyone with whom, and every situation in which, she or he is involved.

Chapter 10 Summary: Keys to Unleashing Leadership

- **Win/win:** The social specialist really does want everyone to win. Even if the social specialist can't articulate it on a conscious level, she or he is aware that the mutually exclusive nature of winning only if someone else loses, as in the control specialist's competitive world, leaves, well, a loser—and probably a sore one at that. The old double-win is one way a social specialist can preserve the peace at all costs. The win-win attitude has also proved very profitable for organizations that embrace it. The social specialist is worth big bucks.

- **Relationships are everything:** Your entire enterprise is built on relationships. There are internal working relationships and external relationships with customers and community. The more successful any of these relationships are, the more successful you are. To neglect any of them will cost you money; how much money depends on which relationships you're neglecting. We'll wager that you might have not ever sat down and actually calculated how much relationships at all levels mean to you in dollars and cents. If not, then you're probably not aware of how much neglect might be costing you. You have some relationship experts on your team right now in the form of social specialists.

- **The wining personality:** The face your organization presents to the outside is extremely important. That's why so much money gets spent on public relations and advertising. But what about the face your organization sees when it looks in the mirror? While you leave much of your external image-making to professionals, we don't necessarily recommend bringing professionals in to deal with internal image issues. With apologies to some of our colleagues in the HR consulting field, we remind you once again that your social specialists are ready, willing, and able to liven up the place. But first you need to appreciate a lively enterprise. Empower your social specialists, and they'll take it from there.

☞ **How others feel:** The social specialist cares about how others feel. But the reason is not so much pure empathy as it can be a desire to eliminate tension and conflict. If the way an individual feels in a team situation isn't going to affect anyone else, the social specialist might just live and let live. Of course, in a team system, the way anyone feels will impact the way everyone else feels to one degree or another. That's the social specialist's invitation to get involved.

☞ **The interaction:** Social specialists interact with the other leadership styles in the same way that the other leadership styles interact with each other. That is, they bring a mostly subliminal influence to the chemistry of the team. A large percentage of the influence the social specialist has on the other team members is beneath the surface, while the other team members might think all they're dealing with is the social specialist they see before them. "Why would a social specialist want control of anything?" they might innocently ask.

Social specialists are great assets to the organizations for which they work. Ringleaders with narrow to broad areas of responsibility would do well to maximize the relational expertise, advantages, and opportunities social specialists present. The degree to which an organization embraces and encourages its social specialists will have a direct impact on the bottom line.

Looking ahead to the stability specialist, you could say that the stability specialist picks up where the social specialist leaves off, or vise versa. The social specialist often takes up social and/or relational issues that the stability specialist is unavailable or unwilling to continue with. On the other hand, the stability specialist takes over with work-related issues the social specialist is not qualified or interested in pursuing.

Of the four leadership styles (control, compliance, social, and stability), social and stability are the most interrelated. When it comes to taming Org and making him a productive member of your organization, the social and stability specialists work hand in hand. Both have their reasons for wanting a participative and productive organizational dragon, as you're about to find out.

Chapter 11

The Stability Specialist

When awareness is completely balanced, communicating with the outside world is instantaneous and automatic. It happens with the touch of thought.

—Deepak Chopra

Leader to Leader

In this chapter, think of the stability specialist in the position of leadership and the other three basic styles—control, social, and compliance—in subordinate roles. Think also of all four in collaborative roles, forming a composite leadership profile; depending on your most immediate scenario. Hierarchical or molecular, they form a composite personality either way.

Stability specialists are guardedly agreeable to sharing leadership responsibilities, if the collaboration will result in more balanced achievement of organizational objectives. Unlike the social specialist, the stability specialist does not seek harmony for harmony's sake. The stability specialist's efforts to keep things operating on an even keel are tied directly to his or her desire to bring about high performance and peak productivity.

If anybody can be counted on to be task-centered, it's the stability specialist, which is not to say that the other leadership styles are never on task. The control specialist is on task to stay in control. The social specialist is on task to keep everybody happy. The compliance specialist is on task to make all the columns add up accurately. The stability specialist is the one most likely to have the big picture, with all of its complex ins and outs, and the organizations overall agenda in mind. The stability specialist considers his or her task to facilitate achievement of the ultimate organizational goals, even if she or he is chewed up and spit out in the process.

Balance: The Substance of the Stability Specialist

"Balance is the perfect state of still water. Let that be
our model. It remains quiet within and is not disturbed
on the surface."

—Confucius

The still mirror pond is an example of liquid conforming to the shape of its container and then settling to peaceful stillness. We gaze on a mirror pond, marvel in its perfect reflection, and feel a sense of serenity. Nature has other ideas, however. Ocean waters are not calm when the wind blows, the storms of November can turn the Great Lakes deadly, as the captain and crew of the *Edmund Fitzgerald* found out. We only regain a sense of peace and tranquility when the water is again calm and smooth.

Stability specialists seek the peace of the still waters, but steadily navigate through the inevitable storms and gales. Stability specialists make terrific pilots because they refuse to be flustered by crisis. It's not that they're not concerned. They are—very much so. Being concerned keeps them alert. But they know that the best chance for survival or anything good coming out of difficult and challenging situations will ride on the shoulders of a calm, collected, and calculating individual.

Quiet courage is often associated with stability specialists, if anyone is paying attention. The fact is that quiet courage is just that: quiet. To disregard danger and plunge ahead boldly is noisy, and it's appropriate in some situations. But that will be the control specialist. Because courage is not the absence of fear, but acting in spite of it, to consider the consequences and act in the most productive manner anyway requires someone that puts the needs of others and the common good ahead of his or her own. Truthfully, the stability specialist is probably so scared in such moments that she or he doesn't have time to beat any drums or grant any interviews.

"Balance, peace, and joy are the fruit of a successful life.
It starts with recognizing your talents and finding ways to
serve others by using them."

—Thomas Kinkade

We think Kinkade is on the right journey, but slightly off course by saying that balance, peace, and joy are the fruits of a successful life. Another way to look at it is that success is the fruit of a balanced, peaceful, and happy life. Many believe that it's not the destination, but the journey we're on that needs to be positive and uplifting. The stability specialist sees balanced and harmonious work behaviors as the best path to success. Vast volumes of research support the stability specialist's position.

Stability and capability

As eager as the stability specialist is to achieve organizational objectives, she or he does not venture far beyond his or her capabilities. Stability specialists will drive themselves past the point of exhaustion, but they appreciate that competencies and capabilities are what they are, and they won't jeopardize the organization's greater good to attempt things for which they're not qualified. The higher the stakes, the less a stability specialist will venture beyond his or her capabilities.

Achievement of organizational goals is the stability specialist's top priority and she or he is liable to do just about anything to get the job done. As a result, stability specialists become Jacks and Jills of all trades and develop very broad capabilities. So, even without over-reaching, they can still overdo it.

Intense is often an understatement when describing the stability specialist. If 50 percent of the people in an organization did 50 percent of the work, the stability specialist would be less of a heart attack candidate. As it is, 80/20 puts a tremendous additional burden on the stability specialist. We should correct that to say, responding to the 80/20 principle, the stability specialist willingly takes on additional burden, rather than being patient and letting others do what they should be doing.

> "I find the harder I work, the more luck I seem to have."
>
> —Thomas Jefferson

Stability and balance

Even though the stability specialist is intent on achieving balance in the organization, she or he can become too intensely focused on balance resulting in, of all things, imbalance. More accurately stated, the stability specialist will contort him- or herself out of shape to compensate for perceived imbalances elsewhere. It's common for the stability specialist to work 80 hours per week or more to get things accomplished that others are paid to accomplish. The stability specialist would love to work him- or herself out of a job. But given the volatility in the workplace these days, that's unlikely.

The stability specialist is cautious by nature and rarely shows just how much of the burden she or he is carrying. As a result, others don't think much about it. When stability specialists wear their emotions on their sleeves, people are usually too concerned with their own problems to notice anyway. Stability specialists try not to be public complainers, but they can allow themselves to become overwhelmed. If you get a glass of wine or two into a stability specialist in what she or he perceives to be a private conversation/confession, you might get an earful of how hard she or he has been working.

Even after a stability specialist erupts, she or he gets back to work with renewed vigor. It's that never-say-die commitment to holding it all together that others come to rely on, and sometimes actually appreciate. Stability specialists will remain stable and balanced when others are freaking out around them. Because they are cautious to begin with, they can remain calm when superiors chew them out for something that's not their fault, then stuff their feelings and go back to work. Stability specialists are not above developing deep resentments and anger. But they rarely allow personal feelings to disrupt their sacred vow to maintain stability and balance.

Stability and steadiness

To keep things moving forward at a steady pace, the stability specialist maintains a steady rhythm. Like the fabled tortoise that defeated the fabled rabbit, she or he sees no value in rushing if it means screwing things up. The stability specialist is a firm believer that, if there is always time to do poor work over again, there is time to do good work the first time. She or he also is aware of all the additional benefits from doing it right instead of fast. Customers who wait a little longer are less hostile than customers who send the work back or start looking to competitors to do a more reliable job.

On a leadership team, the stability specialist will not be the lead in the shoes that a compliance specialist might be. Whereas compliance specialists often point out why things can't or shouldn't be done, and then retreat into their caves, stability specialists lay awake night after night anticipating problems and thinking of ways to address them. Being steady is about getting there in good shape through systematic, rational planning, rather than getting there first and cleaning up the mess when you could be moving on to the next objective.

Stability and strategy

Stability specialists engage in strategic thinking to, among other things, avoid emotional booby traps. The stability specialist might be seething with resentment and anger, on the verge of a stroke, but she or he won't let loose. To a stability specialist, becoming emotional means allowing the inmates to take control of the asylum.

Behind the stability specialist's outward calmness, his or her mind is racing to get ahead of the dilemma, if there is one, and see what's on the other side of it. She or he can't afford to become entangled in the minutia of the moment. Stability specialists can invoke a sort of out-of-body experience when need be to work out solutions, fast. Stability specialists have paid enough attention to realize that, as we quoted Dwight D. Eisenhower earlier, the urgent is rarely important and the important is seldom urgent.

When, in the midst of crisis, you notice a stability specialist working intently and maintaining control, chances are that she or he has already taken a hot air balloon flight, viewed the battlefield from high above, and returned to employ a new strategy based on his or her observations. When there is no urgency, the stability specialist enjoys the lull and thinks ahead. But she or he is ever vigilant to the possibility of disturbances and disruptions. Like the social specialist, the stability specialist has his or her radar on 24/7. Instead of being calibrated to detect unfriendliness, it is set to detect potential disruptions in the smooth and efficient achievement of goals.

Stability and patience

It's not enough for the stability specialist to remain calm in the face of crisis. She or he must do anything and everything within his or her power to keep others as calm as possible. The stability specialist works hard to restore order and regain balance because she or he is painfully aware of how much productivity is being squandered by panic and catastrophic thinking. If someone is too far gone, the stability specialist might park him or her to the side temporarily to get things moving again.

Much of the stability specialist's steadying is done in advance without anyone else's knowledge. In their fore-thinking, stability specialists consider what types of things are likely to set people off and do whatever is within their power to address those situations and influences before they can negatively affect the organization. If things run smoothly in your organization, there is a chance that it's due, at least in part, to the unheralded and tireless efforts of your quiet and steady stability specialists.

Stability and reliability

Stability specialists are as reliable as the day is long. As such, they tend to lull others to sleep, and can cause a sense of false confidence. Either consciously or unconsciously, people come to depend on stability specialists because they never drop the ball. Failing to somehow *make it so* is as intolerable to a stability specialist as conflict is to a social specialist. However, while the social specialist is digging deep into his or her bag of tricks to avoid the intolerable, the stability specialist is pulling every string available in his or her attempt to move the organization toward the successful accomplishment of organizational objectives.

The social, control, or compliance specialist might be engaged in avoidant behavior, while the stability specialist is intending *toward* realization of the big picture. The social specialist takes it very personally if people don't get along, whether or not it has anything to do with him or her. The stability specialist doesn't make it a personal issue when people and/or circumstances throw a wrench into the gears.

As can be expected, stability specialists are disappointed when things go wrong, and ratchet up their efforts to meet the professional challenge. Ask others in the organization to describe the stability specialist and they will probably say that she or he is the *get it done* person.

Stability and being rational

Operating on assumptions is dangerous. The stability specialist is the first person to agree that assuming makes an *ass* out of *u* and *me*. Just as she or he is constantly aware that doing a bad job over again is expensive in terms of money and image, the stability specialist also knows that when even the smartest person assumes, there is an increased likelihood of embarrassment and expensive mistakes. It takes much less effort to pay attention up front and do your due diligence than it does to dance out of trouble that could have been avoided.

Go back to the stability specialist's rational approach and it's easy to see that she or he feels no need to get emotional or take shortcuts. Speed and adrenaline are not keys for the stability specialist; getting the best effort out of everyone involved *is*. That requires forethought and a steady, rational approach. Assumption is the by-product of impatience and/or arrogance, neither of which appropriately describes the stability specialist. To him or her, working smarter, not harder, is eminently rational.

Stability and evaluation

Just as the line between courage and stupidity can be extremely thin, the line between acts of faith and behavior based on fantasy can be nearly indistinguishable. In reality, the stability specialist prefers to evaluate. The trademark persistence of the stability specialist can appear to be loyalty to an organization or ideal. It's most likely the latter. The ideal is a balanced, systemic approach to getting things done in the most effective and efficient manner possible.

Stability specialists are drawn almost religiously toward constant evaluation of process and productivity. Perhaps it's the spiritual nature of believing in overriding principles greater than ourselves that gives disciplined and obedient people, such as stability specialists, a sometimes over-reverent appearance. As Confucius pointed out, balance is at the core of Eastern (and Western) religious philosophy.

If there is an ideal out there for the stability specialist, it takes the form of the task to be accomplished. Trying to engender the best possible performance out of everyone involved is all part of the big picture that the stability specialist tries so hard to bring about. The stability specialist is aware of the positive impact success has on everyone in the organization. She or he looks on success as a multifaceted benefit to all stakeholders.

There are the first-level benefits of reaching stated goals and objectives. There are second-level benefits as the organization's success ripples out into the lives of its team members, their families, and the community. The third-level benefits include emotional satisfaction and increased confidence, both of which set the foundation for future efforts. The stability specialist has faith that all levels will resonate for the collective and individual good of all. His or her hard work is never unmotivated.

Stability and responsibility

By now it should be obvious why the stability specialist is so doggone responsible. If she or he is not, who will be? Not to overstate the stability specialist's responsibility as opposed to others, everybody takes some amount of responsibility for their own activities and territory. That's enlightened self-interest. The stability specialist is no different. But she or he doesn't stop there.

Stability specialists tend to take on responsibility that encompasses much more than they are officially assigned to. Balls that are dropped by less conscientious people, for example, are picked up by sure-handed stability specialists. They will also take on some partial responsibilities that others are being paid to accept. You could say that stability specialists appear hyper-responsible because they are capturing so much responsibility cast off by others. But it's simply against a stability specialist's nature to stand by and let something not get done; especially if the neglect will have an adverse impact on achievement of company goals and objectives.

Be kind to your stability specialists, if they're not working into the wee hours and listening to Org's munching down the hall, they're taking their work home with them. They go to sleep and wake up with it on their minds. Stability specialists have a difficult time detaching and "leaving it at the office." The problem is that, as soon as they do, they return to a crisis. The Serenity Prayer is appropriate for stability specialists. If they can only learn to accept the things beyond their control, and nothing else, their life spans might increase by 10 years.

Stability and dependability

There used to be billboards for a chain of health clubs. The billboards featured a young woman wearing boxing gloves and working over a big punching bag. The "slug" line read: *"Rest when you're dead."* One of the most frequently heard comments in funeral parlors is, "He looks so peaceful." For stability specialists who don't get help with their addiction, a casket might be the first place that they truly find any peace. On the other hand, they're so dependable, you hate to interfere. Being addicted to organizational accomplishment places a nonstop demand on the stability specialist to not let anybody down.

Like anyone else, stability specialists will only feel true peace if they accept responsibility for their own lot in life, and no one else's. Due to their difficulty establishing and maintaining boundaries, driven by their dedication to mother organization, that is rare. On occasion, however, there is a favorable alignment of the planets. When things go well enough for others around the stability specialist, and the demands of the organization and its stakeholders are temporarily light, she or he is left with only his or her own issues to deal with. That's when the true stability specialist is separated from the codependent pretending to be a stability specialist.

The typical stability specialist can be anywhere from slightly to extremely neurotic. Neurotics are characterized as looking inward to find responsibility for things that happen with or without their involvement. Psychotics, even the highly functional ones, are characterized as believing that all problems are created by others and the responsibility never resides with them. Both the neurotic and psychotic's interpretations are exaggerations, although the psychotic is more often credited with being outside of reality. Both the psychotic and the neurotic are predictable.

A psychotic's external focus seldom leads to positive introspection and, therefore, self-improvement. Neurotics sponge up responsibility for things far beyond their sphere of influence and mix positive with dysfunctional elements of self-responsibility and accurate assessment of others. On that you can depend. Neurotics won't go for long before they find someone else's responsibilities to absorb. After all, the world is never quite as balanced and stable as the stability specialist would iike it to be. That means there is always work to be done, and the stability specialist will probably only rest when she or he's dead.

Maintaining Equilibrium

Balance is a natural state. Balance between the stability specialist and other personalities is a constant concern for the stability specialist and he or she will conform in order to maintain that balance.

The stability specialist and the control specialist

The control specialist benefits a great deal from the tireless, behind-the-scenes efforts of the stability specialist. Often, even when the control specialist recognizes the tremendous contributions the stability specialist makes to the organizational success, she or he does not acknowledge it. At other times, the control specialist slaps the stability specialist on the back with an "attaboy," which means that the stability specialist's over-the-top contributions are appreciated *and* expected.

By not challenging the control specialist's power position, the stability specialist seldom instigates friction between these two styles, or any other styles. Friction is not conducive to a well-balanced approach. The stability specialist does not shy away from the friction frequently caused by control specialists the way a social or compliance specialist might. In his or her dedication to staying on task and keeping everyone else firing on all cylinders, the stability specialist will deal with whatever needs to be dealt with in a calm, unassuming manner, seeking only to produce the best outcome possible for the greater good of the organization.

The stability specialist will use whatever means are necessary to achieve maximum performance across the organization, which can include leveraging the power and influence at the control specialist's disposal. Stability specialists can get extra boost for their agenda from the control specialist's drive and ambition. Stability specialists return the favor by tending to details and outside-the-job description tasks that control specialists don't care to deal with.

The stability specialist and the social specialist

In the same way that stability specialists make judicious use of control specialists' drive and ambition, they can maneuver the social specialists' intense desire to build and maintain relationships into the operational strategy of the organization. Social specialists tend to notice how hard stability specialists work because they appreciate the balance and harmony that stability specialists' efforts bring about. Their core motivations are not the same, but the net result is appreciated.

The stability specialist has a similar appreciation for what the social specialist does. The happy and friendly organization so desperately sought by the social specialist for his or her own peace of mind is also valuable to the stability specialist because she or he knows that a work environment free of friction and hostility is a productive work environment. Whereas social specialists wouldn't care if productivity slipped for the sake of a good party, to stability specialists, the party is only as good as the overall benefit it brings to the achievement of organizational objectives. Celebration can play a productive role in the life and well-being of an organization. The stability specialist's chief concern is that the celebration stays in the proper balance with the effort and results being celebrated. A stability specialist is as fast to celebrate effort with no results as a social specialist is.

Stability specialists see no value in arguing. If what's at stake is sufficiently important, though, the stability specialist is not above pleading his or her case. But not everything is that important. The stability specialist will go along with a wide range of suggested solutions if it means moving ahead. How it is done is not as important to the stability specialist as getting it done, within reason.

Unlike the social specialist who will go along to get along, or the control specialist who will go along as long as it's his or her idea, the stability specialist doesn't allow his or her emotional needs or pride to get in the way. If ever you think that a stability specialist is wishy-washy or spineless because she or he is so quick to agree to someone else's idea or strategy, remember that the stability specialist has already been there and back and has advance awareness of whether or not a suggestion fits within a range of acceptable solutions that will contribute to group progress.

The stability specialist and the compliance specialist

The fact that the stability specialist sees the good in everyone as well as their potential to contribute is never more evident than in the case of the bean counters. Compliance specialists have a tendency to throw wet blankets over inspired and creative sessions. When stability specialists manage to get their coworkers to put on their thinking caps and start innovating, you can count on the compliance specialist to stick a pin in the balloon. The stability specialist then makes an unexpected and unorthodox move. She or he endeavors to prop up the compliance specialist's value to the team.

Sometimes, when a compliance specialist huffs and puffs and blows down the teams' marvelous house of cards, she or he emits a nearly undetectable sign of sadistic delight, usually an ever-so-slight smile, visible only to the stability specialist. The control specialist gets angry, the social specialist starts to cry, and the stability specialist gets down to work. As critical as creative and innovative thinking are, explains the stability specialist, it can be counterproductive if it does not lead to concrete opportunities and real solutions.

No one knows better than the stability specialist how the compliance specialist's desire to keep every t crossed and i dotted is an essential element in the overall balance of the organization. As initially annoyed as the stability specialist might be that the compliance specialist picks the worst possible moment to drop the wet blanket, she or he gets over it quickly for the sake of progress. The more experienced and mature the stability specialist, the more likely she or he is to anticipate the compliance specialist's bombshell.

The stability specialist then incorporates the compliance specialist's comments and sub-agenda into the team's strategic design process. A dyed-in-the-wool stability specialist has thought through all but a few scenarios. The most effective stability specialists are balanced on their own leadership motivation inventories, which helps them avoid flat tires on their ability to be effective.

Chapter 11 Summary: Keys to Unleashing Leadership

- **Somebody has to do it:** Nobody has a gun pointed at a stability specialist's head, threatening to pull the trigger if she or he doesn't pick up the slack on the team. Nobody, that is, except the stability specialist him- or herself. Those issues are somewhere in the seven-eighths of the iceberg that's underwater. Suffice to say that you have stability specialists in your organizations and you need to align them with your needs. Their contributions to the composite leadership profile of any team can be profound.

- **Task-centered:** The stability specialist is the one who is thinking of the big picture. Although everyone might give some thought to the big picture from time to time, the stability specialist is thinking big picture *all the time.* As a result, she or he is likely to have the best perspective of what's going on. The task focus of a stability specialist is not such that she or he has his or her nose buried in the task so as not to get a good overview. She or he can see very well, thank you, and is the most likely to have an eye on the future.

- **Balance is best:** Over time, your organization needs to maintain equilibrium like a marathon runner. A control specialist's sudden bursts of energy fizzle out quickly. A social specialist holds back in fear of offending anyone. A compliance specialist is like a marathon runner who stops to check the map regularly in spite of the well-marked route. She or he will finish eventually, but he or she isn't very competitive in doing it. The stability specialist looks for the optimum balance in the effort and the outcomes.

- **Steady as she goes:** The stability specialist seeks balance in approach, strategy, workload, and use of resources—human and other. Steadiness is a matter of application. Things tend to speed up or slow down when reacting to internal or external marketplace volatility. The stability specialist appreciates this need for fluctuation, but attempts to keep the organization steady as a rule rather than allowing fluctuations to be disruptive. Moreover, when there is a call from the outside marketplace to speed up, the stability specialist has the organization ready to speed up quickly in response rather than get up steam only after the opportunity has passed.

- **Stability underscores:** Stability is the foundation upon which the other leadership styles can operate more effectively. Unless there are benchmarks, educated strategies, and informed expectations, who knows where the organizational throttle should be set? The stability specialist is not more important than the other specialists. The quiet-but-powerful underscoring nature of his or work and essential nature is a terrific leveling influence and solid operational foundation.

As we've pointed out several times now, every one of us has a blend of the four leadership styles. No one person is all one thing. There are simply too many nurturing influences and varied experiences throughout our lives. What we address with leadership style is the *dominant style*, with continuing regard for the secondary styles. The dominant style, whether considering an individual leadership profile, the composite leadership profile of a team or organization, or an initiative profile, points us where we need to focus most diligently and commit the best of our resources once alignment between the composite leadership profile and the initiative profile has been achieved.

Keeping the secondary leadership styles in mind, as well as the leadership motivations we'll discuss next, helps us operate with an enhanced knowledge and appreciation of the invisible hand at work in our organizations, and unleash formerly caged leadership potential. If there was ever another way to say *work smarter*, that's it.

Leadership Motivations

Chapter 12

Courage

What characterizes a good leader?
Curiosity, empathy, practical intelligence, and courage.

—Beverly Pearson

The leadership styles (control, compliance, social, and stability) represent your essential nature as a person and how you live day-in and day-out. The five leadership motivations in the ComposiTeam Leadership System (courage, confidence, concentration, passion, and values) are ways that you and your people are likely to respond to change in the form of opportunities or threats. You could say your leadership motivations are some of the primary ways you're *most comfortable* responding.

The first one, courage, can be a complex or a simple concept, depending on how we twist the lens. In the conventional sense, courage is thought of as the opposite of cowardice. In our book, courage does not imply the absence of fear. According to Mark Twain, "Courage is not the lack of fear. It is acting in spite of it." The greater the fear, the greater the courage required to overcome it. Cowardice occurs when fear stops us from doing what we know to be right.

Sometimes there's an extremely fine line between courage and stupidity. Courage is not doing dare-devilish things without regard for personal safety or well-being, or the safety or well-being of others. That's foolishness, irresponsibility, or possibly flat-out ignorance. Courage is about standing face to face with spiritual, physical, and/or emotional peril and doing what is right regardless of the consequence to you. That includes putting the needs of others first. Doing something that results in negative consequences for others, but not for you, is not an act of courage, and it's definitely *not* leading the way you like to be led.

Doing what's right can be a tricky issue. We believe that our better selves know the difference between doing what is right vs. doing the right thing in the Peter F. Drucker sense of it. According to Drucker, "doing the right thing" means following the rules, sticking to the policy manual, following procedure, and so on. Too often this also means hiding behind the rulebook, policy manual, and established procedures instead of making decisions based on what will provide the greatest long-term benefit for the largest number of people.

Doing what is right, in Drucker's context, means essentially the same thing as Dr. Laura Schlessinger closing her program each day by exhorting her listeners to, "Go out and do the right thing." It doesn't matter whether you use Drucker's language or Schlessinger's language, as long as you understand that right is not necessarily synonymous with ritual. Rightness is a matter of conscience, not conformity or compliance.

Courageous leaders don't ignore the spirit behind policies and procedures, yet they will make unorthodox decisions and vector away from the company line if it means serving the greater good. Courage in organizational life never means acting irresponsibly or unreasonably. It means simultaneously keeping a big-picture perspective along with a close-up view of the needs of individual team members and work groups, and then acting on the principle of serving both to the best of your ability. Whether you are working solo, responsible for a narrowly defined activity, or responsible for a large project, courageously leading the way you like to be led is the road less traveled.

Avoidance vs. Attraction

No one does anything for no reason, even though the reason might not be obvious. Although much of our behavior appears to be unconsciously motivated, it is motivated just the same. All human behavior falls into one of two fundamental categories:

> ›   Intentional movement toward something or someone with expectations of positive results.

> ›   Avoidance of someone or something to escape anticipated negative results.

This seems simplistic on the surface, but the ways that we execute our intentional or avoidant behavior are infinite. The inexplicable complexity of human attitudes and behavior resides in whether or not we're attracted toward something or someone, or we are repulsed. To complicate matters even further, there are times when we are attracted and repulsed at the same time. Professional relationships are no exception.

Our leadership styles, be they control-, compliance-, social-, or stability-driven in nature, are rooted in partially conscious, but mostly unconscious, impulses to emotionally and/or physically move toward or away from people, places, activities, relationships, and things. The motivational dimension of the ComposiTeam Leadership System speaks volumes about whether or not we, as leaders, are in a state of attraction, avoidance, or both.

The ComposiTeam Leadership System promotes the use of collaborative team leadership to accept and overcome fear through the combined contributions of diverse and gifted individuals. You're familiar with the concept of strength in numbers. Now consider the concept of courage through collaboration. With the leadership system, and recognition of the team's composite leadership profile, numbers diminish the paralyzing effect that fear can have on individuals facing their fears alone. Dealing with potentially frightening issues in a supportive atmosphere is like turning on the lights in a dark room full of imaginary monsters. Besides, monsters are a lot less frightening when Org's sitting on your team.

Courage and Criticism

For ringleaders in molecular organizations or department heads in hierarchies, making difficult and sometimes unpopular decisions comes with the territory. Sometimes sticking to the straight and narrow when team members want to wander off is the best decision a leader can make for greatest good. At other times, venturing outside of the comfortable and safe boundaries of conventional wisdom is the right thing to do. Either way, the leader might need to take action that will be unpopular and possibly incite criticism.

The criticism can come form the topside, bottom side, right side, left side, inside, outside, or from all sides. Fear of criticism blocks cowardly leaders from doing what is right. Courage is not sheer strength of will, though. It is more than gritting your teeth, tensing your muscles, and absorbing the blow.

Overcoming cowardice also involves wisdom and perspective. If you're a ringleader or a leadership team member, and leaving the safe confines of the proverbial box is your team's problem, try enlightening them with the fact that there is no box except for the imaginary and arbitrary boundaries in their own minds. It's like the man who clung desperately to the windowsill all night until, by first light, he realized his toes were inches off the ground. Knowledge and awareness can make courageous behavior much easier. Knowledge and awareness is what the ComposiTeam Leadership System is all about.

Pulling an unsafe product from the shelves at a great loss for a manufacturer might require a great deal of courage. On the other hand, fear of litigation might motivate a leader to cease an unsafe business practice in anticipation of possibly losing yet more money in litigation fees and damage awards. The decision to keep an unsafe product on the market because a risk analysis has calculated that pulling it will be more expensive than the inevitable legal fees and damage claims is pure cowardice.

Risk vs. Reward

Cowardice and honesty seem to abhor one another. Don't hold your breath waiting for a disgraced corporate executive or government bureaucrat to stand up and say, "The company went under and our investors lost millions, even billions, of dollars, not to mention thousands of jobs, because of fraudulent accounting practices that I endorsed to pad my personal bank account." Such cowardice orbits about as far on the opposite side of the courage spectrum as possible.

Human decisions, intentional or avoidant, are responsible for disasters, yet most of the time no individual is held accountable. When someone is identified as the culprit, it's often a fall guy/scapegoat and not the real perpetrator. Bureaucracy is a haven, if not a breeding ground, for incompetence and cowardice. There are lots of places to hide among those silos. It takes tremendous courage for an organizational leader to tell the truth in today's world. It would be refreshing to hear the head of a federal agency publicly confess, "Changing the system and making it efficient and cost-effective would be like reversing the flow of the Niagara River by hand-carrying buckets of water up the stairs from the bottom of the gorge and pouring them back in the river above the falls." The news itself wouldn't be the most pleasant we've ever heard, but the honesty would be inspiring.

Sometimes spending is the better virtue than not spending. It requires courage in the corporate world to argue for investment in research and development or customer satisfaction over short-term profitability. The best road for all concerned is seldom the easy road. Long-term results require patience and perseverance as opposed to the quick and easy nature of short-term results. Investing in the long-term means delayed gratification in the near-term in favor for higher achievement in the future. That usually calls for courageous leadership to fend off the panicked or greedy desires of shortsighted stakeholders.

The Competent Can Stacker

How do organizations engender incompetence? Consider the shelf-stocker in a grocery store who prided himself in his ability to stack cans in big pyramid displays faster than anyone else in town. He did his job so well that the executives from headquarters made him the store manager. In his new position, he earned more money, but the champion stacker was no longer paid to stack cans. Instead, he scheduled all of the employees for their shifts, dealt with their problems, and processed all kinds of paperwork.

Every once in awhile, particularly when the stacker-turned-manager was feeling the pressures of his expanded responsibilities, a loud crash could be heard from somewhere in the store. The first curiosity-seeker to arrive at the scene always found the fledgling store manager rebuilding the pyramid of cans at lightning speed. How the display was knocked over and why the manager never asked anyone to help restack the cans was a mystery to the shoppers and other employees. Equally clueless were the executives from headquarters who promoted the can-stacker out of his area of maximum skill and competence, and, in doing so, lost a master stacker only to gain a mediocre manager.

The primary objects of fear for leaders in modern organizations are the personal problems that plague individual team members and interpersonal conflicts between team members. Most executives would rather eat shards of broken glass than hear subordinates describe personal and/or family problems. The same applies to tension and hostilities that arise in the workplace because of personality conflicts and warring factions driven by conflicting work styles and ideologies.

Most executives are promoted based on their demonstrated ability to produce results. That makes sense, to a point. People who produce positive results should be rewarded. As we said, rewarded behavior is repeated behavior. However, it makes no sense to reward the individual with increased compensation and, at the same time, remove the person from the very activity at which he or she excelled.

Nevertheless, this is the neverending scenario in organizational life—promoting people out of their range of competencies and mastery into positions for which they have no mastery, and usually no preparation. It's the same principle outlined in Chapter 2: Take stellar sales professionals, make them stop selling, and start managing less stellar sales professionals. Take outstanding engineers and designers and make them stop engineering and designing, and start managing human beings, something they are probably (a) not well suited for, (b) not attracted to doing, (c) not formally or informally trained to do, or (d) all of the above.

To burden people who are well suited to, and successful at, certain things with something entirely different defies common sense. Worse yet, it takes them out of their comfort zones and places them at ground zero, *directly in the crosshairs of fear*. Yet, in organizational life, that is more often the rule than the exception.

The exception is to make a priority out of identifying people who are naturally inclined to deal with the human factor in business, and prepare them for leadership. When the right person is prepared and placed in a leadership position, based on his or her leadership style and underlying motivations, the results are astonishing. The people who excel at doing things they love are rewarded and encouraged to reach new heights and all stakeholders benefit, individually and collectively.

Isolation Is Not an Option

When someone not well suited to dealing with the unpredictable and constantly changing nature of human beings is placed in a position of managing others, the effect can be devastating to the organization. The fear-based lack of empathy, creativity, loyalty, enthusiasm, and energy that results from ineffective leadership ripples throughout the organizational population and all stakeholders wind up paying the price in lower efficiency, productivity, and profits.

Persons in leadership positions do not work in isolation. Organizations are made up of people doing things that affect yet more people. It's basic systems theory at work. The super sales professional, effective engineer, or dynamic designer can, and often do, work semi-independently, but not the leader. Leadership, except when we're self-led, is a public job. Leaders who attempt to isolate themselves are guaranteeing a legacy as leader *in name only*. Everything leaders do, especially attempting to isolate themselves, affects the whole system.

Anyone well suited for leadership recognizes that the role of leader is, by nature, the least isolated and most visible position in an organization. The most enlightened organizations take the role of leader seriously and vigorously protect and enhance the power and effectiveness of the position as a platform from which to support and encourage the growth and development of others. This means placing a high value on courage as a qualification. Courage may or may not have a great deal to do with selling, engineering, and designing, but it has everything to do with leading others.

People who are better suited to working on tasks rather than on other people *as their tasks* do not make good leadership candidates. Similarly, just because someone is naturally gifted at listening to, building up, and encouraging others doesn't mean that she or he is not also skilled at task execution. Leaders need to be skilled at staying on task because organizational designers will seek to ensure that dealing with people is their primary task. The job of leading others is, in many ways, more complex and complicated than virtually any other job, which makes focus, single-mindedness, and other elements of competence and mastery in relationships all the more essential to success.

Hiring and Firing

Courage plays an enormous role when bringing new people into an organization as well as in parting ways. Wise leaders know that the best interests of the organization and its many internal and external stakeholders are best served by recruiting the most talented and capable people available. Managers lacking in courage and opting instead to encircle themselves with like-minded persons, regardless of creativity of ability, will avoid hiring the very people that will best serve the organization. Sometimes these same managers hire Milquetoast in order to avoid the possibility of dealing with the problems spicy types might bring with them. Old nags won't put out the work of racehorses, but they are easier to handle and usually eat less.

When someone is not right for the organization, the thought of terminating that person seems to strike fear into the hearts of most managers. Of all the disturbances that managers try to avoid in the workplace, noisy confrontations rank at the top of the list. Courageous leaders with big picture perspective will recognize the need for the individual and organization to part ways, in the best interests of both. The courageous leader will step up and terminate the team member quickly, quietly, and respectfully.

The cowardly manager will avoid the problem for as long as possible, allowing a problem to fester and abscess, ignoring or denying the damage to the organization and potential losses to its stakeholders. Even then, when action is finally initiated, the less-than-courageous manager will dabble at a solution and probably make the situation worse rather than to act swiftly and decisively. The difference between hiring wisely or poorly can arguably be ignorance rather than lack of courage. Where termination is concerned, those who refuse to act with courage often justify their inaction by denying the gravity of the problem or its true cost.

What Price for Popularity?

A truly courageous leader won't be overly influenced or motivated by popularity. Nobody wants to be unpopular. Despite the John Wayne attitude that some executives claim to possess, which is an "I don't want them to like me, just do what I say," attitude, nobody truly wants to be disliked. Unfortunately, many executives have come to accept lack of favor in the eyes of their team members because they lack the skills to alter attitudes and/or adopt behaviors that might improve relationships. Like fear, this can be a self-fulfilling prophecy, especially when someone gives up before they even get started. Even though it takes genuine courage to venture outside of your comfort zone, nothing will change until you do.

If trust is indeed the number-one component of earning respect from team members, then organizational leaders need to get outside of themselves long enough and often enough to demonstrate that they truly have their team members' interests at heart. Once this is successfully accomplished for the first time, it takes constant effort to keep walking the walk. The manager who skimmed Ken Blanchard and Spencer Johnson's *One Minute Manager* and emerged from his or her office to routinely pat everyone on the back precisely at 2 p.m. every day, and then disappeared back into his or her office, didn't win over the hearts and minds of the department.

The courageous leader will think of what is best for the majority while remaining sensitive to the rights of the minority, making his or her decisions unpopular with one group or the other. Courage is the essential commodity to ensure that decisions are not made based only on popularity. Focus groups and polls have become big business for that unfortunate purpose. They provide decision-makers with data that predicts which decisions will be the most popular or, at least, do the least damage to a leader's popularity. Regretfully, holding a moistened finger into the wind has little, if anything, to do with doing what is right.

Groupthink

When leaders fail to give inspired and enthusiastic support to creative and innovative thinking, they run the risk of encountering groupthink; a condition under which a team seeks internal cohesion at the possible expense of wise and prudent decisions. The attraction to group adhesion is more likely avoidance of conflict. Groupthinkers don't make waves. They go along to get along. When executives surround themselves with *yes* persons, and discourage challenging, alternative opinions, they guarantee that groupthink will choke out courageous thought the way weeds choke life out of more fragile flowers.

Groupthink is fear-driven, and can be powerful because it helps people avoid the often-frightening prospect of taking risks and trying new and unfamiliar things. Groupthink simplifies dealing with difficult issues. Author Irving Janis defines groupthink as the "inability of very intelligent people to make sound decisions." (*Groupthink: Psychological Studies of Policy Decisions and Fiascoes*, 2nd ed, Houghton Mifflin, 1982). Janis cites John F. Kennedy's cabinet in the Bay of Pigs affair, the Cuban Missile Crisis, as well as other historical disasters such as the Korean and Vietnam Wars, the making of the Marshall Plan, and the Watergate cover-up as milestones in the infamous history of groupthink.

Groupthink is an enemy of progressive thinking. Courageous leadership from individuals as well as leadership teams is required to avoid groupthink and its effect of promoting conformity over wisdom. A courageous leader will always seek to do what is right, even if it causes discomfort for him- or herself and even the rest of the team.

Lessons From the Lion

Do you remember the following scene from L. Frank Baum's *Wizard of Oz*?

Cowardly Lion: Courage! What makes a king out of a slave? Courage! What makes the flag on the mast to wave? Courage! What makes the elephant charge his tusk in the misty mist, or the dusky dusk? What makes the muskrat guard his musk? Courage! What makes the sphinx the seventh wonder? Courage! What makes the dawn come up like thunder? Courage! What makes the Hottentot so hot? What puts the 'ape' in apricot? What have they got that I ain't got?

Dorothy, Scarecrow,
  and the Tin Man: Courage!

Cowardly Lion: You can say that again!

As far as the Cowardly Lion was concerned, courage was an outside-in phenomenon. Someone else bestowed it upon you, and once you had it, you feared nothing and nothing was impossible. The lesson to learn from the Lion in the *Wizard of Oz* is that he had it wrong. Individual courage is an inside job. Although there is some comfort in numbers, courage is best developed and nurtured on your own. Then you can share it with your team as added value for your being there. The journey you take with individual courage is a personal and perhaps lonely one. With only rare exceptions, the old maxim that says, "It's lonely at the top," really applies to the ethical, honest, and courageous leader in a hierarchical organization.

As we just said, the increased courage that can result from the proper alignment of natural talents and abilities in a leadership team in a collaborative organization is not necessarily an increase in individual courage. However, the boldness associated with courage can *increase for everyone* on a leadership team when the natural talents of each team member compliment one another. In that sense, there is courage in numbers. The balance of complementary strengths will keep the courageous behavior on track and ensure that the purpose of the actions remains sound.

Ernest Hemmingway described courage (he called it "guts") as grace under pressure. That can mean the Cowardly Lion's notion that courage is a flag-waving, drum-beating concept is also misguided. Courage is a quiet and, to many, imperceptible quality. Most truly courageous acts are never highly publicized. They take place every time an individual stands at his or her ethical crossroads and decides between conviction and convenience, between what's best for me versus what might be best for others versus what is best for all.

True Courage Includes Conscience

People who struggle with courage have consciences. A conscience is often the enemy of sleep. Hemmingway also said that intelligent people are rarely happy people. If you are smart enough to see the many different sides to a story, options in solving a problem, the complexity of achieving true fairness, and equality in human relations, you will have a hard time switching off the white noise and relaxing on cue. Anyone with true courage, as opposed to self-serving boldness and impatience, is constantly being called upon to exercise it wherever unfairness and imbalance exist, which is all around us, all of the time.

Leaders with conscience wrestle with, and agonize over, decisions. Conscientious leaders spend many sleepless nights, while others with a narrower or more self-serving view of the world snooze away. Courage and conscience are not concepts to be taken lightly. If ignorance is truly bliss, which it seems to be, then knowledge, wisdom, and courage are ingredients for a life of deep contemplation and reflection.

Courage Is Not Toughness

Courageous attitudes can appear to be tough and even stubborn. There are elements of both in courageous behavior, but everyone who acts tough and/or stubborn is not necessarily acting courageously. The appearance of toughness is often yet another compensation for fear. Bullies are famous for it. Acting tough works wonders until someone stands up to you. Then what? If there is no courage to back it up, you will back down.

Stubbornness is usually a power play. People who act stubbornly are not usually acting out of principle or deeply held values as much as they are trying to win. To the truly stubborn person, winning is everything, losing is nothing, and there is nothing in between. To them, compromise is losing. A truly courageous leader will give in and allow the stubborn person to win if the issue is of little or no consequence. A courageous leader is committed to achieving the best for the most and is little concerned with who is perceived to be "right." A truly courageous leader will admit to being wrong when she or he is right to do so.

"Nuts"

Courageous leaders are often quiet and unassuming individuals. When Nazi General Luttwitz demanded the American soldiers in Bastogne, France, surrender in December of 1944, the American commander, Brigadier General A.C. McAuliffe, sent his reply: *"Nuts"* was all he said. Unlike his contemporary, George Patton, McAuliffe was not known as a loud and flamboyant commander. He was a quiet, businesslike, get-it-done kind of person who probably never expected to be surrounded and greatly outnumbered by the enemy.

Yet, there he was. He could have surrendered, but he considered the big picture and what surrendering would mean. He could have saved his own scalp and the lives of his troops by raising a white flag. In the end, McAuliffe's irreverent reply was not meant to be a message to the Germans as much as it was a message to everyone fighting against Hitler and the oppressive Axis powers. McAuliffe knew that the odds favored the Germans and, in all probability, he and his entire garrison would be overrun. But even at the cost of their own lives, the power of their courageous act would inspire others.

Courage Requires Effort

If you agree that anything worth doing is worth doing well, you'll also agree that excellence takes effort. Courageous leaders know this and are understandably suspicious of anything or anyone that promises something for nothing. This is especially true of human development. Because a leader's primary responsibility is the growth and development of his or her team members, a full appreciation of the costs associated with growth is necessary.

One of the most common scenarios for leaders is for team members to present ideas that do not account for the real costs in personal or financial resources. Many people in positions of leadership classically respond that every new idea costs too much. They sound like a broken record. Wise and courageous leaders will be realistic about the financial implications of a new suggestion or plan, but they will be acutely aware of the human cost that accountants rarely consider, much less understand.

Tired Fins

Courageous leaders are generally full of the energy that emanates from enthusiasm and commitment. But they can still get tired. It's not easy swimming upstream. Nearly everyone in organizational life that has a functioning moral compass finds him- or herself from time to time swimming against the current that usually flows away from conflict and adversity toward quick and easy solutions.

Leaders that take the awesome responsibilities of leadership seriously won't find it easy going much of the time. The best solution is to do what engineers did to the Chicago River in the late 19th century. Realizing that the river was carrying much of the city's waste into the pure waters of Lake Michigan, the city's primary source of drinking water, a series of locks and dams were built that reversed the flow and carried Chicago River water away from the city and the lake.

Effective leaders invest tremendous time, energy, and resources into developing and sustaining a culture of virtue and excellence in their organizations. It doesn't make much sense to try and run a values-based organization without addressing the core values of the whole. Changing the way people think, act, and do business is a Herculean task, and it calls for remarkable courage. Doing what is right usually means taking the road less traveled by and dealing with the reasons folks prefer the easy road.

Reward Courage

Charles Schwab said, "The way to develop the best that is in a [person] is by appreciation and encouragement." One of the most direct ways that leaders can encourage courageous behavior throughout their organizations is to reward it. It's all too common for the whistle-blower to become the target rather than illegal or unethical practices and those that engage in them. It requires an all-out and sustained effort to place courageous behavior high on the totem pole of organizational values and then keep it there. As the old proverb says, etch the mistakes people make in sand so the healing effects of time can erase them. Carve their positive accomplishments in rock so they can be praised forever.

Once the internal and external communications mechanisms carry the message that courageous behavior is a highly regarded virtue, leaders need to seek it out. We frequently see plaques on walls of restaurants or other businesses with a picture of the employee of the month. We assume that their peers, supervisors, customers, or some combination of all three chose them for the honor. Usually *not* included is the criterion under which the selection was made. That would really complete the honor.

If company newsletters, Websites, displays, and other points of communication also featured a brief story of how the team member demonstrated courage, the message would be powerful. Even if it was a seemingly insignificant act of customer service, when the employee could have chosen more selfishly or cautiously, recognition and reward for making the tougher decision will go a long way to establishing a courage-based culture.

Courage Is Contagious

In *The Fountainhead*, Ayn Rand wrote: "Don't work for my happiness, my brothers—show me yours—show me that it is possible—show me your achievement—and the knowledge will give me courage for mine." Never forget that a single act of courage can inspire other acts of courage, by other people. When people in your organization begin to accept that their courageous behavior will be supported, even if they fail, you'll see a lot more people trying things they otherwise would shy away from.

We have historically given a great deal of acclaim to NASA astronauts. Thanks to the Ron Howard–directed film *Apollo 13*, the engineers, scientists, and others who represent the many layers of support for the highly publicized exploits of the astronauts received long overdue recognition for their acts of selflessness and courage. Firefighters and police officers were acting bravely long before September 11, 2001. So many people every day and throughout history have made enormous sacrifices only to receive little, if any, recognition. They didn't do what they did for the recognition. The recognition, as much as we can give, will inspire similar behavior in others.

It takes real courage to give something up. The line between boldness motivated by selfishness and boldness to bring about the best and most good, even at personal expense, can be as nearly indistinguishable as the line between true courage and stupidity. Giving things up is a constant practice of effective leaders. At the top of the list is recognition. You've heard it said that a good leader takes the blame when things go wrong and gives the glory to his or her team when things succeed. That's big. It takes tremendous courage to step out of a spotlight and put someone else in it. It takes just as much courage to take the bullet when you could so easily pass the blame.

Being a courageous leader means knowing how to hold things in an open hand. Instead of gripping power and possessions tightly, the courageous leader shares with those whose efforts brought about the rewards. The surest way to the top of an organization is to have the support of those with whom you work. Hording the goodies is not going to make friends and influence people. Those who have learned to trust courageous leaders will push them up the corporate ladder. In the end, giving something up can lead to gaining something bigger and better.

On leadership teams, collective courage is evident when team members share the workload and the limelight. True courage is always selfless.

A team can act as selflessly as an individual. The best operating environment for a team is sharing the good as well as the unpleasant. Leadership teams can model courage to the rest of the organization as effectively as courageous individuals.

Chapter 12 Summary: Keys to Unleashing Leadership

- **Leading with an open hand:** Part of leading with an open hand is encouraging everyone in your organization to excel without worrying that they might steal your thunder. There will always be executives, driven by fear, who will surround themselves with puppets that will never outperform the *great man*. The puppets will continue to serve as operatives in support of their boss's climb to the top. A courageous leader has the best interests of the organization and its many stakeholders at heart. With that perspective and agenda, it's in the leader's best interest to promote the growth and development of as many team members as possible. The best way we know to do that is to spread the expectation and responsibility for leadership across the organization and as close to the task as possible.

- **Look to the next leader:** Identifying and rewarding courageous behavior is a start. Becoming a champion of continuous learning and development is another way to promote excellence. It takes an outward focus to build others up. Such an outward focus is another component of courage. Leading the way you like to be led includes being given the opportunity to participate at the most profound level to which you are capable.

- **Change the lead spot often:** Courageous leaders actively seek out and groom others for leadership positions, even their own. This is not merely for succession purposes, but also to keep leadership fresh. They want their organizations to fly like a flock of geese, not a herd of buffalo. This doesn't mean finding someone who will carry on just as you have. It would be better for the organization as a whole for someone to take the best of what you have accomplished and build upon it. Many in positions of leadership have their identity as human beings too tightly wrapped up in their positions. For such people it's no wonder that they are reluctant to turn over the reins. Releasing the tight grip and opening the hands takes courage.

☞ **Collaborative courage:** The concept of courage in collaboration emphasizes the combination of complementary talents and abilities, not a gathering of similarly gifted people. If the fears of one individual can paralyze his or her efforts, a group of symmetrical (similar) styles and motivations will only amplify the fears the group members have in common. The proper alignment of group roles and responsibilities with diverse and complementary (contrasting) talents and abilities will create an atmosphere where strengths in certain team members will shore up insecurities in others, and vice versa. If properly aligned, the composite leadership profile of a team and an initiative profile should create footing solid enough for the team not to trip over their individual or collective fears.

☞ **Shared courage:** It takes courage to be the responsible leader and tug on the reins of progress just enough to make sure that everyone's thinking cap is on straight. People in leadership positions who agree to anything and everything as if money and human costs were no object are not assuming ultimate responsibility for their decisions. Such irresponsible behavior is anything but courageous. It's careless. Being careless and irresponsible is not how one goes about defending the best interests of everyone affected. The creative tension in a leadership team is a hedge against carelessness as it promotes accountability and prudence.

Beware of stupidity and selfishness in courageous clothing. You don't want to lose Org's valuable services so soon after his conversion. The fastest way to do that is to lose the conviction and spine behind the change you've been able to sustain. Understanding and acting out of genuine courage, individually and as a collaborative effort, impresses dragons.

Make sure that courage, however much or little you possess, is selfless and sincere. Courage is only the first category in the ComposiTeam leadership motivation inventory. You may rank higher in another category as a means of contributing a diverse quality to your team and your organization. Before we move on to confidence, we give the last words on courage to Ralph Waldo Emerson:

"Whatever you do, you need courage. Whatever course you decide upon, there is always someone to tell you that you are wrong. There are always difficulties arising that tempt you to believe your critics are right. To map out a course of action and follow it to an end requires some of the same courage that a soldier needs. Peace has its victories, but it takes brave men and women to win them."

Chapter 13

Confidence

They are able because they think they are able.

—Virgil

Confidence is the unshakable belief that what you intend to happen as a result of your actions *will* happen. Because ringleaders or hierarchical leaders set the tone, model, and otherwise represent the qualities necessary to bring out the best in others, confidence is a critical element. The highly visible role of leader can't be successfully fulfilled unless the individual in that role demonstrates consistent confidence. If not, what's being modeled are indecision and doubt.

The same is true of collaborative leadership teams. If the expectation for performance matches the capability composition of the team, the group's collective confidence will be high. Remembering that all of us are more capable than any one of us, there is no reason for a well-designed and well-balanced leadership team not to be confident that what they set out to do will be done. In the same way, there is enhanced optimism that, with a team composite leadership profile that's well aligned with an initiative profile, the chances for success are significantly improved.

A team can also suffer from collective low self-esteem. Picture the football, baseball, or basketball team's bench as they are being whipped on the field or the court. If their collective performance is falling short of expectations, or worse, if their poor performance is consistent with their expectations, confidence will suffer.

Anthony Trollope, 19th century British novelist, put it this way, "Nobody holds a good opinion of a person who has a low opinion of him or herself." One of the primary functions of individual or team leadership is to inspire confidence in others. That can't be done unless the leaders are the real deal in terms of self-confidence. With confidence comes charisma of sorts. People expect leaders to continue accomplishing things they have consistently accomplished over time, to develop new skills, or both.

Confidence Is Golden

Everyone is drawn to confidence. Voters are attracted to confident political candidates, patients are calmed by confident physicians, and even parishioners are comforted by the confidence in their religious leaders. One of the qualities top executives admire most in those in positions of responsibility throughout the organization is confidence. If you want to get the attention of the brass, be someone who accepts responsibility and—more importantly—makes things happen as planned.

If you're in a position of leadership, which is another way to say position of responsibility, you already know that people who accept responsibility and demonstrate true courage and confidence are worth their weight in gold. You know that delegating responsibility to confident people is a lot less nerve-racking than handing over something important to a self-doubter. If you lead the way you like to be led, you will give eager and capable people every opportunity to demonstrate their value to the organization.

This doesn't apply to top executives who surround themselves with political operatives. They don't want others to operate independently, preferring instead to have everything go through them. Such defensive and avoidant behavior results from *lack* of confidence and courage.

When it comes to rings of responsibility, confident medium-range ringleaders are appointed and supported by confident wider-range ringleaders who appreciate the positive value confidence brings to the way people do their jobs. Confidence is a key ingredient to becoming a leader *in name* and *in fact* because of the effect it has on people swimming ahead of and behind you on the organizational food chain. In team leadership situations, each team member brings confidence along with his or her unique expertise.

Self-Doubt Is a Self-Fulfilling Prophecy

> "If you doubt you can accomplish something, then you can't accomplish it. You have to have confidence in your ability, and then be tough enough to follow through."
>
> —Rosalyn Carter

True confidence and a negative attitude can't occupy the same space. John Christian Bovee said that "Self-distrust is the cause of most of our failures...they are the weakest, however strong, who have no faith in themselves or their own powers." Although you don't need to have extraordinary powers to be confident, you do need faith in your own ability to draw upon whatever sources of power are available to get things done.

Confidence comes more from the ability to find information quickly than it does from memorizing everything there is to know about anything. The truly confident leader knows that she or he doesn't need to control everything to make things happen. The greatest confidence-builder in the world is the experience of putting together a coalition of ordinary people to accomplish something extraordinary. Strong and reliable relationships bolster confidence because they are the building blocks of effectiveness.

Confident people tend to associate with other confident people. That is one way the ComposiTeam Leadership System can help increase confidence throughout your organization. When people are recognized for their unique talents and abilities, and not arbitrarily expected to operate outside of their comfort zones, the foundation for confident behavior is established.

If you're not surrounded by confident friends and associates, you might want to take a moment and ponder the reasons. More than likely, if confident persons do not seek you out and connect with you on a personal and/or professional level, it could be that you aren't exuding enough confidence to attract them. If you think that you're reasonably confident, yet others don't share your view, you're probably not as confident as you think. Check to see if you are operating from within your comfort zone.

If you frequently question the wisdom of your own decisions and wonder if you're doing the right thing, chances are good that you're mired in self-doubt. In most cases, people who are in doubt, simply *don't*. People who avoid taking action for fear the results might not be good are likely to worry themselves into a state of paralysis. As a result, the ineffective person remains ineffective, the powerless person remains powerless, and those who question their own ability to get things done give themselves no reason to think any differently.

Confidence and Competence

As much as we've harped on the fact that competency should not be the only criterion for selecting team members, proven competency has a powerful impact on confidence. Flights of fantasy and magical thinking regarding competency do not constitute genuine confidence. Getting on a lucky streak now and then might build a false sense of confidence, but it won't lead to genuine confidence over the long haul. A false sense of confidence will be shattered the first time the imaginary competency fails. In the case of gamblers, new fantasy confidence always seems to rise from the shattered remains of the last failure. Magical thinking is not a good basis on which to build an organization.

Where there is little competence, there will be limited confidence. Self-doubters can be comfortable in their inability to successfully solve problems or to make lasting and meaningful changes in their work habits and environments. Wallowing in problems is usually accompanied by blaming others for one's lack of success. To many, the fact that problems exist is reason enough to be overwhelmed by them. Some people believe that unsolvable problems provide job security. But do you know of anyone who lost his or her job because she or he solved problems too fast or too well?

When team members share the belief that solving problems too fast or too well will cost them their jobs, the paradigm is due for a shift. For individual leaders or members of leadership teams, there is no such thing as successfully working your way out of a job. Successful work leads to broader responsibilities and new challenges.

If members of leadership teams are not properly aligned with their natural strengths and competencies, as reflected in their composite leadership profile, team confidence will suffer. Real confidence increases as real competence increases, especially where natural talents and abilities have formed a foundation. Belief in the ability to do something is greatly bolstered by experience in doing it. Practice might not make you perfect, but it's bound to make you a whole lot better. Building competence through experience is a good way to approach confidence-building. Just believing in oneself for the sake of believing in oneself is a warm and fuzzy thought, but it's never going to take the place of competence as a foundation for confidence.

Just as confidence is increased with strengthened competence, it is also increased with support from others. Effective leaders know how powerful their support can be, especially when someone in their sphere of influence is stepping out of his or her comfort zone. This is particularly important if you value creativity and innovation in your work processes.

Problems and Opportunity

The difference between a confidence-building behavior on the part of leadership and another brick in the wall of self-doubt is often a matter of mental perspective. Self-doubters can easily have their negative thinking reinforced by superiors and even peers that live in a world of gloom and doom. If you don't think you can do it, your boss doesn't think you can do it, and nobody else seems to offer a contrasting opinion, chances are very good that you won't succeed. Nobody will be surprised, either—especially you.

Positive-thinking people look at the world as a wealth of unrealized potential. If that sounds like fluff, consider the alternative. What personal or professional good can possibly come from thinking that the best is behind you and there is less hope in the future than there was in the past? Confident leaders always look for the best; the best methods and techniques, the best ways to team up the best people, the best ways to inspire and lead, and so on.

Nobody gets through a day without facing some sort of problem…much less a lifetime. To the confident leader, a problem is an opportunity to do something better than it has been done before. Problems are learning opportunities, and confident leaders believe in lifelong, continuous learning. In that light, problems are not to be feared. Problems shouldn't shake confidence, but rather be looked upon as confidence-building opportunities.

Realistically, problems are never going to be welcomed with open arms like prodigal children. But they can help demonstrate the difference between a confident leader and a self-doubting leader. For the most part, problems won't wipe the smile off a confident leader's face, while very little will bring a smile to the self-doubter's face. Problems will bring about a surge of energy in a confident leader. She or he will naturally ratchet up a notch when a problem appears. The excitement and accelerated heartbeat are not produced by the appearance of the problem, but by the chance to craft a dynamic solution. Confident leaders love solutions.

Essential Nature and Confidence

In organizational life, the confident leader raises his or her hand and asks for the assignment when a problem threatens the company. Taking an inventory of leadership styles and underlying motivations gives organizational designers the knowledge to cast people in roles that will best serve the organization as well as fulfill the individual. When you need a basketball put through a hoop, you want the ball in Michael Jordan's hands. If you suddenly lost your partner for the member-guest golf tournament and you ran into Tiger Woods in the parking lot looking for a game, your problem would be solved.

If you are a truly confident leader, you want the powers that be to call *your* name when a problem arises in your organization. If your team has been built from confident individuals who are cast in roles consistent with their natural talents and abilities, they will be eager to take on whatever challenge comes their way. It is possible for people to be skilled at things other than what they have a natural inclination to do. The true test of a person's alignment with his or her essential nature is his or her eagerness to address problems.

"As If"

Playing the game "as if" the worst that could happen did indeed happen also positions the mind for confidence. The issues of fear and courage are intertwined with confidence. Nothing attacks and erodes confidence faster than fear of personal failure. While Tommy Lasorda's "Hit it to me" baseball players with can-do attitudes eager to make the big play, there are others who fear that they might fail if the ball comes in their direction.

Many people appreciate the need to step up and contribute to the effort of the team. They even want to. But they still struggle with the fear that, when the moment arrives, they might fail. This timidity encourages them to back off and observe more than participate, pass rather than shoot, and hide in the shadows rather then step into the spotlight.

Although *as if* thinking builds confidence, anticipate problems and challenges by going beyond thinking in terms of *if* a problem will arise. Instead, go ahead and contemplate your response in terms of *when* a problem arises. This method of mental framing will make your overall sense of confidence, and your team's collective sense of confidence, even more unshakable by diminishing the fear and anxiety factor.

Action Planning

Many confident leaders have a bias toward action. They do not enjoy sitting around and waiting for things to happen. They prefer making things happen. Like the courageous leader who can be more impatient than practical, be careful not to equate just any kind of action with effective leadership. All effective, confident leaders favor action over inertia. However, not all leaders addicted to action are effective or truly confident. Some people think that activity, directed or undirected, purposeful or not, is an acceptable substitute for a well-thought-out strategy.

A great deal of confidence can be built upon the practice of planning. It's impossible to fully plan for every possible contingency. Those who try will ultimately plan to the point of paralysis. To those who don't want to make a mistake or be caught in a compromised position, planning is essential. Take a lesson from pilots, who don't generally get a second chance if they mess up.

Pilots plan more thoroughly than perhaps any other brand of professional, with the possible exception of, hopefully, surgeons and demolition experts who work with explosives. Any pilot will tell you that a good landing begins with a good approach. How many chances does a demolition expert get at blowing up the same building? Unfortunately, one story about a surgeon going *back in* to repair something not planned well in the first place is one story too many.

The stakes the rest of us play with are not usually as dramatic as these examples, but the underlying principle is the same. Time spent planning builds confidence in the outcome, with good reason. Confident leaders are champions of planning.

Shaken, Not Stirred

When outcomes are not what we expect them to be, confidence can be shaken. Confidence that is shaken now and again can serve as a gentle reminder that genuine confidence needs to be built upon a foundation of competence, which includes well-reasoned and intelligent behavior. There are many reasons that outcomes vary from our expectations. Unexpected, outside events can interrupt expectations. There is no way to anticipate everything. However, confident leaders always anticipate something.

What we expect to happen because of our planning and actions can also be corrupted and altered by mysterious forces beyond our detection. If you've been paying attention, dragons in the custodial closet won't be a "mysterious force" anymore. But we never fully comprehend the potentially devastating effect of a computer virus until it strikes. Once we recognize the virus is present, it has already begun to destroy our work, ability to communicate, and possibly vast stores of information.

If your confidence is shaken easily and often, you need to consider the degree of competence you possess and how much you can increase it. Your style and motivation data will be essential to an accurate assessment. You might also reflect upon the wisdom of your actions. Confident leaders are not afraid of advice. They seek counsel whenever it is available and practical. Style and motivation data, combined with wise observations and counsel make for winning individual and composite leadership profiles.

Coaching and mentoring are terrific ways to breed wisdom. But who coaches the coach? Confident leaders are aware that they need advice and counsel just as much as the people they are counseling and mentoring. Wisdom is knowledge refined by experience and common sense. Nobody has a corner on the wisdom market. Effective leaders are always seeking as much exposure to wisdom as possible. Those with the most intense desires to grow and develop personally and professionally want to be awash in wisdom; to devour books, films, and other media that hold accumulated wisdom.

Restoring Damaged Confidence

Like corrupted or lost files on you computer, it's a lot easier to lose confidence than it is to restore it. But you won't get an on-screen error message when your confidence is slipping away. It is said that 50 positive experiences are required to undo a single negative experience. That might be extreme in some cases, depending on the severity of the negative experience, it also might be understating some negative experiences from which you might never recover. Better to remain alert, plan well, and minimize negative experiences whenever possible than to be in a constant state of recovery.

When confidence needs to be restored, the process is similar to overcoming phobias. Systematic desensitization essentially means taking baby steps toward the object of fear until you're standing face to face with it; at which point it's not as frightening as it was at a distance in your imagination. Restoring confidence is achieved the most rapidly through the development of competency.

Developing genuine competency requires persistence, practice, and discipline. In other words, it takes time. Competency does not come quickly. Beginning with the proper style and motivational data will provide a tremendous head start over those who are potentially working at odds with their essential natures.

Restoring confidence that has been shaken is accelerated by revisiting the *as if* mentality. Anything that helped to build confidence in the first place will help in its reconstruction. While fear is in your face, anxiety seems to lurk around corners and just over the horizon. Staying in the moment, and on task, helps to restore confidence. Keeping an intense focus on task will make little victories seem more significant, which, collectively, they are.

How quickly and thoroughly you are able to restore shaken confidence has much to do with whether or not the confidence-shaking event was external or internal. If you find yourself slipping in conviction and/or resolve, you might shake your own confidence. Are you aware of how well you stand up to pressure? Have your will and resolve really been tested? If whatever shakes your confidence is internal, then overcoming it is an internal job.

Confidence Takes Responsibility

In his book *Good to Great* (HarperBusiness, 2001), Jim Collins talks about his "Window and the Mirror" concept, pointing out that the best leaders look to something or someone outside of themselves with which to credit success. According to Collins, it is a matter of humility, among other things. Taking credit for success that results from the efforts of others is the deed of a small person, and definitely not a leader *in fact*. Effective leaders find a specific person or group of persons to applaud for the success of their organizations. Members of leadership teams spread the credit around. Leadership teams or individual leaders—either way, it takes confidence to applaud others.

Just as important as it is to look out the window and find someone else to assign the credit for a job well done, when the job falls short or fails in any way, it's time to look in a mirror and take responsibility. This is how Collins articulates the need for leaders to get outside of themselves if they are to be truly great:

> Level 5 leaders (his highest rating) channel their ego needs away from themselves and into the larger role of building a great company. It's not that Level 5 leaders have no ego or self-interest. Indeed, they are incredibly ambitious. But, their ambition is first and foremost for the institution, not themselves.

Author Leslie F. Brandt wrote similar thoughts about other-centered leadership as a spiritual principle in her book *Jesus/Now* (Concordia Publishing House, 1978):

> In the eyes of the world, leadership is usually associated with power and prominence; it is often sought after by very egocentric people. Such people want to be coddled, even idolized; they want authority and they enjoy lording it over their constituents; they want to be served by them.

Brandt goes on to say that those who are chosen to be leaders get their greatness and effectiveness from serving others. Even though the concept of servant leader is not new, it continues to be more exception than rule. The difficulty in finding true servant leaders is caused by an epidemic lack of confidence in leaders. Confident leaders have no problem accepting responsibility because they are aware of how diligently they will work to produce better results, not pawning the responsibility off on others.

In the case of the servant leader, it takes great confidence to graciously give credit to others for success while taking the heat personally for mistakes and failures. Such confidence is definitely an internal job. Effective leaders never blame lack of success on bad luck or random circumstances. They know that much can be learned from mistakes. And you learn the most when the mistakes are *yours*.

When thinking and reasoning are flawed, the results are often bad. Yet, many decisions are based on irrational, unsubstantiated, or magical thinking. There is no substitute for experience and common sense. Courage rooted in experience and reason is much more unflappable than false confidence rooted in imagination. If a plan fails to materialize, it is likely that you, as the leader, failed to properly lead your team's thinking process.

Most good things are a result of effort. And effort completes the process that began with solid thinking. It takes courage and confidence, rooted in natural ability, to give credit to others for accomplishments that you played a major hand in creating. Part of the thinking that anchors courage and confidence is the knowledge that awarding credit is not a zero sum game. When praise is due, there is enough to go around twice. Giving credit to others is the best way to ensure that you'll receive some yourself.

Ain't Braggin'

That unshakable belief in self that upholds a genuine sense of confidence is enough to go on for an effective leader. Skimming some praise off the top for yourself before handing it out generously to the team is unnecessary. Self-confidence is not self-aggrandizement. It is pretty much the opposite. Jay Hanna "Dizzy" Dean said, "It ain't braggin' if you can do it." But a leader *in fact* has neither the time nor the need for "braggin'" at all.

Humility and hard work are the most powerful methods of self-promotion possible. We're not saying that you need to work in a closet and hide your accomplishments. (Before Org came around and joined the team, there wouldn't have been enough room in there anyway.) Good work usually calls attention to itself. Leading as they like to be led, great leaders constantly monitor their radar sweep searching for good work, and they actively seek out those responsible. If there is good work being done in your organization and leadership doesn't know about it, and worse yet, isn't aware of who is doing it, you have a major leadership breakdown. If you ask effective leaders, "Who does the best work in your organization?" they will give you names in a New York minute. Moreover, the people doing the good work know that their leaders know.

Coaching Confidence

Effective leaders constantly coach the confidence in their people, and coaching is made more effective with the knowledge base the ComposiTeam Leadership System provides. Great leaders value others as they value themselves. All people deserve respect, even when they don't do much to promote respect through their thoughts and deeds. Nevertheless, all relationships should begin with respect until circumstances dictate caution. Everybody has strengths that can make a solid contribution to the team's efforts. Finding those strengths and aligning them with the appropriate responsibilities is a tremendous confidence builder for leaders and team members.

We're sure you've heard it said that you should attack problems, not people. The same principle holds true with criticizing what people do rather than criticizing the people themselves. We believe that criticism, at its core, is rarely helpful and is nearly impossible to use as a tool for building people up. As human beings, we are sensitive to rejection.

Criticism is a form of rejection. Rejecting a person's work is touchy. Rejecting the person is devastating. On the other side of that coin is the notion of limiting your praise for the individual and focusing instead on the individual's accomplishments. Psychiatrist Heim Ginot first recognized that the self-esteem of others is ultimately beyond our control. How people feel about themselves in general results from a complex composite of experiences, starting in early childhood. There is very little we can do to improve it. However, we can pour a great deal of gasoline on the fire through criticism. Sometimes, even with encouragement and praise, the best you can do is keep the person on an even keel. In the best of circumstances, they'll avail themselves of the rich environment we provide and use the opportunity to grow.

Ginot's insight was that, if a person does not possess a positive self-image, then praising the person is a form of mockery. The person feels deep inside that you don't know him or her very well, because if you did, you wouldn't say such complimentary things; especially in public. In some cases, the individual with low self-esteem will feel compelled to do or say something to set the record straight and prove that she or he is really not all that wonderful. If you have ever praised someone in your organization only to get a negative response, it's probably because the person didn't feel deserving, and you were left thinking to yourself, "Where did *that* come from?"

You can save that person, and yourself, a lot of bother by not making a habit out of lavishing praise on people directly. By praising the individual's work and accomplishments, rather than the individual directly, you avoid stepping on a hidden land mine that might result in a little pop or a major explosion. Even people who do not value themselves very much can give themselves credit for doing something right now and then. By praising their work, you give them a chance to feel good about themselves and build some self-confidence without giving them reason to straighten you out. Style and motivation data provide you with your first evidence of where praise and encouragement will be most appreciated.

Breaking Through Barriers

As always, build confidence by building competence, but don't put unnecessary barriers in the way. A coach can build up a person's positive sense of self or tear it down. It is a lot easier to tear down than it is to build up. The 50:1 ratio of negative experiences to positive experiences applies here. It's 50 times easier to damage a relationship than it is to strengthen it, especially if you don't know what kind of ego strength with which you're working.

Some leaders think that the way to motivate productive and even creative behavior is to strike fear into the hearts of everyone in the organization. Worse even than Ken Blanchard's seagull managers are the ogres and screamers. They equate being feared to being *respected*. If people in leadership positions have a low self-opinion, they will assume that no one likes them anyway, so why not be ugly? Everything they do seems to throw up a roadblock. Every comment stops somebody in his or her tracks. To an intimidation-based manager, the sight of people laying around, wounded and bleeding, means that the manager is doing his or her job.

It's the leader's job to eliminate roadblocks for people. That's why it's important to master special skills that are essential to effective leadership. You've learned about leadership style typology in this book, in part, so that you can become better skilled at building up and less likely to tear down, even by mistake. You will become increasingly aware that, if your confidence turns to conceit, you will be throwing up invisible barriers to others around you. Although the barriers are difficult to see and can be easily denied, they are real and they will hamper the growth and development you are supposed to be inspiring and nurturing in others. Good leaders inspire people to have confidence in them. Great leaders inspire people to have confidence in themselves.

Do What You're Good At

> "Whatever you are by nature, keep to it; never desert your own line of talent. Be what nature intended you for, and you will succeed; be anything else and you will be ten thousand times worse than nothing."
>
> —Sydney Smith,
> 19th century English essayist

To be aware of, and follow, the path of your natural competencies is a sensible policy for several reasons. It will lead you to the type of activity with which you will potentially make the greatest impact and contribution. More than that, it will lead you into the type of activity that will likely produce the greatest self-confidence. When you are naturally good at something, you can depend on a more reliable outcome from your actions, which is one basis for self-confidence. The late Arthur Ashe echoed Franklin Roosevelt's earlier thoughts when he said, "Start where you are, use what you have, do the best you can." Be who you are, get better at it, and reap the rewards.

Madame Curie said, "Life is not easy for any of us. But, what of that? We must have perseverance and above all confidence in ourselves. We must believe that we are gifted for something, and that this thing, at whatever cost, must be attained." As leaders, this is not only critically important information about us, it is extremely important information about the people within our influence. In team leadership situations, it's our job to help everyone discover what their gifts are, even if that means coaching them to change careers.

This is a sensitive area for some people because they want to believe that they are masters at something for which they're not well suited. Perhaps the greatest example is leadership. Jean Baptiste Alphonse Karr, 19th century French critic and novelist, said that "Every man has three characters—that which he exhibits, that which he has, and that which he thinks he has." Many people fancy themselves cut from the same bolt of cloth as Lincoln, Roosevelt, Churchill, Reagan, or some other notable leader. Many fewer claim to be leaders in the tradition of Gandhi. Yet the natural servant inclinations of Gandhi suit themselves to effective leadership more than thoughts of greatness and grandeur.

In looking around your organization for leadership potential, do not overlook the quiet, unassuming people who seem to be naturally inclined to consider the needs of others. These folks might not be as inspirational or flamboyant on the soapbox as your top salesperson, and they might not seem to have the tough-minded *get it done and make the numbers look good* attitude. But they will draw more out of people in terms of realized potential over time. People who are genuinely other-centered can have outgoing, friendly attitudes. They can also be quietly confident.

Sell the Way You Like to Be Sold

As with courage, confidence not only attracts others, it will help instill similar thoughts in people with whom you have contact. Think of customers as everyone you deal with, as you consider the words of Elbert Hubbard from *Fra* magazine (March 1916):

> I do not believe in governing by force, or threat, or any
> other form of coercion. I would not arouse in the heart of

any of God's creatures a thought of fear or discord, or
hate, or revenge. I will influence others, if I can, but only
by aiding them.

Wading through the somewhat dated verbiage is worth the trip for
that last thought. How many people in positions of leadership are constantly struggling to sell ideas to their people through coercion? We have
all probably had that experience at one time or another. Yet, Hubbard
has an answer for us that's remarkable in its simplicity: to sell people
products, services, ideas, or anything else, you must *help them.* If we
confidently engage in consistent customer service, in other words, cater
to the needs of our people, they will be glad to join in our agenda. It
sounds simple. Admittedly, there will probably be a wrinkle here and
there, but ultimately it is not that complicated. Honey attracts more flies
than vinegar. We'll go so far as to recommend, "Sell the way you like to
be sold."

Confidence Built on Character

In addition to competency and natural ability, confidence has a great
deal to do with character. Consider what Will H. Hays said about trust
and confidence in business:

> We hear a good deal about business confidence, which
> means confidence of business in itself, in its government,
> and in its capacity for expansion. But confidence is only
> another way of saying that people believe each other, keep
> their promises, pay their debts, and regard their duty to
> society. As long as business observes these rules, it will
> have the confidence of the community and it will be safe
> from all of the irresponsible attacks of its enemies.

What happens when the attacks become responsible? What happens
when the attacks are warranted? Confidence is lost. In government, in
business, in individuals, when there is no longer a basis for confidence, it
erodes away. Daniel Webster said that others cannot be compelled to
have confidence in us: "Men cannot be forced to trust." The point that
Hays and Webster made about the confidence we, as consumers, place in
institutions is a mirror of our individual confidence. We must be credible
people if we are to be truly confident people, for all of the right reasons.

Chapter 13 Summary: Keys to Unleashing Leadership

- **Confidence is contagious:** Confidence is always accompanied by a positive attitude; and positive attitudes are contagious. A person doesn't need to walk around chanting positive affirmations to have a positive attitude. Quiet confidence, like quiet courage, is often reflected in a deep and abiding belief that the future holds tremendous potential. Sometimes it's evident in a person's eyes. The more serenely confident you are, the more permission you grant to those around you to be confident as well.

- **Practice practical optimism:** Optimism for the sake of optimism, like self-affirmation that is not anchored in core values or practical application, does not strengthen any true sense of confidence. The future is what we're all working for. Without a future focus, what would be the point of putting out any effort in the present? As confident leaders, we need to value and protect our sense of future and help others within our sphere of influence do the same. When people in your organization know from experience that they can count on your support and encouragement, even when trying new and innovative things, their confidence levels increase.

- **"As if" thinking:** Knowing that there is fear of failure in each of us, we need to be courageous, face the fear, and act in spite of it. To be confident leaders, we must frame our approach to issues and problems, especially human factors, *as if* the worst that could happen did happen. Anticipating and being prepared puts us in the proper frame of mind by getting our thoughts all the way around the otherwise fear-provoking issues. Once the mind has fully anticipated the worst-case scenario, the fear doesn't loom quite so menacingly on the horizon.

- **Confidence knocked off track:** If your confidence is shaken by external events, how solid was your confidence to begin with? How well aligned were you with your natural talents and abilities? Any normal or even a heightened sense of confidence can be shaken. But just how fragile your confidence is depends on the amount of experience and wisdom it is based upon, as well as your essential nature. If outside events are unexpected and you're taken by surprise, the experience will no doubt take its toll on your sense of confidence. In the end, restoring confidence that has been shaken by external factors is still an internal job. It's your personal sense of anticipation and solid footing in a shaky world that will help you weather the unexpected.

☞ **Be careful with compliments**: Praising work is how to give credit to someone in a safe and meaningful way. Praising the work won't drag proverbial fingernails across the chalkboard of a person's self-image. If the person is a closet narcissist, praising his or her work will just be interpreted as praise for the person anyway. You can't lose by praising accomplishment. The same goes for the team. Talk up what they all do and how well they do it, rather than what a swell bunch of people they are. As in most things, there are many ways to get a similar message across, not all of them equal. One mark of an effective leader is to distinguish between ways to say or express something and the best ways to say or express something in order to give the recipient the greatest opportunity to benefit in the most ways.

And so, we bind our courage to our confidence and anchor them both in a higher authority and/or a greater purpose to be served. If we ourselves are the alpha and omega of our sense of courage and confidence, we're on shaky ground. A single strand of rope doesn't make a very effective cargo net. But numerous ropes, all with relatively equal integrity can be relied upon to do things a single rope cannot.

Our sense of courage and confidence must be based on the notion that we are part of something bigger than ourselves. If not, how can we get outside of ourselves to become refined and effective leaders? The leadership team, with its composite leadership profile, is part of what's outside of us. How far you take the concept into the spiritual realm, is up to you.

In any context, leading is about other people. When it comes to our relationship with other people, our success or failure will ultimately come down to issues of character and our essential natures. Knowing who we are and what makes us tick is vital to acting with genuine confidence. Before turning the page to examine the concept of concentration, we close this chapter on confidence with a final thought from Franklin D. Roosevelt:

> "Confidence...thrives on honesty, on honor, on the sacredness of obligations, on faithful protection and on unselfish performance. Without them it cannot live."

Chapter 14

Concentration

Concentration is my motto—first honesty, then industry, then concentration.

—Andrew Carnegie

The ability to concentrate and to use time well is everything.

—Lee Iacocca

The two primary issues that relate to concentration as a significant leadership characteristic are (1) the ability to stay on task, and (2) the persistence and determination to keep going in the face of adversity. These are characteristics that we like to see in our leaders and, when in positions of leadership, we should all aspire to. Depending on the level of dedication you have to your task and the temperature of the fire in your belly, a simple distraction can sometimes be enough to bring you to a grinding halt or at least slowly roll you to a stop. Even when you're moving along at a good clip and feeling good about your momentum and progress, encountering a major and unexpected obstacle or stiff resistance to your efforts will have the same effect.

There is much to be said for just stickin' to your knittin'. The 2002 film *Summer Catch* had a line that expressed the same thought almost as eloquently. To paraphrase: The Indian rain dance worked because they never stopped dancing until it rained. This is one of those concepts that's so simple and basic that we tend to toss it aside with scarcely a thought, or we diminish the significance of the idea because it seems too elementary to warrant much consideration. But time has never failed to prove it.

John D. Rockefeller weighed in with, "Singleness of purpose is one of the chief essentials for success in life, no matter what may be one's aim." Singleness of anything is getting harder to achieve as our lives become increasingly complex. The modern age of digital communications was supposed to shorten our workweek and simplify our lives. The opposite has occurred as faster and farther-reaching connectivity makes it possible for us to entangle ourselves in more activities with more sources than ever before.

The same communication capabilities that make it easy for us to access everything, all the time, also make it possible for others to bug us. Opportunities for procrastination and distraction have never been greater. It seems that the secret to staying focused on anything these days requires shutting off the computer, unplugging the telephone, removing the battery from the cell phone, relocating to a cabin in rural Montana, and posting a Beware of the Dog sign in the front yard.

The Lightbulb vs. the Laser

"When every physical and mental resource is focused, one's power to solve a problem multiplies tremendously."

—Norman Vincent Peale,
influential clergyman of the 20th century

The average person's ability to focus is like a lightbulb when compared to the laser-type concentration of energy great achievers can produce. Diffused light is easy on the eyes, but it never burned a hole through anything. The complete elimination of distractions will probably never be completely possible without completely isolating yourself from everything and everybody. Even when you are completely alone, if there's a deck of cards handy or a computer, you'll probably end up playing a game instead of starting that book you've been meaning to write.

It's human nature to procrastinate. But the potential to increase our effectiveness as leaders holds great promise when we consider how much improvement can be made by doing nothing more than sharpening focus. It's remarkable how many great thinkers and writers speak so passionately about the value of concentration. (Probably because they've spent so much time playing solitaire in mountain or seaside cabins.) So, if we're *really* listening, why aren't we doing more about it?

Og Mandino, author of the timeless classic *The Greatest Salesman in the World* (Bantam, 1985), gave hope to the average person of ordinary abilities when he wrote in his sequel, *The Greatest Secret in the World* (Bantam, 1997): "I will persist until I succeed. [I] will be liken to the rain drop [that] washes away the mountain; the ant [that] devours a tiger; the star [that] brightens the earth...[I] will build my castle one brick at a time for I know that small attempts, repeated, will complete any undertaking."

Persistence can transform the seemingly inconsequential efforts of the ordinary person into profound accomplishments. Channeling or concentrating energy over time has a greater effect on our abilities than just temporarily increasing pressure at the point of contact. The exercise of concentrating also engenders internal benefits. Earl Nightingale, famed radio commentator, observed that "The more intensely we feel about an idea or a goal, the more assuredly the idea, buried deep in our subconscious, will direct us along the path to its fulfillment." Intense focus on a task will release additional energy and passion for fulfillment.

The fact that small efforts, repeated over time, will produce enormous change has been proven as much as any law of nature throughout history. We don't even pretend that one day there will be no gravity or that water won't freeze at 32°F. Nevertheless, we often give up on certain efforts because it seems that continuing will do no good. The truth is, we're usually just demonstrating our lack of discipline and patience. Persistence shows no favoritism. It works for anyone who works it. Persistence is the equalizer for those short on luck.

Keep in mind that persistence and futility are two different things. We agree that banging your head against a stone wall isn't a good way to remove the wall, no matter how motivated and persistent you are. However, whacking the stone wall with a sledgehammer a gazillion times will ultimately produce change. But then, the stone wall isn't engaged in resisting the change. To get a shopaholic to stop shopping by nagging is futile, and will probably end your relationship long before it convinces him or her to modify any other behavior.

How many times have you heard that doing the same thing repeatedly and expecting a different outcome is insanity? Sometimes it is, sometimes it isn't. If your goal is to overcome active resistance, good luck. If you're simply trying to continually place yourself in the path of luck when it comes your way, there's a good chance that luck will eventually be on your side. If you give up and don't continually place yourself in the path of luck, you are *guaranteed* to miss it.

The Zone

Just as writers often refer to being in a state of *flow*, athletes want to be in *the zone*. Athletes are constantly seeking to achieve the highest performance possible for whatever length of time the game is played. A sprinter in track and field competition, whose event lasts but a few seconds, ideally reaches the optimal level of physical and psychological preparation the moment the starting pistol fires. At that instant, the roaring crowd, the other runners, the TV cameras, the shoe endorsements, and everything else cease to exist—hopefully. The only thing left is maximum mind/body coordination in an explosion of every focused ounce of energy the sprinter has to offer.

Tiger Woods and every other PGA professional on the Tour aspire to block out the many distractions surrounding a major PGA tournament from Thursday morning until Sunday afternoon. It is said that golf only requires complete and absolute focus for five seconds at a time. Even so, staying in the zone for as long as the competition is engaged is vital for ultimate success. Baseball players need maximum focus from the time the ball leaves the pitcher's hand until it crosses the plate 90 feet away, which, at 95 miles per hour, isn't very long. What about defensive performance in the field? What about all of those hours in the batting cage? Clearly, the champion in any sport must stay on task; eating, sleeping, and dreaming the particulars of the game if he or she is going to be the best—or even truly competitive.

Writing a book requires focus hour-by-hour at the computer keyboard, week-in and week-out, for months. The focus changes in nature from the researching, to the planning, to the writing, to the editing. But it's all concentrated effort. Writing allows for breaks and rests more than the physical focus of an athlete for the duration of the contest. But the principle is the same. When focus is lost, the intended result is lost with it. Books don't write themselves any more than home runs and holes-in-one hit themselves.

Any task will have unique qualities and requirements for success. We doubt there is any task best accomplished by ignoring it. In writing, as in many predominantly physical endeavors, the act of concentrating doesn't merely release inner energies and thoughts, it also stimulates new thoughts and ideas. Ideas not only flow in the zone, they are created. When you're in the zone, time seems to stand still; until you look at the clock and realize how much time has elapsed. In a philosophical and ethereal sense, operating in the zone is like functioning outside of time. Operating in the zone is like operating in a state of heightened consciousness. Your surroundings seem to disappear and energy increases. Writers often forget to eat and sleep when they are in flow. It's intense concentration, free of distraction.

In the Details

The hammer strike is not as important to the sculptor as where the chisel is placed. One blow with the hammer is as good as another. The same amount of effort can produce dramatically different results if the proper focus is applied. In his book *Managing Your Time* (Zondervan, 1978), Ted W. Engstrom pointed out that "[By] concentrating on the essentials, we will then be accomplishing the greatest possible results with the effort expended." This is another way to say work smarter, not harder. A lot of hard work, on the part of many people, can be swallowed up in failure if a few important details are ignored.

Even though we make a strong case for attention to details, we're not saying that needless complication holds any merit. People often allow themselves to be bogged down in endless details as a way to procrastinate and avoid taking full responsibility for producing results. Complexity is the friend of the procrastinator (and any professional charging by the hour). Still, complexity is sometimes unavoidable. Engineers and great leaders know that simplicity is the ultimate sophistication. Simplicity is the best assurance that energy will be used efficiently in maximizing results.

Mother Nature prefers simplicity. Her most powerful forces are direct and to the point. Gaining the most from expending the least is nature's reward for genuine simplicity. The simpler something is, the nearer to perfection. The Maytag Company built the most dependable washing machine, requiring the fewest repairs, by continuously simplifying it. Each new generation had progressively fewer moving parts until appliance service people started calling them "gutless wonders." Achieving simplicity at Maytag took tremendous focus and concentration over time on the part of their highly regarded research and development team.

Focus, like gravity, should be thought of as a law of nature. Part of what we admire about great thinkers and spiritual leaders is how they express profound ideas and concepts in simple terms. Who will ever forget the master's wise instructions to the student in the film *The Karate Kid* (1984): "Wax on. Wax off." Remember that line when you are giving instructions to your team members. Keeping it simple is not a way to impugn their intelligence. It is a way to release the best possible performance. The most powerful and timeless economic theory imaginable can be expressed in four words: "Buy low. Sell high." Complicating that one only shrinks your bottom line.

The Grand Conspiracy

Concentration and focus, if not assaulted by natural causes, will likely be attacked by guilty and/or jealous associates. If you feel as though internal and external pressures are conspiring to kill any chance for concentration, you're probably right. Not every distraction you experience in your professional endeavors is innocent, despite protestations to the contrary from the distracter. There are unexpected events and circumstances that will interfere with your ability to concentrate. There are genuine emergencies that require your undivided attention. But there are also distracters.

One thing that a focused, hard-working individual does is make less focused, less hard-working persons around them nervous and even resentful. The focused individual doesn't really cause the others to feel anything. The less focused and less dedicated *choose* to feel mocked and humiliated. They then remedy the perceived imbalance through the time-honored tradition of cutting the hard-working person down to size.

Sometimes they plead with hard workers not to work themselves into an early grave. Sometimes they threaten the focused worker outright. Most of the time, the distracters hang out in gaggles and mumble their dissatisfaction with the hard worker. If anything, they use every opportunity to sabotage the focused individual's efforts. There are many books and seminars available that teach how to minimize distractions and overcome procrastination. Depending on your situation, they might be a wise investment.

Parkinson's Law

From one extreme to the other, from dropping out of high school to earning a Ph.D., men and women, adolescents to senior citizens, come face to face with Parkinson's Law, which simply holds that work expands to fill the time available. Parkinson's Law is the opposite of concentration. When concentration tapers off, gaining maximum results for minimum effort becomes minimal results from maximum effort. Which would you choose? As a guiding principle, "Wax on. Wax off" is as fundamental to successful living as "Buy low. Sell high" is to economics. Peter F. Drucker said, "Concentration is the key to economic results. No other principle of effectiveness is violated as constantly today as the basic principle of concentration." As a principle of effectiveness, few things have as much direct impact on your economic health and well-being as your ability to concentrate.

Leaders Have the Hardest Time

Leadership only magnifies the challenge of concentration. Leaders often have more discretionary time than their team members, which can translate into more opportunities for distraction and procrastination. You might have an approachable leadership style that attracts a parade of people seeking help with their problems or simply seeking your attention. Either way, you'll be hard pressed to concentrate.

Your leadership style might lead you to interfere more than you should with your team members' activities; in which case, you're probably disrupting *their* concentration. One of the problems in promoting people who are not naturally inclined to promote the growth and development of their team members occurs when the new boss gets lonely or bored. She or he then bugs his or her subordinates to keep him- or herself company or to micromanage activities that the boss misses doing or is too insecure to leave alone.

Team members often look at their leaders and envy what they perceive to be luxurious freedom from responsibility. The reporter seeking an explanation for "Rose Bud" in Orson Wells's classic film, *Citizen Kane* (1941), politely asks a top executive if he has time to answer a few questions. The executive smiles and says, "I'm the chairman of the board. I've got nothing but time." Maybe at that level, he's right. But Hollywood has helped propel the myth that, the higher you rise in business, the less you have to do.

Few top executives outside of those portrayed in Hollywood films would ever say such a thing. If their time is not invested in concentrating on the essentials of success for their organization, it's probably invested in putting out fires. Whether or not someone is a truly effective leader, anyone who can honestly say that they have nothing but time is retired, or ought to be.

People Focus

People. People. People. Growth and development of the organizational population, both individually and collectively, are top priorities for a leader. Therefore, effective leaders are constantly trying to both strengthen their abilities to concentrate and to coach the same in their people. We have yet to meet a leader who doesn't agree that people are his or her most complex challenge. Internal or external customers, they're all people. When leadership becomes an expectation of everyone, the need for concentration skills is that much greater.

Hockey great Wayne Gretzky warned against skating to where the puck is. By the time you get there, it will be gone. Skate to where the puck is *going to be*. Instead of dwelling on where your people are, concentrate on where you *want them to be*, and unleash all of the energy and creativity that bubbles up when they are truly focused. Your team members will tend to focus on the immediate tasks before them. Leaders have that multiple awareness of past, present, and future. As a leader, you must spend some of your time in the future—the future of your organization.

A Pound of Feathers

The first time someone asked you, "Which weighs more, a pound of lead or a pound of feathers?" you had to think, at least for a nanosecond, before you recognized the trick in the question. How would you answer if someone were to ask, "Who has more to do in a hierarchical organization, the lower-, middle-, or upper-level leader?" The lower you are on the leadership food chain, the more likely you will be saddled with busy work. The higher on the leadership ladder you climb, your busywork might reduce somewhat, but the consequences for making a mistake increase. Money and corner offices aside, which do you prefer, busywork or an anvil suspended over your head?

In our efforts to regulate problems out of our organizations, we burden leaders (and everyone else for that matter) with system-imposed minutia. Unfortunately, leaders at all levels who point out that policies and regulations intended to reduce problems and paperwork cause *more* problems and paperwork, are usually labeled "problems" themselves. Most people seem a lot more enthusiastic about making rules than they do about taking them off the books. It's almost as though bureaucrats make a nest out of shredded minutia and crawl inside where nobody will bother them.

Whether or not that's true, the usual scenario is:

1. A rule is made to address a certain problem.

2. The problem ceases to be a problem (whether or not the rule had anything to do with it).

3. Although the problem is gone, the policy, procedure, regulation, or whatever, still exists.

Welcome to hierarchical organizational life. In molecular organizations, everything is subject to review as the work cells revolve and performance is continually scrutinized. Minutia that distracts people from concentrating on important work is spun off for Org to eat. Good riddance. Bon appetit.

Which takes more time, dealing with external customers or internal customers? As with feathers and lead, it shouldn't matter. If people are the number-one job for the leader, it shouldn't matter which stakeholder is involved. The leader's focus needs to be on serving everyone's needs. More specifically, the leader needs to concentrate on creating and sustaining an environment in which internal customers take care of external customers and each other.

It's ironic that, during hard times when organizations need to get the most from people, training and development is one of the first items cut from the budget. One of the purposes of training and development is to enhance concentration and skill sets that improve efficiency and lead to higher productivity and profitability. Cutting training and development programs during difficult financial times is truly throwing the baby out with the bathwater. In the same breath that we defend the responsibilities that executives face, we're not going to ignore that ivory tower mentalities also exist.

Pecking Order

Chickens peck for their food. The intensity of their pecking depends on the scarcity of the food. When food is plentiful, they peck casually. When food is harder to find, they peck harder and even scratch at the ground. In organizational life, the pecking order is established by job title and/or labor grade. Those at the bottom typically starve first and the roosters are the last to suffer, if they suffer at all. If the roosters act quickly enough, no more than a reasonable number of chickens will need to die before the problem is solved and life gets back to normal.

Those with ivory tower thinking rarely have to peck or scratch. If they are sufficiently disconnected from the day-to-day operation of their organizations, the organizations are more than likely functioning *in spite* of the top people instead of under their effective leadership. That's why you often find top executives distracted by their media appearances, pet charities, golf tournaments, and travel. If they are not going to *actively concentrate* on developing the people in their organizations, the people actually running things are just as happy to have them otherwise occupied.

Never Bored

Leaders that are actively involved in the growth and development of their people are never bored. Few things in life are more exciting than contributing to the growth and development of other people. If you allow people to distract you from your work because your work is boring, then your work does not involve helping people in direct and tangible ways. If this is a difficult concept to embrace, make it your goal to study how you can make people a higher priority in your life and your work. You will never be bored.

If you prefer not to deal with other people in any capacity, then leadership of anyone besides yourself is not for you. Your focus might be better spent on achievements that can be accomplished in isolation. There is a place for every type of personality style in the blueprint of success. Much of the time we spend consulting corporations is spent ensuring that the correct personality types are matched with the roles and responsibilities of key positions. We also help organizations correct their alignment of personalities and job functions if they've never before attempted to structure the organization based upon suitability.

In organizations that want to unleash the diverse leadership potential of teams, we introduce the alignment of composite leadership profiles to initiative profiles. It bears repeating that one of the primary benefits of the ComposiTeam Leadership System is that it forces everyone from the policy-makers, to the initiative owners, to the leadership team members themselves to concentrate on the institutive; from its inception through its execution. The power of the focused concentration alone is remarkable. There is nothing more vital to organizational success than the contributions made by your people. Why wouldn't you do everything possible to keep them focused?

Don't Overconcentrate

Beware of extremism in any cause. Becoming too involved with your people is as much of a mistake as ignoring them. This is more than just being a micromanager or busybody. As in anything else, there is an optimal degree of involvement, even when completely well intentioned. Think of it as balance. Proper concentration will never be accomplished at the expense of, or to the peril of, important matters. Concentration does not mean putting on blinders. It should never be used as an excuse to avoid responsibility to yourself or others.

A socially oriented leadership style can be driven by a need for connection and affirmation, and concentrate on nothing but that. A compliance specialist might hide behind excessive concentration to avoid dealing with people inside or outside of the organization. A control specialist might get fixated on defeating the competition at all costs, and we do mean *all costs*. A stability specialist might become obsessed with balancing the workload to the point that she or he is throwing everything off schedule.

This kind of overthinking can be an invitation or temptation to let organizational goals and responsibilities slide for the sake of getting your personal needs met. It's possible that you can concentrate on meeting your own needs to the exclusion of the needs of others, and the organization itself. This is a common problem that is amplified in organizational life. If leadership is truly other-centered, then the temptation to focus too much on personal needs and desires will be kept in balance. The principles of effective leadership, especially as expressed by a diverse leadership *team*, will not allow for abuse of concentration.

The Proof Is in the Lightbulb

You shouldn't allow a failure now and then break your concentration and focus. Thomas Edison is famous for, among many other things, taking a fresh look at failure. Once he had developed a filament that worked in his lightbulb, he didn't look back at all of his unsuccessful attempts as failures. He realized that every experiment that didn't work brought him closer to the correct solution. The only way that he, like us, would have failed would be to quit before he found the answer. Edison's mantra was, "The answer is out there. Find it."

He also said, "Many of life's failures are people who did not realize how close they were to success when they gave up." That's like saying, "Good-bye cruel world, I'm tired of being poor," and jumping off the Golden Gate Bridge—with the winning lotto ticket in your pocket.

Concentration fixes, specifically, the *persistence* aspect of concentration. When you give up too soon, you rob yourself of the opportunity to succeed. Super Bowl–winning coach Mike Ditka says that you shouldn't consider yourself a failure until you quit trying. *Then* you can call yourself anything you want to. "Never, never, never, never give up," was how Winston Churchill articulated his bulldog tenacity. Negative thinking is essentially the same thing as giving up before getting started. According to Ditka's logic, negative thinking makes us failures from the start. Negative thinking positions us to exist in a constant state of failure.

Instant Gratification vs. Concentration

Why doesn't everyone apply these principles and stick to their knittin' until their ship comes in? Instant gratification is basic to human nature. To purposefully delay gratification requires maturity. Concentrating is also basic to human nature. The question is, "What are you concentrating *on*?" As we mentioned earlier, human beings have a natural tendency to dwell on the negative. If it requires 50 positive experiences to balance out a single negative experience, then sticking to a journey that is loaded with disappointments and setbacks requires a special kind of maturity and drive.

Being obstinate and persistent are two different things. Obstinacy is about the will, right or wrong. Obstinance can be stubbornness. But persistence is about want. Persistence is driven by a desire for something so passionate that the desire is sustained through distractions and obstacles. We doubt that many people ever earned a Ph.D. through sheer obstinacy. As with all things, concentration helps carry dreams to fruition.

Institutionalized Impatience

Attrition is the friend of the focused. The longer you stay in the race, the more people will drop out. Barring any substantial influx of new players, time is on your side. It is said that 80 percent of all sales are made after the fifth sales call. That doesn't mean that every fifth prospect buys something, it means calling on the same person five times, on average, will result in a sale. That takes time and patience, focus and concentration. Relationships are built longitudinally. Any type of success you seek, if it deals with people, will be based on relationship.

If it's that simple, why isn't every salesperson in the world widely successful? Because, even with the knowledge that redundancy increases sales, only 20 percent make the fifth call. That's one reason the ladder of success gets narrower toward the top. Why do 80 percent of the salespeople drop out after one, two, three, or four calls? Impatience. They keep looking for the customer who will buy on the first call.

The world we live in prides itself on getting results fast. The microwave oven has revolutionized the way we prepare meals. Going out to a movie, while still an enjoyable experience, isn't necessary when a flick of your television remote will bring you a wide choice of entertainment.

Investors want rapid returns, or they'll move their money. Executives demand instant results, or they make radical changes in personnel and policy, few of which help, but the flurry of activity shifts the spotlight away from them. Impatience has a domino effect. The executive's impatience is fueled by the investor's impatience. The investor's impatience is fueled by the desire to increase wealth quickly. Investors are often seduced by stories of an unusually high return happening somewhere other than where they have their money. They then want the same thing to happen for them, no matter how impractical. It seems that the only organizations that are immune from customers' impatience are government bureaucracies and monopolies.

Relational impatience is typified by divorce. More couples get divorced after staying married less time than ever before in history. Dropout rates in schools have reached epidemic proportions. Automated teller machines have replaced waiting in line at the bank, or even going inside a bank. Look around and you're sure to see example after example of how we have been socialized to be impatient. That means the number of people that are willing to invest the time, energy, and *concentration* to succeed is getting smaller. The advantage to the patient person *willing to concentrate* over time is increasing.

Courage and confidence are required to fend off impatience. When less courageous and confident people get impatient or nervous, they tend to blink and give in to impulse. Effective leaders have just as much desire to pop and react as the less patient, but they know the value of waiting. Organizational leaders might have personal patience and discipline for not shooting from the hip, but others around them usually don't. Dealing with the impatience of others is a constant leadership challenge.

Outlasting the Competition—Maybe

Another dimension to the *advantage over time* approach is that new people enter the race. A professional baseball player or golfer won't get to the top of his or her field by simply waiting it out. In time, the physical requirements of the game will shift the advantage to younger, less experienced players. In business, compensation, status, and benefits tend to improve as you move toward the top.

This attracts new competition. Just when you think that you might be one of the sole survivors in line for the rewards of promotion, in come new troops, full of vigor, ready to battle it out with you for the position you've been waiting decades to open up. Concentration and focus are among the best habits to form to ensure future rewards. But they're not an absolute lock by any means. If you're known around the organization for superior concentration and focus abilities, the new kids shouldn't threaten you much. If you don't concentrate any better than a coed fresh off a kegger, your job could be up for grabs.

Too Much Information

To say that all things come to those who wait might be an overstatement, but those who are willing to wait will get more than those who aren't. One benefit of concentration and focus is exposure to more information, and potentially more knowledge. But knowing how to handle and prioritize information is essential. Quality information requires time and energy to process, refine, and consider. Overanalysis can lead to that proverbial paralysis. Too much data can contribute to inertia.

Concentration, in its proper context, seeks to balance information with progress. When building confidence through increased competency, a tremendously disciplined ability to focus and concentrate is required. A major factor in building competency is to develop the ability to distinguish between information that's relevant and important and less important information. No matter how skilled you become, making such distinctions will always be a guessing game to some degree. But the more competent you become, the more efficient you will become at selecting and processing data. Some of the most successful people got that way because they could separate the important from the urgent, leaving the unimportant stuff for Org to eat.

Darkest Just Before Dawn

During times of difficulty and confusion, you need the powers of concentration to keep you focused. Those skilled at concentration will be able to successfully lead their organizations out the other side of the most troubling times, while those who find it difficult to concentrate, won't. Those with the ability to concentrate through the hardship and distraction will also enjoy longer-lasting change. The leader's ability to concentrate will be noticed by doubters in the organization, causing more of them to climb on board.

Assume that you successfully initiate change in your organization and enroll Org to help you sustain it. If you only get that far, you're ahead of the field. As true transformation begins to take place, all the forces of the status quo will be marshaled against you. This is natural and expected. Before the actual breakthrough takes place, the breakthrough that elevates your organization from a temporary remedy to a lasting change, you might feel as if the weight of the world is on your shoulders.

The vultures are circling; naysayers are lining up and licking their chops, ready to say, "See, we said all along that it couldn't be done. Nothing will ever change around here." Negativity loves company, so the negative people will usually gang up on the most visible targets: leaders or leadership teams. We're not saying that failure loves failure. But failure doesn't threaten or convict itself. A string of failures, as Edison pointed out, can lead to success. *Negativity* hates success and will sabotage it at every opportunity.

Leaders Sell the Future

Being an effective individual leader, or a member of a leadership team, is a lot like playing three-dimensional chess. We've pointed out that effective leaders—those who lead the way they like to be led—consider the truth of the past, the irreplaceability of the present, and the promise of the future. It is important for all leaders to maintain the ability to transcend the moment to remain mindful of their responsibility for the future.

It's easy to become wrapped up in the moment and in current events. If leaders don't look to the future, who will? Those leaders who fear looking into the future do a great disservice to their stakeholders. Organizations are like organisms; they are constantly changing internally, and so are their environments. A future-focused leader will anticipate difficulties, challenges, and opportunities.

Although leaders sell the future, they don't get lost in it. Leaders must not become so intensely focused on the future that they leave a leadership void in the present. Concentrating solely on the future can be as damaging as concentrating solely on the past. The most effective leaders intentionally distribute their consciousness between the past, present, and future. As they concentrate and stay focused on accomplishment, relevant past, present, and future ("as if") information is all part of the mix.

Trying vs. Succeeding

To wrap up the issue of concentration, we remind you that concentration alone does not guarantee success. But success over the long term, and progressively higher levels of success, require the ability to concentrate. Staying focused and not allowing yourself to be distracted and pulled off task are invaluable abilities that need to be in the toolbox of any effective leader.

Put everything else together, except concentration, and you're likely to wind up with a good, college try. Without the concentration to carry you and your organization the last mile, over the hump, through the swamp, and so forth, what you'll have is a failed attempt. You can learn from failed attempts, the same way Thomas Edison said he learned from his "successful failures." It was concentration and focus that helped Edison string together all of his lightbulb experiments into one, large lightbulb *experience*, with an outcome that changed the world forevermore.

A Lesson From Nature

> "I never could have done what I have done without the habits of punctuality, order, and diligence, without the determination to concentrate myself on one subject at a time...."

> —Charles Dickens

Water can be diverted, but never distracted. Its natural tendency is to move lower. As long as there is lower, it will want to move. Even if it has to carve a path through solid rock over millions of years, water will never stop trying. Human cognitive concepts such as honesty and industry are reflected in, and even eclipsed by, the natural universe's inability to lie, and the instinctive, unstoppable will of living creatures to do what they were created to do. Concentration, focus, and staying on task are some of the most useful lessons we can learn from nature.

Chapter 14 Summary: Keys to Unleashing Leadership

➛ **Step by step:** Tasks often fall short of their desired outcomes because they are incomplete. That's another major reason that concentration is so essential. A magnificent brick mansion is only one brick laid upon another, and then another, and so on. Great things are composed of smaller, less sensational (yet extremely important) components. "It is not the straining for great things that is most effective; it is the doing the little things, the common duties, a little better and better," said 20th century American novelist Elizabeth Stuart. This is one reason that we don't pay as much attention to the details as we could. Leaders need to focus on the big picture and think about things on a grand scale, but never to the exclusion of the intimate details that make the grand scale possible.

- **Freedom and concentration are natural enemies:** College students are expected to concentrate more than they ever have before, while at the same time experiencing the greatest freedom of their lives. That is not just a problem with college students; it's a reality of adult life. Many complain later that they should have socialized more in college because their nose is now too close to the grindstone to really enjoy life. Others regret that they didn't finish college because they enjoyed life too much at the time and the necessary focus wasn't there. Ideally, in college as in the rest of our adult lives, the ability to concentrate *when necessary* allows us more guilt-free time to enjoy the fruits of our labors. Nature loves balance, and *you can't concentrate all the time*.

- **Leading the concentration:** Challenges to concentration, as well as challenges to courage and confidence accompany leadership. Being in a position of leadership is a greater-than-average challenge in organizational life to begin with. Add to that your personal struggle with concentration, and focus becomes a daily, even hourly, priority. More than dealing with your own concentration issues, as a ringleader, entrepreneur, or department head, you need to protect your team members' time and ability to concentrate. Don't needlessly bug them and don't let anyone else do it either.

- **Winning by attrition:** When businesspeople get together and discuss how to beat the competition, just as when they contemplate how to succeed in life, they seldom consider attrition as a key strategy. Successful living is a marathon of sorts. A large crowd begins the race. With each passing mile, more competitors drop out. If you are willing and able to stay with it, the number of people you must compete with shrinks. Winning by attrition is not glamorous or flashy. It's not the kind of thing that will make headlines. But in certain instances and situations, it works. Coasting to the finish line rather than finishing with a full head of steam is risky. The danger is that a vigorous and speedy newcomer might join the competition in the late going and clip the ribbon ahead of you. If you're planning to win by attrition, keep on eye in the rearview mirror.

- **Praise effort; reward results:** Effective leaders promote concentration by rewarding results. They encourage people to try, and support their attempts, but save the goodies for those that demonstrate the *concentration* and *focus* to get it done. If people are rewarded equally for trying, all behavioral incentive to go the distance is lost. If trying is considered equal to succeeding, then succeeding is devalued. If a successful outcome is not important, how important can the effort be? Successful outcomes are very important. That makes the trying important. In the end, the results are what matter most.

We've never encountered anyone whose work wasn't enhanced by improved concentration and focus. True to the nature of diverse leadership styles, however, some people are more inclined to focus and concentrate than others. Avoid the temptation to expect the same level of concentration and focus from everyone. That's like expecting the same amount of creativity from everyone.

People are, thankfully, different. In your initiative profile, and the team composite leadership profile you align with it, expect the more impatient to resist allowing anyone to overthink. Expect also for your focused concentrators to rein in the "no boundaries" folks. Somewhere in the middle, there's maximum productivity, performance, and profit.

With the concepts of courage, confidence, and concentration under your belt, you're ready to take on the last two categories in leadership motivation: passion and values. This is where Org can actually learn to do tricks. When the fires of passion are kindled, as only recognition of a person's essential nature can, the spirit of the team is invincible. Have you ever seen a dragon wag his tail? The values, of course, keep the passion focused without getting in the way.

> "The jack-of-all-trades seldom is good at any.
> Concentrate all of your efforts on one definite chief aim."
> —Napoleon Hill

Chapter 15

Passion and Values

Before water generates steam, it must register 212 [degrees Fahrenheit] of heat; 200 will not do it. The water must boil to generate enough steam to move an engine. Lukewarm water will not run anything. Lukewarmness will not generate life's work.

—Unknown Author

Courage, confidence, and concentration are the cars that make up the ComposiTeam leadership motivation train. Passion is the fuel that runs the engine, and values are the tracks on which it runs. Remove passion, and the train will slow down. If it's not running downhill, it eventually grinds to a halt. Remove values, and the train has no tracks to run on. To use an old maritime analogy, without fuel, the ship's propellers stop. But, even at full speed, without a destination, where the ship winds up is anybody's guess. We don't know many organizational stakeholders that don't care where the organization winds up or in what condition.

It's rare for each element of the ComposiTeam style and motivation inventories to be present in equal numbers. Yet, they all must be present in adequate quantities and in relative proportion to one another to achieve enough balance to make the system work. No element can be missing entirely. We hope that passion will be abundantly present. Alignment of passion and purpose is the key to making people the best they can be.

What is passion? "It is surely the becoming of a person," according to British filmmaker and editor of *Projections* (Faber & Faber, 1992) John Boorman:

Are we not, for most of our lives, marking time? Most of our being is at rest, unlived. In passion, the body and the spirit seek expression outside of self. Passion is all that is other from self. [The] more extreme and the more expressed that passion is, the more unbearable does life seem without it. It reminds us that if passion dies or is denied, we are partly dead and that soon, come what may, we will be wholly so.

Passionate Passion

Passion sustains effort. Focused effort leads to excellence. Passion and excellence are never far apart. Commitment and enthusiasm are the two principal by-products of passion. Being committed to a course of action is one thing, staying committed to it is something else. Nobody seems to have a problem with motivation over the short term. But maintaining resolve over the long-term will thin out the crowd considerably.

Enthusiasm is also something that is plentiful in the moment, but is hard to sustain over time. In both cases, passion is the driving, sustaining force. Passion itself, as much as everyone is capable of it, is nevertheless scarce. Most things that people start are never finished. Sometimes the task becomes too difficult. At other times, distractions siphon away energy and focus, never to return. In most cases, they simply lose interest. There isn't enough gas in the tank to go the distance.

If passion is real, it probably won't stay away forever, even if it dwindles in intensity from time to time. Infatuation will flicker and go out. Passion is more like the party favor candle that can't be blown out. Julia Child said, "Find something you're passionate about and keep tremendously interested in it."

Passion Can't Be Created

Because nobody really knows where passion comes from or what it's made of, human hands can't create it. Passion can no more be intentionally invoked than love at first sight. Like unexpected love, passion has a life and will of its own. You could ponder endlessly whether passion is rooted in nature or nurture. In the end, it simply *is*.

You can either go with your passions or attempt to suppress them. If you move away from your essential nature, unanswered passion will torment you. Although passion cannot be created, you can search it out and identify it. Finding and identifying passion can unlock untold potential within you and others. True passion is a terrific indicator of what your essential nature truly is. Recognizing and accepting what you have been designed and naturally equipped to do is the first step to becoming fully actualized.

Unfortunately, like unanticipated love, much of what you have a passion for is not necessarily practical or particularly helpful. Passion is not the same as addiction. The two can appear similar to the point of being indistinguishable. The $64,000 question is whether passion leads to addiction, or the other way around. Some would say that addiction and passion are uncorrelated, despite their similar power to shape behavior. Given the immense influence and longevity that addiction and passion both demonstrate, they might be anchored in the same part of the psyche. We can't say for sure.

"Passions are vices or virtues to their highest powers."

—Goethe

Benjamin Franklin understood the potentially counterproductive nature of passion when he said, "If passion drives, let reason hold the reins." Ralph Waldo Emerson had a similar perspective when he acknowledged passion's simultaneous power and lack of focus by pointing out that "Passion, though a bad regulator, is a powerful spring." Passion is similar to fire in that it can save your life or kill you, depending on the circumstances.

Alfred Lord Tennyson might have best articulated the importance of making passion a personal competency when he said, "…happiness…[in] this life does not consist in the absence, but in the mastery, of [passions]." Consider the alternative to passion—lethargy. Without passion you're doomed to live our lives in Thoreauian quiet desperation.

Unfortunately, most of us develop mastery of our misery instead of mastery of our passion. It's easier. It comes more naturally to follow the path of least resistance. Following our passion is often a risky business. It might come as a surprise to many that identifying and pursuing passion has practical value. This knowledge is particularly important to effective leaders, if for no other reason, it unleashes passion in others.

According to John C. Maxwell, in his book *The 21 Indispensible Qualities of a Leader* (Nelson Books, 1999), "When a leader reaches out in passion, he is usually met with an answering passion." Isn't that the type of reciprocal energy you want to permeate your organization? Passion building on passion is a by-product of collaborative leadership—when leadership is expected from everyone. If you like to be led with passion, then lead with passion. If you want your people to be at their most passionate, align what they do best with what your organization needs most.

Harnessing energy

Although the true origin of passion remains a mystery, you know what it can do, and it can help you to do good things. In the film *City*

Slickers (1991), when Jack Palance (Curly) held up one finger and told Billy Crystal that the meaning of life was "one thing," he didn't mean that you should arbitrarily choose one pursuit to the exclusion of all others. If that is all a person does, that individual will no doubt become extremely proficient at whatever that one thing is. But the singularity of a pursuit doesn't guarantee passion.

Curly's advice makes much more sense if he meant that you should isolate the one thing you feel most passionate about and somehow parlay *that* into a career or lifelong activity. Many people would agree that being able to work in the field or at the activity for which they have the greatest passion would be heaven on earth. For many who have done just that, heaven on earth is how they describe their occupations. We've all heard the advice to identify what you would do, even if you were not paid for it. Identifying our essential natures through style and motivation is a road map to passion, and vice versa.

George Burns put it simply, "I'd rather be a failure at something I love than a success at something I hate." That must be a formula for low stress. Look at how long he lived. What do you do when personal responsibilities and/or the agenda of others aren't taking precedent? That activity is probably something you feel passionate about. What do you daydream about doing when you're being paid to do something else? To what activity do your thoughts wander when focus on other things gets fuzzy? Thoughts about the object of your passion are never fuzzy. They are distinguishable by their crystal clarity.

If not what, then where?

It's not enough to determine what you feel the most passionate about. What comes next? The late Dr. David Viscott said, "There is some place where your specialties can shine. Somewhere that difference can be expressed. It's up to you to find it, and you can."

Dr. Viscott's words are simple and straightforward, and identifying the best environment in which your specialties can shine might not be too difficult, once you know what your passion is. This is when those personal responsibilities and/or the agenda of others rear their ugly heads. Sometimes the sacrifice required to pursue your passion is too much and, depending on your family situation, would hurt any number of other people. That's when decisions must be made—life decisions that will affect you every day for as long as you live.

As a leader, you must endeavor to align your own passion with your leadership responsibilities, large or small, molecular or hierarchical. Next comes the leadership responsibility to familiarize yourself with the personal styles of all the people within your sphere of influence, and to align them with the most appropriate job responsibilities, in the correct environment. If you're dealing at the initiative level, then aligning the initiative profile with the team's composite leadership profile is in order. What you do, where, and how you do it are interdependent issues when dealing with passion.

Pain and Gain

A military definition of pain is "weakness leaving your body." We agree that sacrifice, no matter how unpleasant, is a leadership necessity for organizational goal attainment and should be considered value-driven behavior. Leaders are often called upon to make sacrifices as they help others to identify and pursue their own passions. When it comes to sacrifice, the leader is always the first in line. If the leader is the last to suffer in your organization, motivation will be a problem.

The pursuit of passion is not painful. Working through the layers of emotional debris or outright barriers that have passion bottled up can be very painful; so painful that most people never manage to release their passion from its prison. Add that to the human tendency to stay with the familiar rather than to venture into the unknown and people have even more reason to avoid passion. Despite the fact that releasing passion could lead to a life-transforming experience, most prefer to settle for the life they have, thank you very much.

Leaders often find themselves struggling to introduce people within their sphere of influence to their individual passions when those folks aren't necessarily interested. More likely, they are frightened by the unfamiliar pursuit of passion. Yet, organizational leaders aren't necessarily attempting to help others identify their passions out of a sense of altruism or devotion to self-actualization. They know the greatest power to innovate, solve problems, and achieve high performance will be released when people put their passions to productive use. That's the purpose of the ComposiTeam Leadership System. We can't name a single organization that ever *suffered* because its people felt alive and brimming over with enthusiasm and purpose.

Extrinsic vs. Intrinsic Rewards

The rewards for passion affect the individual and the organization. Super achievers will improve the overall performance of the organization and feel terrific in the process. A person who is genuinely happy at work is a person who is genuinely happy at home. When happiness and satisfaction are based on a proper alignment of passion and purpose, the results carry through all phases of life. Leaders benefit from mastery of passion when they help others identify and release their own. Emerson said, "It is one of the most beautiful compensations in life that no man can sincerely try to help another without helping himself."

Personal and professional lives are enhanced for leaders that successfully help people identify and align passion. This assumes that the leader's goals include helping people grow and develop, which all leaders should be. Think of it in opposite terms. Would you want a leader to be passionate about something other than helping others grow and develop, succeed and prosper? This issue folds back on proper alignment of personality and role. If a person is passionate about engineering, one of the worst things you could do is to force him or her to shift focus away from engineering to managing people.

Such a misalignment of passion, personality, and purpose will have the opposite effect of proper alignment. Misalignment will damage the individual and the organization. The fall out will be internal and external to the individual *and* the team. In domino fashion, misalignment of passion and professional position affects the individual, the stakeholders closest to him or her, the stakeholders nearest to them, and so on, extending outward to external customers and the community.

Success and Succession

Passion is an important factor in the organization's future. The style of leadership that brought the organization to where it is might or might not be what is called for to move forward. That decision can only be reached after extensive and deliberate research, reflection, and discussion. At its core, the decision of what style of leadership is most appropriate for the long-term goals of the organization must be accompanied by identification of the passionate individual who will work tirelessly to unite the efforts of the organizational population toward achievement of those goals.

Mobilization and inspiration of an organization is a job for a skilled people-centered leader. Yet, the most common approach is to align top executives with the particular industry or discipline the organization represents and then, when seeking their replacements, to search out and recruit clones. Any highly skilled people-centered leader will be able to assimilate enough knowledge and understanding about any industry to effectively lead the organization to ultimate success. Leaders with passion for the industry first, and the growth and development of other people second on their list of priorities will inevitably waste precious talent, time, and energy that a skilled people-centered leader will unleash immediately through the alignment of composite leadership profiles and initiative profiles.

A people-centered leader will spend his or her efforts on building and developing the strengths of the organizational population. You could think of it as constantly tuning the engine to ensure the smoothest and most fuel-efficient performance. The non-person-centered leader will do what nine out of 10 leaders do: step on the gas to drive the organization forward. When the performance stutters and starts to miss, they stomp even harder on the pedal.

When non-person-centered leaders discover that square pegs don't fit smoothly through round holes, they set out in search of bigger hammers. People-centered leaders understand that round holes call for round pegs, and they set out to find them. They might even sand the edges off the square pegs when necessary and appropriate. None of this is about being a warm and fuzzy leader. It's about getting the most productive and profitable performance out of the organization possible.

You can tell which type of leader is in charge by observing how the organization behaves over time. If the people are excited and enthusiastic about what they are doing, achieving results, and looking for more, the leader is committed to supporting them. If people are invested in the success of the organization and work cooperatively with one another, across disciplines, to ensure the best possible organizational performance, they are, no doubt, aligned with their natural strengths and abilities and being led as their leader likes to be led.

If an organization is divided into rigid silo-type departments and a militaristic, bureaucratic hierarchy, the leader is not thinking of his or her people first. If there is bickering, divisiveness, fictionalization, lack of enthusiasm, and low morale and productivity, the leader's primary focus and passion are not on helping others to grow and develop. The properties of a well-oiled organization, firing on all cylinders, will only be present when the person in charge is *passionate* about the success of everyone in his or her charge.

"Let the beauty of what you love be what you do."

—Rumi

If you hold a major stake in the success of an organization, how can you justify placing someone other than a passionate people-centered leader in charge; someone who loves helping people grow and develop? Leaders who are passionate about people can bring dead organizations back to life. It happens all the time. Have you ever come back to some activity in your life and said to yourself, "I forgot how much I enjoy this." Effective leaders know that in even the most depressingly unproductive organizations, there is tremendous untapped leadership potential. Unleashing it will launch a miracle comeback. A non-person-centered leader won't even go looking for it.

Avoiding Passion

It's possible to intentionally avoid passion. Many people are aware that they have passion for something lurking about in their psyche, but they do their best, sometimes going to great lengths, to keep it locked in the attic. Passion demands performance and commitment. Many people are content with mediocre performance and avoid commitment like the plague. One of the philosophies driving lethargic attitudes is "nothing ventured, nothing lost."

There is a certain pathetic logic to such thinking. Any professional gambler will tell you that the surest bet is the one that stays in your pocket. There are times when discretion is the better part of valor. But, to a degree, life itself is a gamble if you intend to realize more from getting involved than you can expect from sitting it out. In reality, venturing nothing probably means losing a great deal.

Board Room Reports

Many organizational executives live by the credo "Play it safe." Listen in on board or executive committee meetings at some organizations and you're likely to hear:

"What ever happened to so-and-so?"

"He's still here."

"Are you sure?"

"Yes, I just saw him coming out of the restroom last week."

"Has he ever screwed up anything big?"

"Not that I'm aware of."

"Then, how about putting him in this open slot?"

The exact conversation might vary, but you get the point. People that remain unengaged and rarely venture out of the bathroom stall of life often wind up running organizations. Others, in their ambitiousness and/ or enthusiasm, cause commotions, get themselves fired by envious superiors, or simply leave in search of greener pastures; leaving vacancies that get filled by the only person left standing. When the person at the helm of the organization got there by avoiding passion, how much passion in others can you expect him or her to inspire?

"Love, passion, and compassion, are all welded together."

—Carson McCullers
20th century American novelist and playwright

Values: Laying the Tracks

Before locomotives could begin hauling railroad cars full of people and freight from the Atlantic to the Pacific, the tracks had to be laid. It was one of the greatest achievements of modern civilization. It is also a good metaphor to describe the value of values. Tremendous movement was made possible by the construction of a road, a patch, or a byway. There was somewhere to go, a way to get there, and for each traveler, a reason to make the trip.

Accepted values in organizational life provide a clear sense of direction, preferred methodologies for getting there, and reasons to act. Without these things, much in the way of time, energy, and resources will be wasted in an effort that might take you someplace you had no intention of going, at a price you had no intention of paying, and with more unintended than intended consequences. Accepted or not, values will determine where the organization goes and how it behaves. Like passion, the entire issue of values in organizational life has real and practical application and consequences.

Paradigm Happens

In our discussion of passion, we alluded to the fact that passion is a good thing as long as it is properly channeled. Values constitute the channel. Any organization that is willing to expend valuable resources without clearly defined and articulated values is essentially rolling the dice. How responsible is that? Margaret Wheatley, author of *Leadership and the New Science* (Berrett-Koehler, 1992), says, "Organization happens." If you don't intentionally and proactively design and set about to build you organization, it will form itself, and you'll have a big, fat, not-so-friendly dragon to contend with.

We say, "Values happen." Your organization will be guided by values, whether or not you deliberately decide what those values are. It can't be assumed that naturally occurring values will be desirable. Leaders who ignore their responsibility to shape a values-based organizational culture are asking for trouble. Edmund Burke, an 18th century British political philosopher, said, "The only thing necessary for the triumph of evil is for good men to do nothing." If you don't intentionally decide what set of values you want to guide your organization, you'll have to deal with what comes. If you don't have a guiding philosophy about your organizational values, how are you going to attract the kind of people dedicated to moving in the direction you want to go?

Whose values?

There are certain timeless and ubiquitous values that guarantee the best outcome for the greatest number of people in any given situation and/or culture. We believe that these values are all rooted in the notion of treating others in ways that you would like to be treated, as in lead the way you like to be led. In essence, that means extending respect and regard to others, regardless of merit. Begin with good thoughts and friendly behaviors toward others until and unless the way they treat you calls for another approach. In most cases, the respect and regard should continue regardless of how they treat you.

We don't recommend, as W.C. Fields said, being a damn fool about it. There is a point where fair treatment crosses a line and becomes an issue of forgiveness. We're saying go for the good, and keep going for the good for as long as possible, hopefully forever. In the world of psychology, the golden rule is referred to as "mutual regard," or "other regard."

It is the place that leaders should start from when attempting to direct the formation of organizational values and beliefs.

"The time is always right to do what is right."

—Martin Luther King Jr.

The Spirit of the Matter

Just because something is not illegal doesn't mean it is the right thing to do. We remind you again of the difference between following procedures and doing what is right. Former congressional representative J.C. Watts of Oklahoma describes having values as doing the right thing when nobody's looking. The concept is not that far-fetched. If you stop and think about what your community would be like if the majority of citizens had no virtuous values to guide their behavior, the picture would not be pretty. There are very few criminals, relative to the population, who will break into your house and steal, or run into your car and speed away, or intentionally harm you or anyone in your family.

The vast majority of citizens in our nation are responsible and demonstrate virtuous values, even when nobody is looking. If the fear of being caught were the only reason not to shoplift, store shelves would be cleaned out. If your neighbor stole you blind every time you left home, you would have no possessions left. Values give us a way to be; a way that benefits the most people and protects the rights of the majority and the minority.

Curse of the rulebook

The rulebook, although intended to serve a useful purpose, can backfire. Rules, policies, and procedures are, by nature, designed to eliminate waste, fraud, and negligence, as well as to standardize the way things are done. Unfortunately, rules are designed for the lowest common denominators. So, following the rules is an invitation for everyone above the line to do what is required of them and nothing more. Those who fall short of complete compliance with the rulebook create an enforcement problem for administrators who would rather not deal with such things, and generally ignore them.

At the end of the day, policies and procedures have diminished overall performance for those who would have been far more productive if left to their own devices and personal leadership. At the same time, policies and procedures failed to force universal compliance, thus leaving the people for whom the rules were written below the curve. The 20 percent that account for 80 percent of the work are, as they have always been and always will be, working based on personal values that transcend the rules.

Effective leaders are not intimidated by the threat of dealing with problems or the people who have problems. As a result, effective leaders put aside rulebooks in favor of what is best for the organization and its population in the here and now, as well as the future. Leaders who make a difference are guided by their values and actively attempt to make those values resonate throughout the organization. Values are part of the on-going dialogue that effective leaders keep alive.

The Unspoken Language

Although values and beliefs are discussed openly and regularly in an environment of effective leadership, they also fill the air. Team members work hard alongside one another in an atmosphere of trust that is made possible in large part by the existence of a value system. In large organizations, with multiple geographical locations, a strong value-based culture will make any branch office feel like home to a traveling team member. A team member from Disneyland in California has an instant bond and mutual understanding with an employee at Walt Disney World 3,000 miles away, or in Tokyo half a world away. The Disney culture is that strong.

Some organizations are complex systems; mazes where people can get lost and never be heard from again. No matter how complex and far-flung an enterprise might be, a strong, value-based culture will knit the team members together and keep them working in concert with one another, toward uniform goals, even when they don't see or speak to each other.

We remind you again of the airline example, and how a company culture, or shared values, keeps thousands of arrivals and departures every day, in hundreds of cities, in dozens of countries, involving more than 50,000 employees operating smoothly—and overcoming a thousand problems a day, from weather to terrorist threats. No single leader or team of top executives can make that happen. Fifty thousand people aren't sitting around with their noses in a rulebook. Org is tossing luggage on board, serving your pretzels, taking your reservations, all the while guided by the invisible hand, created from the collective spirit of all those people. Their shared values and purpose cause things to happen; things so complex and extensive that no individual person could possibly keep track of it all. And, tomorrow morning, it will all start over again.

Published rules can't help but be specific and situational. Values are ubiquitous and tend to be made up of timeless principles. Fraudulent business practices and practitioners of fraudulent business tactics are popular villains with the popular media. What the media does not report on with any regularity, if they report it at all, are the deeds of values-based citizens and the performance of ethical businesses. Easily, 90 percent of businesses are ethical, values-based enterprises. That's a lot of news going unreported each day. How many entrepreneurs and corporations do you do business with each day? How many of them would you call unethical?

Lack of values means trouble

Those who call values politically incorrect are acting on a set of values. In the absence of virtuous values, individuals and organizations become vulnerable to harm. Assuming that people will conduct themselves in accordance with *virtuous* values is a common way to be taken advantage of. If there are people in the organization that intend to deceive or defraud, your non-stand on the issue of organizational values leaves the door open to claims that in the absence of a governing authority, anything goes.

An organization can't tolerate internal contradiction and dissonance for long. Ambiguity leads to chaos and, worse yet, anarchy. In bureaucracies, where accountability is practically nonexistent, the absence of unifying values will go undetected and unreported. Organizational life in the private sector, although fraught with waste and corruption itself, is still more or less self-correcting and can't defy virtuous values for long before it shakes itself out. In the meantime, qualities such as confidence, concentration, and passion can be put to effective use by confidence artists that prey on the good nature of those who assume everyone in the system is virtuous.

Intentional deceit is not the only danger. Don't forget those who unintentionally do immeasurable harm in the name of virtue. Sometimes values just aren't enough without a modicum of common sense. Just like passion needs to be tempered and guided by values, everything you think and do should fall within reason. The parameters of common sense vary from individual to individual. That's why effective leaders deal with what is sensible and reasonable in their ongoing dialogue and continuous learning cultures.

Culture gone bad

Just as Margaret Wheatley pointed out that organization happens, cultures happen. If leaders don't become the conscious architects of values-based cultures within their organizations, whatever values exist naturally will become galvanized. Unfortunately, a few bad apples can sour the sauce for everyone. The worst odor comes from apathy and complacency. Leadership is required to guide and inspire a culture based on virtuous values. That leadership can be collaborative team leadership, if it's guided by an intentional leadership system.

Culture is also a practical issue of dollars and sense. The enthusiasm with which people do their jobs has a tremendous impact on productivity and profitability. A strong values-based culture will reduce expensive shrinkage and waste. If someone stops and bends over to pick up a piece of trash in the company parking lot, don't you think that same person will report a hiccup in the system, step up to correct a problem, or act quickly to resolve an issue that is costly to internal and/or external customers? Values affect your top line *and* your bottom line.

> ## Chapter 15 Summary:
> ## Keys to Unleashing Leadership

- **Passion won't die out:** A passing fancy, fad, or infatuation won't last. If you make the mistake of misdiagnosing one as passion, you might lose your belief in passion. Don't be fooled. Passion is more like an inexhaustible fuel cell than an internal combustion engine. Passion comes from a mysterious, unknown place, much like the early stages of falling in love. Its power is unparalleled. No one can explain it. Nothing can contain it. Although it can fade in and out like a distant radio station, rarely does anything sustain effort over time in the way that undying passion can.

- **Passion begets passion:** It takes passion to identify and encourage passion in others. When you find someone who is passionate about identifying and encouraging passion in others, you've found a tremendous candidate; either for an individual leadership position or for a spot on a leadership team, contingent on how he or she affects the composite leadership profile on that team. When leadership is an expectation of everyone, it's time to start unleashing passion company-wide. Passion, no matter where it's located, will have a positive impact on the rest of the system.

☞ **Values happen:** We fully agree with Meg Wheatley that, when two or more people get together, voluntarily or involuntarily, for whatever reason, they will begin to organize themselves. Intentionally or unintentionally, organization (the verb) will happen and organization (the noun) will result. They will bring with them, intentionally or unintentionally, their values and beliefs. The collective values and beliefs of the new organization might parallel the values and beliefs of the individuals, or they might be shaped and altered in the combining. Either way, the organization will have values.

☞ **Right is right:** You can stay out of trouble by following procedures. But did you help anyone? Sometimes doing what is right goes beyond the operating manual. The rules can't account for everything, all of the time. There are times when judgment is called for, especially for those in positions of leadership. When there are no clear tracks to follow, your values keep you straight. If there are no clearly defined values in your organization, where are you going? How are you going to get there? Will there be a high cost in lost trust from your internal and external customers? Remember, it takes 50 positives to counteract one negative.

☞ **Values happen:** If organizational culture is left to self-formation, it will run to the lowest common denominator and form its own restrictive and counterproductive rulebook. If you didn't consciously adopt virtuous values and intentionally base your organizational culture on them, and reinforce them with continuous learning and an expectation of leadership performance, the culture you wind up with will probably not be receptive to progressive thinking. Friendly dragon or unfriendly dragon, the choice is yours.

Courage, confidence, and concentration, when fueled by passion and guided by virtuous values, are an unstoppable leadership system that can stand up to any adversity, distortion, or assault.

> "Truth, self control, asceticism, generosity, non-injury, constancy in virtue—these are the means of success...."
>
> —Mahabharata

AMEN.

Index

A

abuse, substance, 18-19
accuracy, compliance and, 178-179
action planning, 234-235
Albertson, Joe, 33-34
aligning what people do best with what is needed, 58-59
alignment priorities, 118-119
alignment, composite leadership profile/initiative profile, 108-110
analysis, compliance and, 176-177
anxiety vs. fear, 145-146
application, the art is in the, 60-62
avoidance vs. attraction, 214-215
avoidance vs. intention, 143-144

B

barriers, breaking through, 240-241
Belasco, James, 32
blame game, the, 38
Blanchard, Ken, 163, 164
Blueprint for Leadership, 35-36
Brandt, Leslie F., 238
Buffalo, Flight of the, 32
Burns, George, 267

C

can stacker, the competent, 217-218
carefulness, compliance and, 179-180
Carlzon, Jan, 34
changing culture, 19-21
character, confidence built on, 243
chart,
    money, 21-22
    organizational, 21-22
City Slickers, 266, 267
Collins, Jim, 60, 237
competence, confidence and, 231-232
compliance
    and accuracy, 178-179
    and analysis, 176-177
    and being methodical, 181-182
    and being systematic, 182
    and carefulness, 179-180
    and details, 177
    and facts, 179
    and mathematics, 177-178
    and precision, 180-181
compliance specialist, 175-186
    and control specialist, 166-169, 183-184

and social specialist, 184
and stability specialist, 184-185,
208-209
compliance, 103
composite personality made
simple, 52-53
composite personality,
calculating, 86-88
culture =, 51-54
the power of, 53
three easy steps to, 60
ComposiTeam Leadership
System, 49-50, 61, 76, 125
concentration vs. instant
gratification, 257
concentration, 104-105, 246-263
confidence and competence, 231-232
confidence, 104, 229-245
coaching, 239-240
restoring damaged, 236-237
true courage includes, 222-223
contagious, courage is, 226-227
contamination vs. enrichment,
131-134
control, 103
and commanding, 161-162
and competitiveness, 164
and controlling, 160
and determination, 163
and dominance, 163-164
and fearlessness, 159-160
and impatience, 162
and power, 158-159
and taking charge, 164-165
and vigor, 165
control issues, 156-165
control specialist, 155-174

and compliance specialist,
166-169, 183-184
and social specialist, 168-169,
193-194
and stability specialist, 170-172,
206-207
corporate culture, 15
courage, 104, 213-228
and criticism, 215-216
includes conscience, true, 222-223
is contagious, 226-227
Requires effort, 224
Cox, Danny, 32, 141
creative tension, 59-60
culture = composite personality,
51-54
culture,
changing, 19-21
corporate, 15
cynical corporate, 15-16
culture gone bad, 277
cynical corporate culture, 16-17

D

dawn, darkest just before, 259-260
Dean, Dizzy, 239
details, compliance and, 177
development as a system,
leadership, 25-26
diet, changing Org's, 20-21
DiSC Profile, 48
Disney, Walt, 59
dream, the impossible, 172
drill, the hurricane, 142-143
Drucker, Peter F., 28

E

effect, silo, 22
empathy, the power of, 40-41
end to isolation, an, 23
energy, harnessing, 266
enrichment, contamination vs., 131-134
expectation, leadership as an, 28-43

F

facts, compliance and, 179
fear,
  promoting, 139-140
  vision, and leadership, 147-148
fear as friend, 140-141
fear factor, the, 137-151
fear vs. anxiety, 145-146
fearlessness, the myth of, 138-142
fins, tired, 224-225
first rule of leadership, 29-30
focus, people, 252-253
followership, Leadership is revealed, 36
freeze up any organization, lack of knowledge can, 67-69

G

gain, pain and, 268
gain vs. loss, 142
Giuliani, Rudolph, 148
Good to Great, 60
groupthink, 221

H

hand, the invisible, 44-63
hierarchies, traditional, 21-24

hiring and firing, 219-220
honesty is the best policy, 70-72
hostage, leadership potential held, 54-55
hurricane, the drill, 142-143

I

iceberg, tip of the, 30-32
impatience, institutionalized, 257-258
initiative
  profile principles, 102-105
  profile, the, 96-122
  style profile, 109-110
  naming the, 100-101
  owning the, 99-100
  profiling the, 99-102
Inside/Outside, 144-145
instant gratification vs. concentration, 257
instructions, initiative profile, 105-108
intention vs. avoidance, 143-144
Inventories, 67-95
  filling out the, 72-74
  filling out the, 74-76
  peer-reporting, 81-82
isolation, an end to, 23
isolation is not an option, 218-219
issues, control, 156-165

J

Janis, Irving, 221

K

keys to unleashing leadership, 26-27, 41-43, 61-63, 93-95, 123-124, 135-136, 150-151, 172-174, 185-186, 196-197, 227-228, 209-210, 244-245, 261-263, 277-278 knowledge, tools for gaining and using, 69-72

L

Lasorda, Tommy, 33
law of inertia, 22
Law, Parkinson's , 251
lead the way like you like to be lead, 29-30
leader in name vs. leader in fact, 31-32
leadership as an expectation, 28-43
leadership development as a system, 25-26
leadership is a specialization, 39-40
leadership is revealed in followership, 36
leadership motivation inventory, see *LMI*
leadership potential held hostage, 54-55
leadership style inventory, 69
leadership styles, 56-57
Leadership, Blueprint for, 35-36
leadership,
 first rule of, 29-30
 keys to unleashing, 93-95, 123-124, 135-136, 150-151, 172-174, 185-186, 196-197, 209-210, 227-228, 244-245, 261-263, 277-278
 vision, and fear, 147-148
Leonard, Stew, 34
Lightbulb vs. the laser, the, 247
lightbulb, the proof is in the, 156
limitations, dealing with, 129-130
lion, lessons from the, 221-222
LMI, 69, 70, 74-76

loss vs. gain, 142
LSI, 69-70, 72-74
luck, good and bad, 17-18

M

managing the team, 125-136
mathematics, compliance and, 177-178
MBTI, 48, 53
McAuliffe, General A.C., 223, 224
measuring personality, 47-49
meet your Dragon, 13-27
Mehrabian, Albert, 30
methodical, compliance and being, 181-182
molecular organization, the, 24-26
Moments of Truth, 34
Myers Briggs Type Indicator, see *MBTI*
myth of fearlessness, the, 138-142

N

natural vs. unnatural teams, 55-56
Newton, Sir Isaac, 22

O

Org, 13-27
 and why he's cynical, 16-17
organization, the molecular, 24-26
outlasting the competition— maybe, 258-259
overconcentrate, don't, 255-256

P

pain and gain, 268
pain vs. leadership, 146-147

paradigm happens, 273-274

Parkinson's Law, 251

passion and values, 264-278

passion, 105
  avoiding, 271
  passionate, 265

personality as a strategic weapon, 50-51

personality typology, 47-49

personality, 44-63
  measuring, 47-49

planning, action, 234-235

pleasure vs. pain, 146-147

popularity, what price for, 220

power vs. influence, 159

precision, compliance and, 180-181

price for popularity, 220

principles, initiative profiles, 102-105

priorities, alignment, 118-119

problems and opportunity, 233

procedures, standard operating, 149

profile, initiative style, 109-110

profiles will differ, 119-122

profiling the initiative, 99-102

promoting fear, 139-140

prophecy, a self-fulfilling, 148-149

public or private, 101-102

R

rankings, leadership style and motivation, 77-81

relationships of social specialist, 187-193

relationships, internal and external, 165-172

reporting, 130-131

reports, board room, 271-272

responsibility, ring of, 23-24

reward courage, 225

reward, risk vs., 216

rewards, extrinsic vs. intrinsic, 269

right, the customer is always, 34-35

ring of responsibility, 23-24

risk vs. reward, 216

rulebook, curse of the, 274-275

S

Santini, The Great, 140

Scrooge, Ebenezer, 18

shaken, not stirred, 235-236

silo effect, 22

silos and subversion, 21-22

skepticism, healthy, 182-183

Smith, Adam, 44

social specialist, 187-197
  and compliance specialist, 184, 195-196
  and control specialist, 168-169, 193-194
  and stability specialist, 195, 207-208

social, 103-104

Specialization, Leadership is a, 39-40

speed is on your side, 97-98

stability, 104
  and balance, 200
  and being rational, 203-204
  and capability, 200
  and dependability, 205-206
  and evaluation, 204
  and patience, 202-203

and reliability, 203
and responsibility, 205
and steadiness, 201-202
and strategy, 202
stability specialist, 198-210
    and compliance specialist, 184-185
    and compliance specialist, 208-209
    and control specialist, 170-172,
        206-207
    and social specialist, 195, 207-208
Stayer, Ralph, 32
steps to composite personality,
    three easy, 60
styles, leadership, 56-57
subordinate, who is the, 29
substance abuse, 18-19
success and succession, 269-271
Summer Catch, 246
supermarket, Joe Albertson's, 33-34
symmetry, 89-90
system, leadership development as
    a, 25-26
systematic, compliance and being, 182

T

team for the wrong reasons, the
    wrong, 110-117
team,
    managing the, 125-136
    not reinventing the, 127-130
    size of the, 127-129
Temperment Sorter, Keirsey, 53
tension, creative, 59-60
Titanic, 31
torpedoes, damn the, 149-150

traditional hierarchies, 21
truth, moments of, 34
trying vs. succeeding, 260-261
typology, the language of
    personality, 47-49

U

unleashing leadership, keys to, 41-
    43, 61-63, 123-124, 135-136, 150-
    151, 172-174, 185-186, 196-197,
    209-210, 227-228, 244-245, 261-
    263, 277-278,
unnatural teams, natural vs., 55-56

V

values, 105, 272
valuing people, 126-127
Viscott, David, 267
visible, making the invisible, 47-49
vision, leadership, and fear, 147-148

W

weapon, personality as, 50-51
weighting, 134-135
Wheatley, Margaret, 15, 273, 277, 278
Wizard of Oz, 221
world,
    the compliance specialist's
        perfect, 176
    the perfect, 117-118

Z

Ziglar, Zig, 32
Zone, the, 248-249

About the Authors

John Hoover, Ph.D., is a human and organization development specialist, author, popular speaker, and recovering idiot boss. He is a former executive with the Disneyland Entertainment Division and, as managing partner of the second firm in the United States to publish commercial audio books-on-tape, he produced programs featuring authors including Herbert Benson, Ken Blanchard, Harold Bloomfield, Jack Canfield, Danny Cox, Terrance Deal, Peter F. Drucker, Dean Edell, Lillian Glass, Mark Victor Hansen, Tom Hopkins, Irene Kassorla, Norman Vincent Peale, Larry Peter, Al Ries, Robert H. Schuller, Jack Trout, and Zig Ziglar. Since selling his audio/video publishing company to McGraw-Hill and serving three years as general manager of McGraw-Hill audio and video publishing, he has consulted on a wide variety of projects for clients including Boeing, Delta Air Lines, Hilton Hotels, IBM, Motorola, Printronix, Sanyo Fisher, and Xerox.

Dr. John has authored or coauthored six books prior to *Unleashing Leadership*. He is cofounder, with Angelo Valenti, Ph.D., of the *ComposiTeam Leadership System*, a new online system for mapping projects and initiatives in behavioral terms, aligning the composite personalities of teams with project and initiative maps, and tracking initiative and team progress. His background also includes six years as a California Board of Behavioral Sciences–registered marriage, family, and child counseling intern, street gang counselor for the Orange County Probation Department, life skills counselor for homeless families in transition, and adolescents in crisis. Dr. John is a Tennessee Supreme Court Rule 31 civil mediator.

A former member of the California Association of Marriage and Family Therapists, he currently belongs to the American Society of Training &

Development and the Society for Human Resources Management. Dr. John holds a master of arts in marriage and family therapy from Azusa Pacific University in addition to his master of arts in human and organization development, and a doctorate degree in human and organizational systems from the Fielding Institute in Santa Barbara, California. In addition to his personal and executive coaching and consulting, he is an adjunct faculty member at Aquinas College and the Aquinas Adult Studies program in Nashville, Tennessee, and Middle Tennessee State University.

Angelo C. Valenti, Ph.D., received his graduate degree from the University of Georgia in 1976. At that time he joined the faculty of Oklahoma City University as an instructor and shortly thereafter was named chairman of the Psychology Department.

In 1980, Dr. Valenti moved to Memphis to become a staff consultant with the psychological consulting firm of RHR International. In this position, he conducted organizational studies, psychological assessments, and consulted with management in a variety of industries.

Two years later, Dr. Valenti came to Nashville to establish a private consulting practice, The Company Psychologist. Since that time he has served as a psychological consultant for a client base consisting of publicly traded organizations, private companies, and family owned businesses in a variety of industries including insurance, publishing, healthcare, retail, financial services, manufacturing, printing, inventory control, transportation, and distribution.

Dr. Valenti is a public speaker, a published author, and is active in many civic and professional organizations, including the American Psychological Association (Division 13 – Consulting Psychology). He is also an avid golfer. He and his wife, Ginger, have three children.